Puzzled

Puzzled

Secrets and Clues from a Life in Words

DAVID ASTLE

P
PROFILE BOOKS

First published in Great Britain in 2012 by
Profile Books Ltd
3a Exmouth House
Pine Street
London EC1R 0JH
www.profilebooks.com

First published in Australia by Allen & Unwin
www.allenandunwin.com

A CIP catalogue record for this book is available from the British Library.

ISBN 978 1 84668 542 2
eISBN 978 1 84765 816 6

Typeset in Palatino by MacGuru Ltd
info@macguru.org.uk

Printed and bound in Britain by
Clays, Bungay, Suffolk

The paper this book is printed on is certified by the © 1996 Forest Stewardship Council
A.C. (FSC). It is ancient-forest friendly. The printer holds FSC chain of custody
SGS-COC-2061

FSC
www.fsc.org
MIX
Paper from
responsible sources
FSC® C018072

For the girl whose name is hard to spell

Contents

Puns

Reversals

Spoonerisms

Rebuses

&Lits

Hybrids

Mini Puzzles

INTRODUCTION

How the Bug Bit

Forget Batman. My hero as a kid was the Riddler. Every afternoon after school I longed to hear that cackle coming from the television. I adored the lurid jumpsuit, the bowler hat: the whole puzzle package. How his crook-like cane was shaped like a question mark, and his henchwomen – Query and Echo – were smart, verbal babes trained in combat and repartee. And no one got hurt. Or killed, at least. Murder wasn't on the Riddler's agenda. His mayhem of choice was bank jobs and wordplay. True, the guy was a psycho, but my kind of psycho, a villain after my six-year-old heart.

His obsession of course was the riddles, those brain-curlers he left scattered round Gotham City. Puns were his calling cards. (*What people are always in a hurry? Russians. How many sides has a circle? Two – the inside and outside.*) Where Batman had the muscle, the stamina, the entire Bat-armoury, he often struggled to match the limber brain of my lime-green pin-up.

Where is a man drowned but still not wet? That's another riddle I recall, a coded warning for the caped crusaders. Quick, the clock was ticking. I dreamt up a vat of liquid honey – is sticky the same as wet? Or maybe talcum powder. Can a man drown in fabric, or dust, or fairy floss? By the time I'd stumbled on quicksand, so had Batman, literally, drowning in the Riddler's booby trap. If not for a Bat-grapnel we may have lost him.

The routine was relentless, every caper a fresh string of clues, and I loved it. Somehow I fancied puzzles might be a calling. (Bear in mind I was six at the time.) Just imagine, living on a wordplay salary. And why not? The idea felt no less weird than selling sea monkeys or X-ray spectacles.

At my local library, I dug out jokes and limericks, riddles and knock-knocks: a menace in search of ammo. I revelled in embarrassed zebras and ducks quacking up. Pity my family, nightly copping the dandy-lions, the sand-witches and every other groaner in the book.

On top of puns, I nagged Mum for puzzle books, the rainy-day kind with dot-to-dots and spot-the-difference pictures. I circled French towns in seek-a-word boxes. I filled the blanks and built pyramids out of letters.

By late primary school, I started to see secret messages lurking in food labels. Eta Mayonnaise, I saw, held the sentence 'I annoy a mate' in reverse, and did I bug my family with that discovery. Shades of the day I found the fluke hiding in OVALTINE:

'No one's leaving the table until you solve a puzzle,' I told my younger siblings.

'Not another one,' whined Kate, Sister One, a future psychologist.

'Pass the milk,' said my brother, Richard, a defiant spirit to this day.

'Is this like a game?' wondered Sister Two, Lib, a multilinguist-in-the-making, barely out of nappies.

'What two colours are inside Ovaltine?' I slid the tin across. 'You have to use every letter once, and once only.'

'*Grnfff*,' said Kate, her mouth full of Weetie Puffs.

'Huh?' said Lib.

'Violet,' said Rich. 'Can I go now?'

Escape was never so simple. I stole my brother's spoon, pointed to the Ovaltine label as the only ticket to freedom. 'Is tin a colour?' asked Kate.

'The tin is green,' observed Lib.

Richard was seething. 'You want some Ovaltine on your head?'

'Tan,' said Kate. At least she was trying.

'Tan and …?'

'Who cares?' they replied.

To say I was a pain in the neck is a fair summary of those days growing up. But puzzles were a virus in the blood. Even the fact that ASTLE, our surname, held a dozen different five-letter words seemed to validate my calling as a mix-master. Most names are lucky to produce one or two words, whereas mine carried its own trove, from STALE to STEAL, from mill streams (LEATS) to the Serbian whizz behind the radio (TESLA), from SLATE to TEALS, from TELAS (weblike membranes) to TAELS (40 Chinese grams), from a memorial pillar (STELA) to bristly (SETAL), from TALES and, lastly, LEAST. Likewise I loved the idea that DAVID could lose his head to become AVID, and as long as I was losing myself in letters, I felt impassioned.

A billboard near my nan's house showed a butcher standing at his block. *Pleased to Meet You*, ran the caption. *Meat to Please You*. Smitten, I recited the slogan like a mantra, the ad a kind of scripture for a punster on the rise.

The taller I grew, the deeper the mania. Staying with Jessie, my maternal grandmother, I burrowed into her *Webster's International*, a burgundy-bound dictionary too heavy to lift. Inside were cross-section diagrams of hydrants and spider orchids, camshafts and Spanish galleons. I dug up words like wittol (a tame cuckold) and had to check what cuckold meant. The book was a universe in alphabetical order.

Most visits, Jess and I played Scrabble, matriarch versus

punk. The board was a turntable I ended up inheriting once Jessie drew her final tiles. But back then, with a pile of arrow-roots on a plate, I played ridiculous words like ITE and CAL and NAE, and Jess spent half the game combing *Webster's* to see if her grandson was precocious or desperate. Possibly both.

My parents bought me crossword magazines just to shut me up: the quick American variety where little words like ADIT (a mine entrance) and ORT (food scrap) ruled supreme. My fingertips turned black from the ink of umpteen grids. I grew familiar with baseball abbreviations, New York mayors, and people with vowel-heavy names like Oona Chaplin, Yoko Ono and the architect I. M. Pei.

I doted on Scrabble tiles. The game came with two dozen dice inscribed with letters instead of numbers. I blew week-ends just rolling the cubes across the carpet. (Of course I also managed to break a nose playing under-12 rugby, fall in love with Katrina Ferguson, play bad tuba, ride my bike, but all this was downtime from the alphabet's thrall.) Shaking the cup, rolling out the cubes, I moved the letters into words, the words into knots of criss-crossing Zs and Vs to maximise my score.

Genetically the letter-bug stems from Mum, an avid reader still, and long-time lover of Lindsey Browne, the man who made crosswords for the *Sydney Morning Herald* and the *Daily Telegraph*. For Heather, come day's end, nothing beat a Gordon's gin and a wrestle with the clues of LB. I envied her rapture, in a way. Still just a kid, I could only shrug at the private dialect of cryptic puzzles. *Cat bites philosopher. Correspond with a Spartan almost*. What the hell did it mean? I blamed the gibberish on adulthood, a code to master once you knew how to drive, or hang a door, or talk to the opposite sex without your face catching fire.

The first cryptic clue I solved was at our local drive-in. The bill was a James Bond double, and the car teemed with siblings. Amid the chaos I can still picture the *Herald* folded to the puzzle page.

This was the summer between two schools. Sean Connery had just saved Jamaica and Dad was off getting ice creams. Seizing her moment, Mum tried to finish the puzzle but had no chance of solitude, not with a tweenage verbaholic leaning over her shoulder.

Burning silver and blue, read one clue. Mum took her time, doodling in the margin. Next she wrote AGLOW in the grid. The best I could muster was 'Why?'

'Chemistry,' she said. 'You'll do that in high school.'

'Chemical what?'

'The symbol for silver is Ag, which leaves us with blue.'

'Hang on. What are you talking about?'

'Not just the colour. What else does blue mean?'

'Don't ask me. A mistake?'

'That's right. Or a brawl. Or here,' she tapped the page. 'Blue means sad, or low.'

'So?'

'Put them together and you get a word for burning – AGLOW.'

'Oh.'

Thus the flame was passed from one cryptic nut to the next. Mum went on to explain how a disrupted MONDAY spells DYNAMO, or flower can mean a tulip as well as something that flows. She said that WONDER makes RED NOW when turned the other way, or AGLOW was called a charade, since the word is broken into smaller pieces, just like the parlour game breaks movies into syllables. 'Get it?' she asked.

'Give me another clue.'

'Here's one.' And she read the clue aloud: *'Follow in green suede shoes (5).'*

No surprise, the Riddler sprang to mind, his dapper costume, though his shoes of choice were plimsolls.

'You've fallen for the trap,' Mum warned. 'Don't think literally. Ignore the shoes and concentrate on the words.'

'That's what I'm doing, isn't it?'

Bond by now was chasing Blofeld on a skidoo, and the rest of the family was shushing, but Mum persisted. *'Green suede.* Look inside the letters. What do you see?'

'Sue,' I said.

'Stretch it out. What's a word for 'follow' that ends with SUE?'

'Pursue,' I said.

'Look deeper – it's all there.'

'Where?'

'Forget about the shoes. Look at the letters.'

'ENSUE?'

'Voila.'

The buzz outlasted the movie, the drive home, the next day. Suddenly a month of summer camping became a retreat devoted to the cryptic art. Little by little I learnt to spot anagrams, homophones, red herrings. Early mornings I'd wait for the ferry, her cargo the latest LB crossword, plus answers to the puzzle from the day before.

I started high school, a culture shock entailing Latin and straw hats, where a man called Snags sealed my fate. To this day I don't know why Keith Anderson, my English teacher, had that nickname, but back in 1974, my first year of high school, Snags was good for two favours. One, he fostered my creative writing, and two – he caught the flu in August.

Enter Max from geography, a fill-in teacher who took the helm one morning with a newspaper under his wing and no idea what class he was supervising.

'English,' we replied. Year 7, we were suck-ups.

'English, eh?' Max opened the *Daily Telegraph* and flicked through the pages. 'Here y'are.' He stabbed the puzzle section. 'Make me a crossword.'

Methodically, I did. Max was amazed. Or maybe furious is a better word. His task was meant to be a time-sponge, but a few ticks before the bell here was some smartie submitting a 15-by-15 grid with symmetry and clues and the whole caboodle. Damn – now he'd have to run off copies.

That maiden puzzle – a crisp Xerox circulating the corridors – put a new spring in my step. With only one problem. Max had neglected to run off the solution, meaning I fielded enquiries from all levels of the academy.

'Hey Astle, what the fuck is PERFIDY?'

'How d'ya spell OCCURRED?'

If this was the puzzle life, I wanted more. To think half the playground was taking my name in vain, enmeshed in my logic. I felt like the Riddler, curbing the urge to cackle my glee.

At home, instead of drawing pie charts and Venn diagrams, I drafted grids and wove words inside them. I began collecting names and phrases. Overnight a drab textbook on Australian explorers gave up such gems as ERNEST GILES (SINGLE TREE) and TANAMI DESERT (TAN + AMID + gnarly TREES). In my own small way I felt in step with the explorers, my landscape a sprawl of untapped language. I kept up the headway with LB on the train. And come 1979, amid final-year exams, I sent a parcel to the man himself, care of the *Herald.* Ultimo 2007.

Inside was a monster grid, hand-drawn and pencil-shaded, coinciding with the newspaper's milestone. CONGRATULATIONS SYDNEY MORNING HERALD, read 1-Across, with the baseline adding: TEN THOUSAND CRYPTIC CROSSWORDS NOT OUT.

In many ways the gesture was a tribute to the man for his years of mental bedlam, since I knew he had crafted most of those 10,000 crosswords himself. Or then again, it was my painstaking way of getting noticed, a tentative plea to join the fun.

LB took the bait. He sent me a reply, enclosing a copy now busy with arrows and stars, circles and crosses: lessons in the art of clue-building. Margins teemed with comments: *nifty anag, less abbrev.* And slowly I rose to the challenge. A correspondence bloomed. Every month a slew of raw puzzles would return to my letterbox with LB's sage appraisal. We became pen pals in the same city, chatting about grids and the Moscow Olympics, what anagram potential RONALD REAGAN might offer. But we didn't meet in person till 1982, some three years into our exchange.

I remember the day in living colour. Driving down the leafy ridge of Greenwich Point, a millionaire's row of barristers and mortgage brokers, I nursed the butterflies of a blind date. At 21, an adult on paper, I was due to meet a crossword god, aged 66, in his secret puzzle palace. But really, there was little blindness involved. I'd been entering the LB mindscape six days a week for almost a decade, divining clues as personal insights into their creator. I knew the man's humour (punny), his gripes (bureaucracy), his loves (cricket, classical music). And to a lesser degree, he knew mine.

First thing I noticed, his house was not a palace. The million-dollar view was a spray of jacaranda against a paling fence. The garden steps crunched with snails. I rang the bell and heard the footfalls. The man who opened up was every inch the mad professor, broad in the shoulders and with caterpillar eyebrows. We shared a pot of tea and ate some chocolate hedgehogs on the patio. His office was a kitchen nook, a lifetime of battered books and graph sheets strewn across the bench. I felt honoured to share his company and spooked at the same time.

Hindsight has helped me explain that unease. As a protégé you sense your future self in your mentor, just as your mother-in-law foreshadows your wife. Yet passion in both scenarios tends to quash the doubts. Fatally, I had no choice but to tamper with words. If my career path led to this kitchen cranny, so be it. And perhaps LB detected that mutual flaw, anointing me with a *Herald* debut a year later, in 1983.

SCAFFOLDING was my first 1-Across – *Back off in burning metal framework* – and I've been 'constructing' for the paper ever since. Anonymously at first, as was the house style, then later using my own initials. Those two letters – DA – are how most people have come to know me. *Don't Attempt*, swear some solvers. *Dangerously Addictive*, the other camp.

But before mapping out the book, let me finish my Riddler confession. After twenty-five years of crafting clues for a wage, I feel the time is right to lose my workaday clothes in order to reveal the lime-green leotard underneath. In many ways this book is a coming-out exercise (*'Yes, I make puzzles and I'm proud of it!'*), as well as a chance to lead you through the oddity of Cryptopia. In the coming pages you'll see how different clues operate and why each style throws new light on the words around us.

You may think that you know English but I'll show you its flipside. Across twenty-five years I've found some extraordinary features in so-called ordinary words, just as OVALTINE hides TAN and OLIVE. Ready or not, you'll also get to plunge into a Master Puzzle, a multi-level challenge that's waiting to be solved around the corner.

That's right, a single grid is beckoning, each of its thirty-three clues sparking a different chapter on the art of puzzling and the secret lives of words. You'll also read about the peculiar life of clue-mongers, including mine, and the tangled tale of human wordplay, how an ancient itch to toy with letters has led us to this black-and-white curio we call a cryptic crossword. Just be warned: the further you travel down this winding road, the more likely you'll catch the bug that once bit me.

So what's going on?

At first glance the Master Puzzle will seem like any other crossword: a prim block of black and white squares, numbered and clued like any other. But this baby has some stories to tell.

To give you the best tour of Puzzleville I've loaded the box with the twelve key recipes, from anagram to charade, from rebus to container. Solving as we go, we'll encounter puns and codes, homophones and deletions – each clue warranting its own chapter and detours, a solution included.

Expose Ned, Russ, Hector, for example. That's not 1-Across, but Chapter 1, and where we'll start the puzzle, entering the grid and the cryptic story as a whole. Each chapter will help you produce a new answer for the grid, as well as tips on how each formula works. Yet far more than a how-to manual, this book is a mystery tour through language, a master crossword to solve as we travel.

That's our destination – one finished puzzle. Yet as we unravel the clues, we'll also hear about the Pappadam Argument, the Sator Stone, the Accidental Swastika, the Centipede Tower and plenty more puzzling topics.

Lipograms? Signposts? Unches? Clue by clue we'll uncover the tips and traps, the origins of puzzles and the changes over time. See the Master Puzzle as your ticket to strange locations with DA as your guide – tormentor as mentor. Come the final clue a crypt will be opened and a cryptic puzzle cracked.

For the pro, the trip will sharpen your lateral reflexes. For the tyro, take heart: the rewards are wild, even if the head-spin verges on vertigo. Even should you never confront a puzzle again, this trip at least tells you what the whole weirdness is about.

So turn the page and meet the Master Puzzle. If the spirit is willing, solve what you can on your own, filling in what you can, then read the stories behind the challenge. Or better yet, skim the clues on show and see if you feel that dangerous tingle in the mind, the same one I felt as a kid, looking for a way in. *Cockney chaos? Swinger's bar?* What the hell is going on? Here's your chance to find out.

If you've never solved a cryptic crossword before, then make this your first. Or if this coming puzzle is number 10,000 in your life – give or take – then I will make your 10,001st memorable.

MASTER PUZZLE

MASTER PUZZLE CLUES

Across

1 Women's mag covers one Italian painter (6)

4 Press disrupt opening about Russian writer (8)

10 Central period in time-spread one spent! (7)

11 Almost completed month hosting upstart libertine (3,4)

12 Disorientated, guided east of tall grass zone one slashed (10)

13 Pizza centre behind which French grill? (4)

15 Snub regressive outcast (5)

16 Ignorance spoilt nice scene (9)

18 Seafood nibble causing pains for Spooner (4,5)

22 Nebraskan City Circle gives old lady a laugh (5)

24 Decrease anaemia remedy? (4)

25 Discourteous shift is dispatched, subcontracted (10)

28 Swinger's bar for partner pickups? (7)

29 A weir worker set ... (7)

30 ... Twister for openers? (8)

31 Creepy film absorbed in autopsy chopping (6)

Down

1 As mentioned, weather to get hotter? (5)

2 Sucker pens article for website guide (4,3)

3 M _ _ E (4,2,4)

5 Expose Russ, Ned, Hector (7)

6 After boomers it regularly goes next! (3–1)

7 Pacific islander immune to revolution (7)

8 Nation hunting craft in Italian canal, say (9)

9 Giant flower shop online (6)

14 Enhanced means to focus on scatterbrain locus (10)

15 Soundly ushered back and docketed (9)

17 Partial set closer?! (2.)

19 Cockney chaos going to stir green (7)

20 New 24-Across-coated pickup yet to be delivered (2,5)

21 Koran avidly studied by Arab holy leaders here! (6)

23 Early curve superb on cheerleader (7)

26 Outlaw fled outlaw to repeat (5)

27 Dope doubled his $500 in seven days (4)

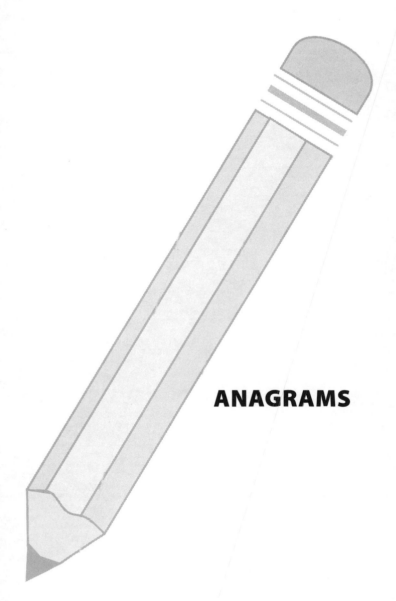

ANAGRAMS

CHAPTER 1

Expose Russ, Ned, Hector (7)

Last year a nephew tugged my sleeve at a barbecue and asked, 'What is God?'

I took a deep breath, stalling for time, wondering how agnostic I felt that week. In the end I dished out some sloppy view of the cosmos only for Simon to interrupt. 'Wrong,' he said. 'It's a mixed-up dog.'

A bright kid, Simon loves *SpongeBob* and *Doctor Who* – but he's yet to discover the pleasure of cryptic crosswords. (I'll give him time – he's nine.) My point being, most of us nurse a knack of juggling language. The day we misspell RECEIVE on paper, switching the middle vowels, or call someone Amy instead of May, or gaze at a STOP sign and see words like POTS or POST – we know how anagrams work. We order and disorder by nature. To see the message ELVIS LIVES scribbled on the subway wall is to get the verbal joke.

To prove the instinct, try reading this: *Tnrinug rdnaom ltteers itno amgnraas ceoms eislay buaesce haunms nluralaty ajusdt cohas itno oderr.* (Or said more plainly: *Turning random letters into anagrams comes easily because humans naturally adjust chaos into order.*) Even if you didn't pounce straight away, I'm sure you grasped plenty. The brain is trained to do so.

Bart Simpson's brain included. Stuck at ten years old, Bart spotted the mix-up potential of The Rusty Barnacle's menu.

Lethally the letters were magnetised, allowing the brat to switch the words with ease. Thanks to one quick shuffle COD PLATTER turned into COLD PET RAT.

Aged nine, I wasn't any better. My dad was an old sea captain who thought our home needed a better communication system. So he put a batch of fluorescent letters on the family fridge, a means for all of us to leave messages or make shopping lists. Imagine his rage when he saw BREAD MILK EGGS turn into guff like MILD GEEK BRAGS or KGB RAIDS ME LEG.

Even now I can't pass a MOBIL sign without LIMBO looming in my head, or pour a glass of PEPSI and not think PIPES. Crazy, I know. A benign affliction in many ways, and one I failed to stifle when dating in my early twenties.

Tragically, her name was Melissa, a psychiatric nurse from Gordon in Sydney's north. She may have laughed, driving to the restaurant, when I said her suburb held the word DRONGO. Perhaps she risked a smile when I noted her birth name could be rendered into AIMLESS. Yet by the time we'd passed a mattress showroom called Capt'n Snooze, and I somehow felt the urge to report that SNOOZE is a blend of OZONES, we both sensed the night to be in trouble. If her grimace wasn't a clue, then the moment I caught her taking case-notes under the table certainly was.

Anyhow, most people, if not Melissa, have the anagram knack. The reflex is latent in our system. And that makes it time to meet three boys called Russ, Ned and Hector: our first clue of the Master Puzzle.

As you've suspected, we're talking anagrams – the oldest type of cryptic clue, and perhaps the most familiar to newcomers. Back in the late 1920s, when cryptic crosswords first emerged in Britain, the anagram was the original trick in the setter's bag. Leonard Dawe, the science teacher who scored the maiden crossword gig in the *Daily Telegraph* in 1928, chose a blend of plain vocab and trivia for his clues. *Incursion*, say, at 13-Across, was RAID. *Visionaries* led to SEERS. *A river in France?* LOIRE. Drawing a steady audience, the puzzle carried a touch of Greek myths and Oliver Cromwell, plus a smattering of new concepts in XRAYS and TNT. But no anagrams. Not yet.

That tack was taken three years later, in league with several other papers across the land, when suddenly Dawe and other setters ignored the obvious definition of a word like OVERLAP, opting instead for *A plover (anag.) (7)*.

Gradually a game was hatched. While the people of America – where the crossword puzzle began in 1913 – still wrangled with clinical synonyms, reading a clue like 'glut' to help reveal SURFEIT, the Brits had other ideas. Dawe, in fact, clued the same word as *Fur ties (anag.)*. Fittingly, in the same puzzle on 7 May 1928, the science teacher added one more anagram clue: *Cheer it (anag.)*, namely HERETIC, as that is how the whole cryptic deviation must have seemed to the US purist.

We'll be talking more about the American Revolution (and British Evolution) of crosswords in time to come, but for now, it's important to see how anagrams and cryptic puzzles go hand in hand. Soon every British offering was marbled with anagram clusters, with no other defining element aside from an order to rearrange.

Yet every good thing has its day, and soon the solving public required a bit more subtlety. Anyone can see that PLUM is a mix of LUMP, so what real joy is lurking in such a pallid morsel as *Lump (anag.)*? Answer – not much. Leonard Dawe and Co could no more depend on the bald and the blatant to satisfy their solvers. Instead compilers had to *disguise* their anagram clues, which leads us back to Russ, Ned and Hector.

For many readers this book's first clue – *Expose Russ,*

Ned, Hector – will represent their first cryptic clue, full stop. In which case, to avoid too many false trails, let's take a step sideways and see how cryptic clues in general are put together.

RUMBA IN BURMA – quick versus cryptic clues

My two pinup poets as a teen were T. S. Eliot and W. H. Auden, those two enigmatic men with initials for names. The first, I knew, was an anagram of TOILETS, the second, I didn't realise, was a crossword nut.

One day, arguing with a pal across the Atlantic, Auden said that despite cryptics seeming more complex than their US cousins, they also happen to be more precise. In other words, while straight clues are more straightforward, cryptic clues can diminish any doubts about the eventual answer. The best way to illustrate the point is to go dancing …

Imagine 1-Across in an orthodox puzzle reads *'Style of dance'*. Sounds easy, but there are dances galore. In the 1960s, for example, the floor was busy with the Watusi, the Yuletide Jerk and the Popeye Waddle. So where does that leave us? Letter count will throw more light on the subject. In this case, our missing dance has five letters, allowing us to cancel the camel walk, the stereo freeze and the doctor's boogie. But then we're stuck in limbo. Wait, is LIMBO the answer? What about WALTZ? POLKA? STOMP? RUMBA? The choices stack up.

Next step – check the grid. Do we have any cross-letters in our imagined crossword – other answers crossing our mystery dance? Let's say no. The grid is empty, with 1-Across awaiting our guesswork.

Fine, let's imagine the dance we need is WALTZ. If that hunch is right, then 3-Down (in a lattice-like grid) must begin with Z, the last letter of WALTZ. And if that's not likely, then

WALTZ must be wrong. (These are the theories you test to limit your answer pool.) So let's try WALTZ: how does 3-Down read, our supposed Z-answer? Let's imagine this next clue reads *African nation (6)*.

Yay. This must be ZAMBIA. So now you enter both answers – WALTZ across and ZAMBIA down – convinced you're on the right track. But hang on. Say the correct dance is SWING, meaning the G works just as well for GAMBIA. Or why can't RUMBA bring ANGOLA into play? Or POLKA and SALSA do the same thing? And if CAPER is kosher as a dance, then RWANDA is up for the rumble too. Suddenly you're doing the Hippy Hippy Shake in a minefield, the words of Auden ringing true.

Despite their name, quick clues often ask for slow and cautious responses. Unless a clue is dead specific, like *young cat* for KITTEN or *Turkish hat* for FEZ, then a solver can never be sold on a single answer. Compare this to a cryptic's generosity, with each clue carrying two elements. Different schools call them different names, but in this book we'll know them as the definition and the wordplay.

Definition, of course, speaks for itself. *Magic stick (4)* is WAND. Orthodox puzzles give you nothing else. A cryptic clue on the other hand does the solver two favours, providing both a definition of your answer and a little word-game to help get you there. The trick is telling the two apart. So let's get back to that mystery dance, and check out these two cryptic clues:

Dance revolutionised Burma (5)
Burma-style dance (5)

As we know, *dance* in both clues is the definition. This leaves us with *Burma* in either case, plus a third word in the shape of *style* or *revolutionised*.

Notice anything in common with these last two? Think

about *style*, the verb. The word means to shape, to make over, in the same way revolutionise means to shake up, or change. Both are labelled anagram signposts in the crossword trade, sometimes called anaginds (or anagram indicators), but I prefer signposts. They're telling you to agitate the adjacent set of letters, in this case BURMA, to reach your answer.

Signposts are vital in anagram clues. A setter needs to plant a word suggesting upheaval or renovation, a word like stir or shock. Seasoned solvers look for these indicators on impulse, mixing the adjacent clues to satisfy the definition. Which here we know is *dance*.

Mind you, *dance* can also be a signpost, as can any word embodying motion, making both sample clues a bit more slippery.

Trickier still, both the likely signposts (*revolutionised* and *style*) occupy the clues' midpoints. Placed there, a solver has to decide which end needs mixing to give up the answer. Ten times easier if the signpost opens or finishes a clue, confining the definition to the opposite end. Let's take a second look at both examples.

In the first example – *Dance revolutionised Burma* – you know the middle word is the signpost as *revolutionised* is too long to be the fodder (or letters to scramble). So your eye then falls on *Burma* as the batch to 'revolt', giving you a kind of *dance* …

In sample 2 – *Burma-style dance* – the chances of *style* holding a word that means *Burma* are next to zero. Besides, what else can *Burma* mean? It's a country, right? Aside from being the old name of Myanmar, what more can be said, word-wise? Making *style* your probable signpost, with *dance* the definition.

And bang, out jumps RUMBA. The jig is up.

Bear that in mind as we go. As opaque as a cryptic clue may seem at first, the opposite can apply. Where a quick setter gives cold definitions, the darker cousin offers two roads to reach the one destination.

As you solve more clues over time, you'll separate the two key elements with greater confidence, recognising where the division falls. Jonathan Crowther, a long-time setter for *The Observer* in the UK, known to most of his fans as Azed, put it best. 'A good cryptic clue', he wrote, 'contains three elements:

a precise definition;
a fair subsidiary indication [or wordplay];
nothing else.'

In other words, every word counts. In the case of anagrams, you'll be facing a definition, plus a signpost and the fodder (which adds up to the wordplay). Though signposts, as you've gathered, may be tricky to isolate. Already in this section we've had a range of words standing in for signal duty: style, stir, dance. What next, you ask. Red, white and blue?

Well, *black and blue* could do the job, despite being a phrase, since those three words capture the sense of being battered. But I hear your uncertainty. Let's open the way to signposts.

SIGN HERE – anagram signposts and surface sense

Tangle
Snarl
Brew
Jolt

If Paul Simon knew 50 ways to leave his lover, the cryptic compiler knows 500 ways to mislead his solver.

Wreck
Wrench
Crazy
Kinky

The crunch is change. Even *crunch* is cool – or crush, or bash. As long as the word embodies an altered state. Yet change – the notion – is fickle in its own right. Words like odd or outlandish can also suggest a deviation. Thus a clue like *Exotic Burma dance* is a valid route to RUMBA.

Compatibility is the key. Setters look for signposts that chime with the other parts. Drafting a clue for CHAIN-SMOKER, say, a phrase that holds HEROIN and SMACK, I may retain the clue's druggy flavour this way:

Smack, heroin, crack, tobacco addict (5–6)

Then again, in composing a food-related clue, I might turn to kitchen words to act as that simpatico signpost. ORANGE, say, is a blend of GEAR ON, making one possible clue:

Fruit gear on bananas (6)

That's the game as setter or solver – to hide or find the signpost. If we stay in the pantry, the options are ample. If *bananas* doesn't work, what about nuts or fruitcake? (You look for terms that serve two masters – the clue's surface sense and the wordplay recipe.)

Cocktail is another option. Or *crackers*. Now we're cooking. Or maybe even *cook* can save the day – a verb meaning to prepare, or corrupt, as in cooking the books. To the same list you can add *stew* or *stir* or *fry* or most chef actions. (Think dice, beat, whip.) Solvers must be alert to that kind of camouflage. Take this gem, crafted by Simon Martin, alias Enigma of the *Independent*:

Response to Warne's spin (6)

A breeze once you know how the elements click, but what a fiendish means of hiding the answer, ANSWER. Much like a leg spinner, compilers rely on subtle variations and artful deception, and this clue displays both: a low-key signpost beside low-key fodder, the whole combining to create a perfect delivery.

For RUMBA, I'd dabbled with other signposts. If BURMA, we agree, is the craftiest anagram (better than UM, BRA, or the dubious MR AUB), then how best to couch the clue? What's the least visible signpost? Perhaps a word like *rock* could fit – a music genre as well as a word meaning sway. Opening the way for:

Burma rock dance (5)

Another idea is *club,* a word that can sidle up to *dance* in its noun guise, as well as carrying its own nasty impact when treated as a verb. Giving rise to:

Burma Club dance (5)

Notice the capital C, a thicker smokescreen for the solver to see through, and not unfair in the grander etiquette of crosswords. Of course a neater RUMBA clue would read:

Burma dance club (5)

But that's a no-no. Can you see why? Because *dance,* your definition, is perched *between* the signpost and what needs clubbing. Signpost and fodder must always be side by side.

By contrast, *Dance in Burma Club* can pass muster as an anagram clue, but why use four words when three do just as well? The answer hinges on surface sense, or how smoothly the clue reads on the page, the same brand of elegance Shane Warne's clue achieves. At the drawing board I tested other maybes:

Improper Burma dance
Dance in Burma resort
Steps around Burma

Different house styles (we're talking papers now, not music) have a bias towards different signposts. One editor may be happy with 'slip' as an indicator to mix, while another might deem slip too sloppy. So what about 'wrong'? Is that all right? Or 'tight' – as in drunk? Too old-fashioned? Surely 'fashioned' is legit, and so on. That's how the arguments ricochet. As for ricochet – that's usable in my book. But now, let's move on from Burma and meet our three amigos occupying 5-Down.

RUSS, NED, HECTOR – Trojan horses and binary thinking

PETER and PAUL lie in PERPETUAL. Just as a tailored MACKINTOSH holds NICK and THOMAS. Or PAEDIATRICIAN nurses twin girls, ENID and PATRICIA. This name-game leads us back to RUSS and NED.

Wait, what happened to Hector? Let me tell you a quick story.

Troy is famous for many reasons, from Achilles' heel to Brad Pitt's six-pack. But the story's clearest image is the wooden horse, the perfect metaphor for a cryptic clue. Just because the creature stands like a horse, and looks like a horse, and casts a horse-like shadow, this doesn't mean it neighs.

Inside the belly, of course, was where the strife began. For the Trojans at least. The gift was a ruse, as Achilles and his mates hopped out of the belly and marauded the city. Yet Hector bravely resisted the Greeks, endowing his name to the English language as a word meaning to bluster, bully or badger. Some legacy, you may think, but a signpost ready-made for cryptic clues.

Some names – of both boys and girls – can deputise well as signposts. *Harry* is a regular starter, the name meaning to pester or ravage. *Pat* is possible, while *Dotty* is a tad dated. *Jimmy* is a candidate, thinking crowbars. *Dicky? Eddy?*

Let's look at the clue one more time: *Expose Russ, Ned, Hector (7)*

If you haven't solved the clue already, you should be giving roles to each word and name. Hector is a classic signpost in both senses, that capital H akin to the big-C Club back in Burma, a curveball to catch you off guard. Giving weight to the signpost theory is the nearby fodder of RUSSNED. That's right, no longer two boys but a clump of seven letters, the tally matching the answer you're after.

Here's a tip: ignore the clue's imagery. No matter how smooth the surface sense, look for the deeper strategy. The key to cracking cryptic crosswords is to think on two levels, to look past what the words evoke and decide what roles they play.

So get hectoring. Bully RUSS and NED and see if you can make a seven-letter word. A word meaning what? Where's the definition? Simple – what word is left?

Expose is a word with several meanings. One relates to risk, where the wooden horse exposed the vulnerability of Troy. Then there's photography, to 'render to the light'. Or a scandal – to wheel a dirty secret into view. Each is a variation of the word's prime meaning, that is to lie bare, to peel away, just as you expose this clue.

Suddenly the wordplay is naked. As the chapter creeps to a close, can you hector RUSSNED into a word for strip? Try synonyms first – DISROBE? UNCOVER? If no joy there, try swirling the cluster. Juggle the boys in the margin. Put them in alphabetical order: DENRSSU. Throw them backwards: DENSSUR. Suddenly NED and RUSS become UNDRESS and the maiden answer is plain for all to see.

RECIPE PRECIS: ANAGRAMS

Anagram wordplay relies on two key elements, the signpost and the fodder. The signpost is any word suggesting renewal, change or error, while the fodder is the adjacent swag of letters in need of swirling. On seeing a possible signpost, check for possible fodder, which must lie adjacent. Words like strange, new, off or out are often used, but the signpost candidates below will help you to see the range of possibilities.

adapt, bizarre, cook, dance, errant, fashion, ground, hack, in a mess, jar, kinky, lousy, modified, novel, odd, perhaps, queasy, resort, sort, terrible, upset, violent, wind, zany

QUIZLING 1.1

Can you double a letter in ASTOUNDING and mix the new eleven to make a word meaning astounding?

QUIZLING 1.2

What three countries, all five letters long, can be separately rearranged into three words that rhyme with each other?

QUIZLING 1.3

If two words for trick – CON and DUPE – lie in POUNCED, can you pounce on the kindred pairs lurking in DUSTMAN, MARTINET and TREATISES? Every letter is used once only.

CHAPTER 2

Ignorance spoilt nice scene (9)

One night, with nothing on TV, my brother and I staged a seance. The deal was simple. We pinched a wine glass from the special cupboard and laid out the Scrabble tiles, A to Z, around the edges of the rumpus-room table. As the elder, aged ten, I played high priest. Looking to the ceiling I asked any spirits in the room to hop inside the glass. We waited a while, allowing the spirits to get comfy, and then gingerly turned the glass over, put our fingertips on the base, and started asking questions about our future. *What would we be? Who will we marry?* Nothing happened. The glass sat inert. We sat inert, and then we gave up. Maybe tried Cluedo instead. But somehow the stunt opened my eyes to the idea that maybe, just maybe, letters held the answers to the great unknown. Besides, why would Rupert, my dead uncle, have any inkling of tomorrow? How would my late Aunt Agnes single out my bride from the masses? Stuff ghosts. Maybe anagrams held the key.

As kooky as the notion sounded, it wasn't original. ONE WORD has always promised a NEW DOOR in the minds of men. History reveals a great procession of loons prepared to invest heavily in jumbled letters and what they murmur.

Alexander the Great, no less, was a sucker for this type of prophecy. One night, back in 332 BC, while squeezing the lifeblood out of Tyre, the general dreamt of a satyr, one of those half-goat characters who rate poorly as portents go. Troubled, the Great One summoned his soothsayers, asking them to interpret this strange vision. The men responded by writing the word 'satyr' in the sand. They mixed things around until they found a version to lull their boss. In Greek, apparently, when SATYR is allowed to stray, you end up with 'Tyre is thine'. So Alexander pounced, and the rest of course is ancient history.

In similar fashion, the entourage of Louis XIII was said to have included a Royal Anagrammist named Thomas Billon, a courtier vested with finding omens in shuffled letters. Across the Channel, the Brits were likewise hooked. When Mary Queen of Scots had her head removed in 1587, a nameless pundit turned the monarch's full Latin title – *Maria Steuarda Scotorum Regina* – into her destiny: *Trusa vi regnis morte amara cado*. ('Thrust by force from my kingdom I fall by a foul death.')

The king to replace Mary was James I, her son, whose name was treated more gently by the Mix Masters of the day. JAMES STUART, as the pundits were quick to report, was truly A JUST MASTER.

Such letter-fixation was spoofed by Jonathan Swift. The Irish writer could spot human folly from a hundred paces. In *Gulliver's Travels*, Swift had his hero call on Tribnia, a kingdom of nincompoops besotted by letter-fiddling. Look twice at TRIBNIA and you'll soon realise the actual kingdom Swift was ridiculing.

With a madness to match, so-called scholars sift the works of Nostradamus. The mystic wrote during the plague years of the 1550s, churning out more than 1000 quatrains. Centuries on, devotees examine the words for deeper meaning, resorting to all kinds of manipulation. PAU, NAY and OLORON, for instance, are three towns mentioned in Quatrain VIII-1, which fans have wangled to spell NAPAULON ROY, alias Napoleon the King. An even longer bow is drawn in the case of Quatrain IX-44. This verse describes a menace named RAYPOZ who 'will exterminate all opposition'. Surely this is Hitler, claim the scholars. The felling of Europe, the seizure of Poland, the death camps … With only one problem: how to change RAYPOZ into HITLER? Easy. You switch the P with an N, then mix the new six and you get NAZROY, King of the Nazis.

This kind of hokum inspired Francis Heaney, one of America's finest anagrammists, to lampoon such verse-tweaking. Early in 2009, the crossword-maker was asked by the History Channel to see if his mixing skills could unmask the mystery figure of Mabus, an agent of wide destruction who's found in Quatrain II-62. Here's the verse in its English translation:

Mabus then will soon die, there will come
Of people and beasts a horrible rout:
Then suddenly one vergeance,
Hundred, hand, thirst, hunger when the comet will run.

Nostradamus junkies had already claimed this mysterious MABUS to be SADDAM, once you restyle the B into two Ds, and swap a vowel for good measure, but Heaney went one better, using the entire quatrain to create his version of the truth:

When Obama one-ups old McCain in two-thousand-eight
    run,
We'll see well-heeled Enron-lovers defend thee,
Antichrist, repellent netherworld deity –
Bush? No … Rush Limbaugh!

Whatever our future holds, the weight of the unknown is clearly too great for twenty-six letters to carry. DIVINATION, we should remember, is a blend of DO IT IN VAIN, just as the opaque prophet MICHEL DE NOSTREDAME (the real name of Nostradamus) can be rearranged into RANDOM ITEMS LEECHED. Our cue to focus on the next anagram clue, 16-Across in the Master Puzzle.

SCRAMBLED SCIENCE – mixing methods and false anagrams

The actor ROBERT REDFORD hides RED BORDER FORT in his name. Given the same treatment, UNIVERSAL PICTURES converts into A TURNIP CURSES ELVIS. Both anagrams feature in the credits of the movie *Sneakers*, a 1992 tech-thriller with a strong emphasis on decrypting. As for why the studio opted for such *lame* anagrams, I'm at a loss to explain. Mind you, ROBERT REDFORD is a tough nut to crack, with those four Rs to handle. Then again, UNIVERSAL PICTURES holds RECLUSIVE PURITANS, which capably describes the geeky gang of code-busters that includes Mr Redford.

The more you indulge in letter-switching, the more you come to appreciate the difference between sleek and clunky. Francis Heaney's mock prophecy, for example, is pure grace, while finding SADDAM in MABUS is not just oafish, but wrong.

Imagine letters as Lego blocks, and therefore a word as being shapes created by those blocks. Sleek anagrams will change the original shapes into new and elegant forms. The best suggest their source by owning a related shape or style, all the more gracious once you consider that the two objects share the same pieces. Consider THE EYES – THEY SEE, or, ENDEARMENT being TENDER NAME. But when you force the formula, bending a word into ludicrous shapes, the anagram art is diminished. MR AUB, say, is a good example of a poor anagram.

The secret to mixing is being awake to the potential of the letters at your fingertips. And just like playing Lego, you're always wise to scatter the blocks in order to see what new shapes lurk in the rubble.

Martin Bishop, the character played by Redford in *Sneakers*, relies on a Scrabble box to crack anagrams. In the film he picks out the relevant tiles and sprawls them on the table.

John Graham, known to most British solvers as Araucaria, relies on the same method, strewing the key letters at his elbow to see what new structure he can make.

Others swear by the benefits of a circle. This tribe will arrange the letters into a wheel and start looking for telltale clusters such as IVE or NCE, hoping the rest will jump out.

Just as many puzzle fans depend on the dash method, mapping the mystery word in a series of blanks and confirmed letters. Once that sequence is sketched, the solver will place her remaining letters into a clump above the dashes, and ponder.

'Whatever works' is the motto. Notably every technique (the pieces, the wheel, the clump, the dashes) involves a strewing of the source-phrase, just as kids rake Lego blocks to see what they have in free-form.

But to get back to crosswords, note that the challenge lies at two levels. First you need to spot the fodder (the letters to mix) and, second, have a rough idea of what the outcome will mean. Not so simple with the current clue we're facing:

Ignorance spoilt nice scene (9)

After dealing with signposts, you should be wary of the role that *spoilt* is playing here. The word looks like a possible signal to jumble, but jumble what? That's the question, since the letter clusters on either side tally up to nine, the same count as your answer.

Sometimes this dilemma – wondering which end is your fodder – suggests a false anagram. You're not sure which clump is yours to stir and which part's the definition.

Perhaps the time is right to make a confession. As compilers, we can take pleasure in planting false anagrams, luring solvers to mix the wrong bunch of letters. For example, a false anagram of MONASTERY could be HOLY PLACE, which could well tempt a solver into treating the phrase as fodder rather than the answer's definition.

The other step in the false-anagram strategy, from a setter's point of view, is ensuring the signpost stands between the other two elements, so causing confusion about which way to look. I fell for this trick myself a few years back, working in a Sydney pub. The clue came from the *Sydney Morning Herald* and seemed simple at first glance:

Serene hold crumpled Tyrol pants (10)

Piece of cake, I thought. You mix TYROLPANTS to render a word meaning *serene hold*. With that conviction I spent a lunch break barking up the wrong tree, musing the likes of PLATYSTORN and TROYPLANTS and wondering why nothing clicked.

Back behind the bar, the light bulb flickered. What does *serene hold* mean anyway? Damn it. All the while I'd been crumpling the wrong ten letters. *Tyrol pants* was the definition, not the fodder. Instead of treating *serene hold* as a legit phrase, I should have seen SERENEHOLD as a cluster. On the spot I made a pair of LEDERHOSEN before you could say 'Yodel-lay-hee-hoo'.

Careful then of the current clue – *Ignorance spoilt nice scene.* You have to decide whether the answer is a synonym of *ignorance* (meaning we mix NICESCENE), or vice versa, where *nice scene* hides in twisted IGNORANCE.

Ask yourself: which is more likely? Are we seeking *ignorance* or a *nice scene*? Which makes more sense as a definition? The odds favour *ignorance*, a word in any thesaurus. Compare that to *nice scene*, which may hint at PANORAMA or ARCADIA or even RIVIERA (if you look at 'nice' twice), but which cluster is the surer bet?

Time to fetch the Scrabble tiles. Or make a wheel. Map the dashes. Whichever method alerts your brain. NICESCENE. Start looking for patterns. Importantly, *ignorance*, your definition, is a noun, ending in NCE, the same trio lying in the fodder. Is SENICENCE a word? CENISENCE?

Of course, you can always solve this clue from the other direction. Do you know a nine-letter word for *ignorance*? There's STUPIDITY, I suppose. And DISREGARD. Yet neither sits in NICESCENE, so you swirl on.

That's when SCIENCE emerges. You may recall your early lab classes, the teacher saying that science stems from the Latin for knowledge, and knowledge of course is the flipside of ignorance. Remove SCIENCE from NICESCENE and you have EN left over. ENSCIENCE? NESCIENCE?

I'm thinking that we've just solved our second clue. The beauty of cryptics is that almost every clue gives you the chance to *confirm* your answer. NESCIENCE means not-knowledge in its barest form, a little like those two numbskull boys and their wine glass. But seriously, put up your hand if you knew the word nescience.

NESCIENCE IS BLISS – the Piñata Principle and rare words

Without betraying too much, I can tell you that NESCIENCE is the most obscure answer in the Master Puzzle. Other entries will be far more familiar, with the possible exception of one Italian.

As a puzzle-maker you're expected to play at either end of the pool, wading in the shallows of pop culture and plunging into the erudite. Neither end is 'better' than the other, yet both are important. For me the perfect puzzle swoops between highbrow and lowbrow, Dvořák and Tupac, with the occasional NESCIENCE to tease the vocab.

Obviously the word 'nescience' is relatively unfamiliar, and hence my choice of the anagram recipe. Veteran setters develop a hunch for knowing when any answer is a challenge to grasp, and so go a little softer in the clue, with anagrams the kindest option of all.

Trust me, I toyed with some doozies before publication. Did you know NESCIENCE, say, combines six compass points and three Roman numerals? That aspect alone could invite a fiendish clue, but I resisted. Why? The answer is the Piñata Principle.

Crossword-making has been described as 'the art of losing gracefully'. In other words, everything a setter makes needs to be *unmade*. Those Lego blocks again. Or, to use the piñata metaphor, consider that a crossword is useless if it doesn't crack open. Forget the frills, the garish paint: if that paper belly refuses to spill its treasure then soon the good people at your party will stop taking a swing.

Roger Squires, the most prolific crossword-maker on the planet (with more than 64,000 puzzles published in more than 470 papers and magazines), regularly applies the Piñata Principle. Known to many as Rufus in the *Guardian*, Squires must have known that ORMOLU lies beyond most vocabs, and so opted for an anagram:

Rum loo embellished with gilt decoration (6)

Scarcely the sleekest of his million clues, but fair. The signpost is clear, the fodder obvious, leaving the last part ('with gilt decoration') as the definition. One hefty clout and the clue bursts open.

Rare words matter in crosswords – solving or setting, quick or cryptic. Just because recondite (which means obscure) is obscure in its own right, this shouldn't jeopardise the word's selection. One reason people turn to crosswords is to have their vocabs exercised, excited, extended. Thanks to Araucaria I've annexed my vocab with such oddities as zori, otary and chasseur. (You've just met, in order, a Japanese sandal, an eared seal and an agile soldier.) Not that every puzzle should teem with archaisms. But now and then, adding a quaint specimen to the usual parade is part of the puzzler's brief.

A good thing, too, if you listen to the makers of the *Collins English Dictionary*. For every new edition, lexicographers decide which words will join the book and which older residents have grown obsolete. In comes Google, and out goes oomancy (divination by eggs). Words resemble muscles; they wither without use.

So in stepped HarperCollins, creating the Save The Last Word Project. For the new edition scheduled for 2010 there was a list of twenty words that were destined to be culled. Among the endangered species were malison (a curse), agrestic (uncouth) and nitid (bright). Writers and celebs were approached to do a stint of verbal philanthropy. Choose a word and foster it. Humorist Stephen Fry was thrilled to adopt fubsy (short and stout), while poet Andrew Motion fell in love with skirr (a whirring of bird wings in flight).

Use it or lose it was the message, making the adoption scheme a challenge of sorts. If any of the chosen words failed to appear across six separate sources, from press to print, online or on TV, before a set deadline, then euthanasia was applied.

When it comes to sustaining rare words, crosswords perform a kindred duty. In recent years I've supplied oxygen to ABSQUATULATE (decamp) and DEHISCE (to burst open), but in the end the people will decide what stays and what goes. Here in the Master Puzzle I've thrown a lifeline to NESCIENCE, the long-lost cousin of ignorance. Whether that's enough to ensure the word's survival, I don't know.

QUIZLING 2.1

What's the *lazy way* of converting these four words into anagrams?

ELBOW   GOTHS   RIFTS   TAPED

QUIZLING 2.2

SEW and RIP sit in WIPERS. Using every letter once only, can you scramble each word (and brand) below to make a pair of opposites in each case?

ALFRESCO   DYNAMITED   THEOLOGIST   STOLICHNAYA

QUIZLING 2.3

What iconic mode of transport is 'parked' in the anagram of VERY COSTLY OLD ROAD MACHINES?

CHAPTER 3

Enhanced means to focus on scatterbrain locus (10)

Ted Validas is an old friend of mine. Like me, he crafts puzzles for the daily press. Or make that crafted – past tense. The guy disappeared in mysterious circumstances some twenty years ago, never to be seen again.

Back when I knew him, Ted made a variety puzzle, with anagrams a common ingredient. Breezy stuff, like mixing common words to find well-known authors – RENEGE for Greene or CLEARER for Le Carré. Should a solver write to him to extend the list, adding STUPOR for Proust, say, or VIOLATER for Voltaire, Ted would write back in good spirit, never missing a beat, always signing off his letter in the same way: *Yours verbally, Ted Validas.*

Now and then, when Ted made a botch of a piece of trivia, calling Daleks robots instead of armour-clad mutants from the planet Skaro, for example, or getting confused between Celtic and Gaelic, then the puzzler would take the flak. He'd vow to get it right next time. *Yours verbally, Ted Validas.*

But after six years of correspondence, he vanished. His puzzles kept appearing in the paper, people kept writing in, but the name Validas fell off the radar. If people tried looking up his name in the directory or calling the switch at the *Herald* to seek an extension: nothing. The man was a ghost, his ongoing puzzles the only trace that he ever existed.

So where'd he go? The answer remains a riddle. One solver sent a Christmas card to the *Herald* in 1991, thanking Ted for twelve months of brain-bending, but the envelope was left to moulder in the mailroom, addressee unknown. Other readers sent mail to nitpick or cajole, offer other ideas, but nothing lured Ted from the void. Instead they received the usual replies, using the same font, the same tone, but this time round the name at the bottom was another character called David Astle, whoever he was.

In case you haven't twigged, you can call off the dogs. There's no need to drag the harbour. Cancel the helicopter. Ted Validas and David Astle are the same animal. Back in 1985, when I first started making Wordwit, a variety word puzzle, I thought it wise to invent an alias. Maybe it was nerves, or modesty – or a fundamental dread that the format would fall on its face.

Thankfully, it didn't. Week by week, learning on the job, I kept tending the small box near the back of Section One, and the feedback kept flowing. Wordwit thrived. It ran birthday competitions and readers' puzzles, played with headlines and punchlines, acronyms and anagrams: the whole verbal toy box, drawing a loyal following as the years rolled on.

Location helped. The feature sat below the daily crossword, which I'd also begun to make around the same era. Stuck on a certain clue, you could give Wordwit a look, or vice versa. The puzzles were natural companions. Now in its twenty-sixth year, Wordwit continues as a Section One diversion, and I continue to make it.

Or Ted Validas did, that first stretch. A daft name in hindsight, but Delta Davis sounded porno, while Levi Saddat had the whiff of zealot. Writers of course have a long tradition of resorting to pen names, with anagrams a common disguise. Theodor Seuss Geisel, best known as Dr Seuss, also plied his trade as Theo LeSieg. Another American, Edward Gorey, wrote a series of macabre books for kids under the manifold egos of Ogdred Weary, Wardore Edgy and Mrs Regera Dowdy.

Then there's Gwen Harwood, the Tasmanian poet who longed to break the male monopoly of published poets in *The Bulletin* magazine back in the 1970s. So Gwen hatched a plan. Before too long the asexual W. W. Hagendoor found great success as a contributor. Though perhaps the most surprising member of this curious club is an inventor.

Alexander Graham Bell felt cursed by celebrity. As father of the telephone, his name was recognised before he arrived, all but eclipsing the person attached to it. Fine if you want the VIP treatment but not so hot if you want to write a paper on lizards.

That's right. When not playing with sound waves, the Scot was looking under rocks. In later years Bell wrote an article on reptiles, but knew that if he submitted his story to *National Geographic* under his given name, then (a) his piece may well be accepted on the strength of his fame alone, or (b) a thousand readers will see the byline and say, 'Hey, what's this talkie-machine chappie doing cavorting with iguanas?'

Hence Bell muddled his last two names to invent a no-name naturalist, his magazine piece running in 1907 under the title of 'Notes on the Remarkable Habits of Certain Turtles and Lizards' by H. A. Largelamb.

Meanwhile, several other writers have kneaded their own letters to coax characters into life, like the mysterious biographer called Vivian Darkbloom who haunts the pages of Vladimir Nabokov's *Lolita*. Almost restrained compared to Richard Stilgoe, the British writer who couldn't be cured from fiddling with himself. In his 1981 anthology, the *Richard Stilgoe Letters*, all thirty stories feature characters drawn from the author's name. We meet Israel Rightcod the trawler boy, Italian Olympian Ricardi Hotlegs and a choirmaster named Elgar I Chordist.

Speaking of music, we have one more side trip before grappling with the Master clue. For this yarn we return to England, home of the cryptic, where a gifted clue-monger and a famous musician shared a talent for orchestrating letters.

HENDRA VIRUS – anagram codenames and solo lyricists

Crossword-makers turn to anagrams like Catholic nuns to rosaries. Neither vocation can quit their sacred fumbling, intoning spells as they go. Consequently, when not teasing solvers with anagram clues, many setters torment their own names in order to create a pseudonym. The custom was illustrated best in the *Listener*, the one-time radio magazine that boasted possibly the most difficult cryptic of its day. Browsing back copies you'll find the works of Robin Baxter (alias Nibor), Richard Rogan (Aragon), Jack Gill (Llig) and Jeff Pearce (Caper), to name four.

Chris Brougham QC was another setter to uphold the tradition. After taking silk in 1988, Brougham spent his daytime hours navigating the byways of bankruptcy law. By night, however, the lawyer entered different corridors, dreaming up crosswords for the *Spectator*, *The Times* and, at one stage, the *Listener*, under the cover of Dumpynose. For all the smirks the alias triggered, Dumpynose was a practical solution, as BROUGHAM offers little in terms of anagrams. (Does RUMBA HOG work?) So the QC chose to jumble PSEUD-ONYM instead.

Editing crosswords for the *Wall Street Journal*, Mike Shenk faced a similar dilemma. Anagram-wise, SHENK is a tough ask, yet Mike as editor saw the wisdom of crafting a fresh byline as contributor. Hence the arrival of two mystery women, MARY-ANNE LEMOT and NATALIA SHORE. Any ideas? Suffice to say that few New Yorkers suspected Shenk had manipulated NOT MY REAL NAME and ANOTHER ALIAS.

Which leads us to Bert Danher, a Liverpudlian horn player who made scores of brilliant crosswords when not performing music. Inventive and witty, this popular compiler wowed *Guardian* solvers under the veil of Hendra. In his prime, Bert provided crosswords for the five major UK papers, with the *Guardian* joining his roster of *The Times*, the *Daily Telegraph*, the *Financial Times* and the *Independent*. All this, and blowing the French horn for the Liverpool Philharmonic. Yet perhaps the most remarkable aspect of this setter's life dates to his childhood.

Bert's mother was Ann McCartney, sister to Jim. Through the tragic death of Bert's father the two families were drawn even closer, the future puzzler spending whole stretches with the McCartneys during the Depression. If jazz wasn't blaring on the radio, then Uncle Jim was teaching Bert the art of cryptics. Not only did those ad hoc sessions nurture a stellar career, the bond they created also saw Bert become the godfather of Jim's first son, a moptop named Paul, the future Beatle.

Sharing a passion for words and music, the two cousins enjoyed a strong rapport, despite the gap of sixteen years. Arguably this lifetime affinity, or the seminal influence of Jim in both lives, helped to fashion one of the finest anagrams in music history.

Paul himself is cagey on the subject, telling reporters that the title of his 2007 album, *Memory Almost Full*, is merely a phrase borrowed from his voicemail, a metaphor for modern life, he said, but other observers favour an alternative theory. Scramble the title – MEMORY ALMOST FULL – and you'll spell FOR MY SOULMATE LLM (or Linda Louise McCartney), Paul's long-time partner and co-founder of the rock band Wings. Linda, sadly, had succumbed to breast cancer in 1998. Is the title a coincidence or a dash of anagram brilliance? The ex-Beatle's staying mum. But there's no question that verbal agility runs through the family. For evidence, turn to Paul's first-cousin-cum-godfather, a stylist known as Hendra, and you'll see the calibre of his mixology:

> *If I tail car carelessly that will be unnatural* = ARTIFICIAL
> *World Cup Team poorly dressing after shower* = TALCUM POWDER
> *Stalling in faulty air contraptions* = PROCRASTINATION
> *Saw three pigs turning aside* = STAGE WHISPER

In my book this fab four is as lyrical as anything Bert's younger cousin composed. And that's just the maestro's work in the anagram category. A tough act to follow, but the Master clue is beckoning.

FAME AT LAST – embedded signposts and Robin Lucas

Where normal people collect beer coasters or teaspoons, I prefer signposts. Not the street-corner kind, but new and sneaky means to indicate an anagram. *Rolling Stones* is one example, and *Dire Straits* another. Most folk see two English rock acts, but I'm inclined to read both bands as sly instructions to make ONSETS and ARTIST. Likewise a *mixed blessing* is GLIBNESS, while *pasta salad* is TAPAS. If the perfect signpost sits cosily beside its fodder, throwing the solver off guard, then how wonderful to find names and phrases that do the job already?

Off guard, in fact, is another good example, bearing in mind that *off* means sick or askew. So suddenly *off guard* is not just a word meaning unwary, but a cryptic pairing that leads to A DRUG. Over years, collecting these covert couples, the list began to look like this:

Off-centre = RECENT
Off-roading = ADORING
Sneak off = SNAKE
Paired off = REPAID/DIAPER

The mania persists today. I'm always on the hunt for new signposts. Like NEW, for instance, a word asking solvers to renovate the adjacent letters, thus giving up such clue tricks as *New Ager* (GEAR or RAGE), *New Orleans* (LOANERS) or *New Testament* (STATEMENT). Then there's the beauty of both elements – signpost and anagram cluster – fusing into one whole. *Newcastle*, say, can pave the way for CLEATS to be clued like so:

Newcastle climbing gear (6)

Likewise, LEDGES comes from *sledgehammer*, and SHORE from *horsewhip*. Pushing the envelope, you could also argue that *spinaches* yields CHASE (as in *spin-ACHES*), and *offensive*, ENVIES (think *off-ENSIVE*). Good old Burma, nowadays known as *Myanmar*, could betray MANY, since *mar* is a crossword-word for *spoil*.

You get the idea. Embedded signposts are fiendish, and therefore not so rife across cryptic puzzles. (We setters do show some mercy, you know.) Nor is the ploy new, as noted in a 1968 collection of *Guardian* puzzles. John Perkin, crossword editor at that time, urged solvers to be watchful of 'decidedly tricky' anagrams. He then provided two examples:

Les Miserables – or Turning of the Screw = WRETCHES
Sweet miscreant = NECTAR

Subtle and sadistic, the best clues test how far a recipe can go, while never losing sight of the Piñata Principle. Now that you're awake to embedded signposts, let's take a new look at the Master clue:

Enhanced means to focus on scatterbrain locus (10)

By itself, *scatterbrain* is a fair signpost, a word suggesting ditzy and disorganised. Then again, *scatter* also does the trick, freeing the word's other half – BRAIN – to combine with LOCUS. And bingo, you have a ten-letter cluster.

Before confirming the answer, let me tell you why I chose this clue – and answer – for the book's central puzzle. The year was 1990. The clue appearing in a November cryptic was a benign anagram:

Robin Lucas tweaked optic gizmo (10)

The answer arrived the following week. The envelope was nondescript. The opening line read 'Fame at last! I was thrilled to be an anagram in your cryptic crossword …'. My eye drifted down to the sender's name and there was the florid signature of Robin Lucas, a solver from Mudgee in New South Wales who'd almost spilt her coffee over the usual breakfast challenge. Even with a pair of BINOCULARS I couldn't have foreseen such a sweet coincidence, where one random answer happened to be the name of a reader who'd confront the same anagram. I said as much in my reply, thanking Robin for taking the time to write. And it being 1990, the last year of my professional camouflage, I ended the letter the only way I knew: *Yours verbally, Ted Validas.*

FURTIVE SIGNPOSTS

Here's a glimpse of a few more furtive signposts I've gathered over the years.

battleground (gives you tablet)
castor oil (coats – when you 'roil' CASTO)
feeding frenzy (feigned)
flesh wound (shelf)
Gordian knot (adoring)
halal butcher (Allah)
hypnotherapy (phoney)
madrigal (grail)
odd couples (close-up)
odd man out (amount)
shipwreck (hips)
shortcake mix (track shoe)
Steinlager brew (generalist)
windowpane (weapon – when you 'wind' OWPANE)

QUIZLING 3.1

Antigrams are contrary anagrams. UNITE, for instance, hides UNTIE. Can you figure out the words that inspired each antigram here?

FLUSTER
MORE TINY
NICE LOVE
REAL FUN
TRUE LADY

QUIZLING 3.2

What two Greek letters can be scrambled to spell two new Greek letters?

QUIZLING 3.3

When ants swarm the rug, a picnicker can be alarmed. To prove the point, can you mix ANTS with PICNICKER to make a hyphenated word for terrified?

CHAPTER 4

Discourteous shift is dispatched, subcontracted (10)

'O fat male,' says the comedian.

The crossword-maker frowns. 'How do you spell oh?'

'O,' says the comic and the audience erupts.

The crossword-maker gazes at the scaffolding on the ceiling. 'Is it Tom Somebody?'

The comic frowns. 'I thought you made puzzles for a living.'

'I do, but this is showbiz.'

'Show hasn't even started.'

Again the audience laughs. 'One more,' says the comedian. 'What can you do with big melons?'

'Mel Gibson,' I say, exhausted, and the audience's cheer is more Bronx than joyous. The pain is over – for everybody. The comedian stows his script. 'Seriously, fella, I thought you'd eat anagrams alive.'

On paper, I felt like saying. In private, yes. Not with spotlights on my head and pancake make-up on my face. The comedian was Paul McDermott, host of the offbeat quiz show *Good News Week*. The anagram game was his idea of a warm-up, tossing me phrases that hid celebs like Meatloaf. Thankfully, the cameras were yet to roll, as the game felt more like an ambush. As cool as VERY COOL TUNE may have read aloud, I'd never spotted COURTNEY LOVE while baking under a 500-watt globe.

To be honest, I was on the show to plug a novel, not cross-words. But flogging fiction can be a hard sell, so the publicist played the crossword card, sneaking me sideways into the *Good News* gig, using the ruse of Meet the Puzzle-maker to smuggle the novel into the conversation.

The very reason I should have seen the ambush coming. Instead of scoffing sandwiches in the green room I might have been wiser playing Scrabble, priming the reflexes, but there's a limit to switching letters under pressure. Next time you visit the circus, don't expect to see Alphonse the Amazing Anagrammer on the bill. People struggle to convert spoken words into anagrams, even those people who make crosswords for a living.

The job is made for pen and paper. If I ask you to find a singer in ONLINE GUY, I'm sure you'd uncover NEIL YOUNG in good time. It's a simpler task. All the bits are there. Much tougher if you *hear* the phrase I'M A JERK BUT LISTEN and try to grope for JUSTIN TIMBERLAKE. Nothing compares to seeing the letters on the page, as well as knowing what shape the outcome might take.

This last advantage is the crossword luxury. (Mix RUSS and NED into a word for *strip*.) Before any disarray begins, the clue pre-empts the result. Then again, away from puzzles, our minds can jumble VELCRO to stumble on to CLOVER without great call for wheels and dashes. The difficulty climbs in sync with the letter tally, making the popular Target puzzle a tricky assignment.

Found in umpteen newspapers, Target asks solvers to find as many words as possible from a scrambled nine-letter word. To spice up the recipe the words must be four or more letters long, no plurals, no proper nouns, and each word must include a nominated letter. Usually that letter is encircled by the remaining eight, much like a bull's-eye inside a target, and spatially a great help with mental acrobatics.

GREAT HELP, in fact, was one cluster I recall. Somehow TELEGRAPH jumped straight out. Target puzzles can topple that way. Other times, like the morning I was on the radio, you'll be staring at alphabet soup.

The interview was set to be an audio tour of a newspaper's puzzle section, telling listeners how the various puzzles are assembled, from Wordwit to Target, plus the number twins – sudoku and KenKen. I'd taken twenty minutes to prepare, going through the day's quick and cryptic clues in case any needed explaining. I'd even filled in the number squares and nailed APOCRYPHAL, the Target word. Perfect – until I glanced twice at the Target diagram. Wait, APOCRYPHAL has ten letters, not nine. I'd made an error. Was it APOCRY-PHA? No, the mix had an L, and only one P anyway. Holy crap, what's hiding in YOYPCHARL?

Seconds before the chat began I started reliving the *Good News* nightmare, the bogus whizz sitting in the spotlight. The small talk started. I must have sounded like a trauma victim, vacantly discussing puzzles with my mouth while my brain was a blur of YOYPCHARL, or CHYLYPARO, but nothing worked.

In my defence, POLYARCHY (government by many) is up there with nescience and fubsy. Not that the interviewer ever asked, knowing better than to spoil the solution. Instead she quizzed me hard about my looming unemployment.

DA: My what?

Radio journo: Aren't puzzles being outsourced?

DA: Imported, you mean? The *Australian* getting its crossword from the London *Times*?

RJ: I'm talking bigger picture. Who needs you, for example, if computers can make the puzzles for us?

DA: Well, sure, um …

RJ: Makes sense, right? Brave new world, and all that.
DA: With anagrams I guess –
RJ: If Deep Blue can beat Garry Kasparov in chess,
    can't a computer be programmed to turn out grids
    and clues?

Rather than record my stunned response, let's leave the whole train wreck and tackle the subject of cyber-clues, not just the software, the anagram engines, but also a seven-letter word that caused a moral shit-storm.

GREAT HELP – machine-made puzzles and naughty subtext

Target is a lucrative franchise, though the people responsible are not so much compilers as software operators. Every day the puzzle is generated by an inbuilt program, the game itself supplied by more than one contractor.

Sudoku is the numerical twin, a brilliant format inspired by the genius of Leonhard Euler, a Swiss number-cruncher back in the 1700s. His Latin squares – a grid of figures adding up to a common sum in all directions – have inspired modern puzzlers to refine the format. The word sudoku is Japanese for 'the numbers must remain unmarried'. As well as being addictive, the puzzle is ideal for any microchip to manage; a simple program is capable of spewing out a million variations before morning tea. Both Target and sudoku are machine-friendly: a closed set of variables within a fixed grid. Sound a bit familiar? A little like crosswords, right?

Perhaps that's what the current mayor of London, Boris Johnson, believed. Before taking public office Johnson was a journo, and part of the radical decision in the mid-1990s to replace crossword-setters with computers.

As deputy editor of the *Daily Telegraph*, Johnson and his colleagues saw sense in the move. Other diversions, like chess problems and pub quizzes, could be drawn from databases, so why not cryptics? Already the paper owned a deep archive of past clues. Rarer words like POLYARCHY may have lacked a companion clue from history, but more common entries were linked to dozens of clues. Keen to save a penny, editors warmed to the notion of human-free grids. And if machines weren't smart enough to craft a decent clue, then why not program the database to fetch and match?

Readers were appalled. Overnight, puzzles lost all subtlety. There seemed to be no pulse behind the pastiche. Recipes duplicated. Puns and words overlapped, or whole formulas were missing. The flak grew so heavy that the *Telegraph* went back to the human touch, while Boris Johnson decided he'd try the relative calm of politics.

No question though, computers have been a godsend for word puzzles, for both making and solving them. Once upon a time, when pen and paper were the lone tools, compilers had to fill grids and wangle anagrams using grey matter only. Mixing, in fact, is what computers do best, on top of helping crossword fans find what words may fit a selected sequence. (FLIPPANT and ELEPHANT, say, share their even letters and thus could fit the same grid entry.) But mixing and fitting are not the same as generating fresh clues, complete with surface shine and deception. This human dimension lies beyond the ken of software commands – so far. Until such time, I still have a job to fulfil, borrowing whatever computer tools I can grab.

Again, as with Target and sudoku packages, the Web abounds in anagram generators. Many are gratis, some need subscription, some you pay to upload. In testing the range you'll come across slow ones, moody ones, shallow and archaic ones. Just like when choosing a car, you'll need to experiment to see which engine suits your anagram lifestyle.

Anagram Genius is one proven vehicle, the first major generator of its type, the software developed over six years by Cambridge entrepreneur William Tunstall-Pedoe. Come release day, back in 1994, Genius enjoyed widespread coverage. Even Johnson's *Daily Telegraph* was part of the hoopla, with the paper bragging that its own masthead could be massaged into DEEP EARTHLY LIGHT, HIGHLY DATA REPLETE or GLADLY PRE-HEATHITE in forty seconds flat. But that was tame compared to the ruckus at the *Daily Mirror*, the paper running a front-page story in 1995 to promote the new device. The article carried a photo of the then Health Secretary, Virginia Bottomley, accompanied by a headline screaming I'M AN EVIL TORY BIGOT.

Other mixers carry such names as Anagram Artist, Anagram Ferret, Nanagram or, one that recently imploded, Errata Among Range (an anagram of ANAGRAM GENERATOR). Personally, I can recommend Wordplay Wizard, a package created by an ex-editor of the *Listener* crossword, Ross Beresford. Thanks to his toy I discovered that DENNIS TITO, the first tourist in space, had TENDONITIS. No doubt the gag-writers on *Good News Week* had similar tools. There's no sin in that. I might spend ten minutes a day just playing with anagram machines, throwing in a phrase like SWEATING BULLETS (because the letters look so ripe) and seeing what flashes back. The anagram clue below, in pre-Mac times, might have taken more than an hour to craft:

Nervous about wellbeing status =
   SWEATING BULLETS

Another game I'll play with software toys is to seek out verbal flukes, like uncovering two eight-legged creatures (SPIDER and CRAB) in CRISPBREAD. Or trying the game in reverse, entering two painters (DALI and MATISSE) and getting ASSIMILATED.

Of course, some anagram engines can be puritan, much like the Target puzzle that refuses to include 'naughty bits'.

Search all you like, you won't find BUM and DICK in certain online crunchers, a fact that has provoked the plea among Target solvers for extended anatomy. Every month, it seems, a paper must face the moral dilemma of ignoring CLITO-RIS in SOLICITOR, or explaining how SPINE can be legit if PENIS doesn't seem to exist.

The practice is a type of bowdlerism, where slang and genitalia have been wiped from the database, just as Thomas Bowdler, back in the early 1800s, circumcised the Bard's 'prick of noon' in *Romeo and Juliet* for the nicer 'point of noon'. Seasoned Target fans don't bother listing ORGASM for IGNOR-AMUS, while AROUSING is borderline. In Target-ville, sex and the twenty-first century don't exist. If you chance upon MODEM in MODERNISM, bad luck. And don't even bother with the C-word in TRUNCHEON – it ain't gonna happen.

Unless the unthinkable happens, and just as many solvers see the smut before any solution is disclosed, as occurred in the *Washington Post* in 2008. The puzzle was called a Scrabble Gram, sponsored by Hasbro, the board game's licence-holders. To reach the maximum score, you had to rearrange four racks – each with seven tiles – into the longest possible word. Here's how the racks appeared

EUTTSXB
AIYDDTK
EEIVLHC
EOODSPP

For Americans at least, rack 2 would be a cinch, the KATYDID (or cricket) part of every US summer. Then come VEHICLE and OPPOSED. Leaving just the top rack for the good people of DC, possibly the hardest of the four. Oh Lord, surely not – BUTTSEX!? Since when has that depravity snuck into Random House? The phones ran hot. The switchboard melted. The paper fell short of placing an apology, though the furore gained a lavish irony in the next morning's solution, where SUBTEXT was revealed.

As one user quipped in a puzzle forum, 'Well, the inventor of Scrabble was a guy named Alfred Butts ....' But enough dirty talk – for now at least. Time to examine 25-Across in the Master Puzzle, our last anagram clue.

RISE OF THE NEW – everyday jargon and subtractive anagrams

Forty years back, a word like 'subcontracted' came with a hyphen. Two centuries before then, the same word didn't exist. Nowadays you can't spend a working week without running into a subcontractor, or subcontractee, or maybe even operating under a subcontract yourself.

As the world changes, so does language. Out with fubsy, in with fax. Until fax turned quaint, getting dumped for text, which has since lost its 'e', and so on. The whirligig never stops. In fact, even 'whirligig' is on thin ice.

Unlike the answer to our current clue, a robust ten-letter term that's growing more robust as each year passes. According to the *Shorter Oxford*, our mystery word was born around 1981, most likely debuting with a hyphen. If so, that coy attribute has since been lost, the term now part of modern conversation. On Google, this mystery word registers close to six million hits, compared to the 150,000 incidences of nescience. And if you want further proof of how ubiquitous this one-time piece of jargon has become, then this chapter has already used the word in passing.

So let's refresh the memory banks. Here's how the clue reads:

Discourteous shift is dispatched, subcontracted (10)

Taken as a whole, the clue suggests the working realm. At

least that's the surface sense: a rude bunch of workers getting the sack, their new employment terms reduced to a subcontract. But don't let the clue's surface distract you. Ignore those images of open-plan offices, and focus on the building blocks.

Where's the signpost? *Shift* looks like the standout, but that's leaving too many letters to disturb. To the signpost's left is DISCOURTEOUS which has eleven letters, while ISDISPATCHED to the right has twelve – and we seek an answer with ten. To use a phrase common to working life: *Help Wanted*.

As a category, anagrams are split into two kinds – the simple and the complex. The first sort we've met in the last three chapters: signpost plus fodder equals answer, as defined by the clue's other part. While *scatterbrain* was tricky for its embedded signpost, the rest of the game followed along orthodox lines. Going one more step, complex anagrams can spread their fodder across a longer phrasing, such as this deft sample from the *Guardian*, composed by John Halpern, a superb innovator known to many fans as Paul:

Ground rich with deep crack = DECIPHER

The words to grind are *rich* and *deep*, to give a word meaning *crack*. Note how the fodder words sit astride *with*, the clue reading much like a recipe instruction: add X to Y to make Z. In complex anagrams, the fodder needs minor assembling before the shake-up can start. That may entail adding – or taking away, as the next clues demonstrate. The first was styled by a setter called Flimsy from the *Financial Times*, while the other is drawn from my own scrapbook:

Tape's broken, not a bother (4)
Wet sitcom broadcast minus copyright (5)

As the label suggests, subtractive anagrams ask you to

remove a few letters from the fodder before anything else can happen. Of course, to keep things fair, a clue must flag both operations. Let's look at that first clue. Can you see the two indicators? *Broken* is your anagram signpost, and *not* – the word – tells you to exclude. Sure enough, if we break up TAPES (not with an A) we make PEST, a word meaning *bother*.

In the second clue, the hint of double-play is also there – to mix (*broadcast*) and to trim (*minus*). Mix SITCOM minus *copyright* (or C) and you'll create MOIST, as clued by *wet*. Let's put the Master clue back in the frame:

Discourteous shift is dispatched, subcontracted (10)

Same deal, just a few more letters to handle. Where are the signs? As you probably figured, the anagram signal is *shift*. Except that now we know that deletion is also on the agenda, as echoed by the word *dispatched*. What word or letter needs dispatching, or sending off, before the mixing can start?

Remember those words of Azed back in Chapter 1: 'A good cryptic clue contains three elements.' And what are they again? A precise definition. Fair wordplay signals. And nothing else. So don't overlook that little word *is*. No clueword appears in vain. That tiny *is*, in fact, provides you with the letters you need to dispatch from a shifted DISCOURTEOUS, the new incarnation meaning *subcontracted*.

I'll make it easier for you: C E U R O S T U D O. (It might also remind you of a certain radio interview where the announcer forecast the downfall of human puzzlers, usurped by software packages.) Certainly the DJ had a point, watching the likes of Target and sudoku falling into programmers' hands, but the day clue-mongers are OUTSOURCED to the microchip will be the day that robots run the asylum.

COMPLEX ANAGRAMS

Usually less tricky than they sound, complex anagrams ask you to scramble letters – with a twist. Perhaps a letter is thrown in before the shuffling, or extracted. Perhaps the anagram fodder doesn't sit primly in one cluster, but is supplied in separate bundles. This duo from the *Financial Times* will help you tune your radar to recognise the tactic.

From Falcon: *Play in match and be beaten* = MATCH + BE = MACBETH

From Styx: *Bonus remuneration removed from dodgy taxpayer* = TAXPAYER – PAY = EXTRA

HALL OF FAME: ANAGRAMS

Les, Tom, Dicky and Harry (6) [Cox & Rathvon, US]
Every second letter an 'a' – bananas? (9) [Satori, *Financial Times*]
Doctor accepted as trainee astronaut (5,5) [*Times* 8559]
An acrostic puzzle in Latin (5,5) [Taupi, *Guardian*]
Being out of one's class in semis, beaten badly (11) [*Times* 8380]
UFO, for example, circling above Britain (12) [Crux, *Financial Times*]

SOLUTIONS: Molest, alternate, space cadet, Costa Rican, absenteeism, abbreviation

QUIZLING 4.1

We know that HER MEN COLLAPSE hides former supermodel ELLE MACPHERSON. Can you refashion each phrase below to fashion a model past or present?

HAILED POSH   UNHINGED CELEBS

SMOKES? TA   VAIN LADIES TANGLE

HELIUM KID   NIGHTLY INSTRUCTOR

QUIZLING 4.2

Scrabble pros don't play BARONET, when REBOANT – meaning resonant – may draw a futile challenge from their opponent. Heeding this advice, we've played these weird sevens on the board, despite the same tiles holding which far simpler words?

AMBONES   SONANCY   FLANEUR   DYELINE

ZINCITE   OOCYTES   PTYALIN   TRISHAW

QUIZLING 4.3

If 'squandered zillions' is LOST LOTS, can you figure out these other anagram pairs? Each coupling involves words of four or five letters.

Loathe warmth   Exorcises?

Start pub-crawl   Eco-lit

Fruit blemish   Mud-brick home

Bedtime story   Ulna locale

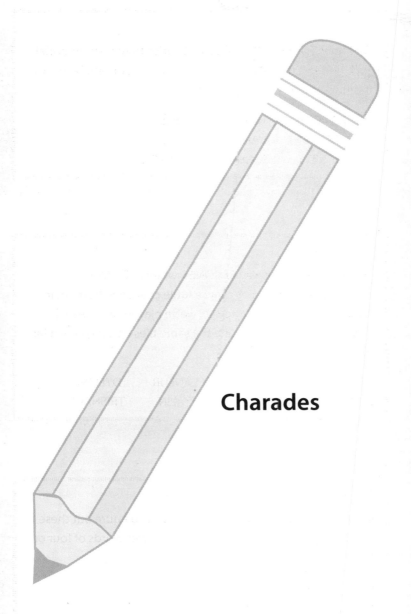

Charades

CHAPTER 5

Nebraskan City Circle gives old lady a laugh (5)

Cornflakes
Goalpost
Trousers
Menace
Lentil
Obviate
Perpetual
Domino

Radar Trap is a code puzzle I make every week for the *Herald*'s Metro section, a list of eight words or names encoded into symbols. Usually the topic is declared, like Famous Stutterers (Porky Pig, Aesop, Noel Gallagher) or Things You Shake (Polaroid photo, drug habit, Etch-A-Sketch), while other weeks the task is twofold: cracking the code, and then determining the theme that unifies all eight.

What links friendship, say, with mozzarella, truth, limousine, hamstring and imagination? (All can be stretched.)

Or these five movies: *X-Men*, *Muriel's Wedding*, *Notting Hill*, *Forrest Gump* and *Rear Window*? (Each film has a main character in a wheelchair.)

So how about our opening list? What quirk links 'Cornflakes' and the rest? This was the challenge facing

Sydneysiders in 2008, trying to find a common thread with a prize up for grabs. Search engines most likely came to the rescue, with rescue the operative word.

How well do you know your history? All eight words were code names for World War II operations, from bombing runs ('Obviate') to propaganda mail-outs ('Cornflakes'). Hardly household names, but the terms were urgent business some sixty years ago. And once you solve our current Master clue you'll have a ninth code name for the list. But instead of turning to codes or anagrams, this clue entails a new formula.

Players of charades, the popular mime game, will know the rules already. You get a name like Liverpool, say, and you break the city into halves, pointing to your liver, then acting out a swimming pool. Breakdown, in fact, is the crux of charading.

Potentially, any movie or famous name can be broken into pieces – sounds or syllables or smaller words. At first glance, Mahatma Gandhi looks a nightmare to dismantle, but then you unpick the seams and see five fragments: MA-HAT-MAG-AND-HI.

To illustrate how crosswords have adopted this game, let's choose a WWII operation. MENACE looks perfect, the coupling of two smaller words, MEN + ACE. Clue-wise a setter may go this way:

> *Guys superb when facing danger (6)*

Guys are MEN. *Superb* is ACE. Marry them and there's a synonym of *danger*. So what is *'when facing'* doing? The cryptic term is linkword, namely any word helping to bring the other two elements together. Seldom desirable, sometimes linkwords are unavoidable. This may run contrary to Azed's dictum – two elements in every clue and nothing else – but wordplay and definition won't always mesh. It's best to view links as visible stitches that keep two panels compatible.

Selecting linkwords has its own art. Choose the right one, and the word will not only describe what's happening in a wordplay sense (since *men* and *ace* are physically *facing* each other), but also contribute to the clue's overall surface meaning.

Let's try Operation Two, a naval attack on Sumatran oil-fields code-named LENTIL:

Pulse fast – close to 49 (6)

Here the marriage is cosier, as LENTIL can be defined as *pulse*. Pair that with *fast* – not just the essence of Lent but also a word supporting the notion of heart rate – and the cardiac trap is sprung. For added bait, the leftover IL translates as forty-nine in Roman numerals, the figure supporting the pulse idea. As the linking phrase, *close to* means both 'beside' and 'roughly', serving the needs of surface meaning as well as wordplay command.

Now we move on to DOMINO, the last operation listed. The clue below was styled by America's best cryptic setter, Henry Hook, a gifted recluse from New Jersey. You'll see more of Hook's handiwork as the book unfolds, but for now consider this gem:

Monk in oxygen mask (6)

Unlike my first two efforts, Hook has avoided a linkword. The best charades work this way. Here the wordplay side (*monk in oxygen*) spells out DOM+IN+O, where Dom is the common title for a Catholic monk. Yet the stroke of genius is how neatly the word *oxygen* – or O – sidles with *mask*, not forgetting that dominoes are not just spotty blocks but also those half-masks that the Riddler fancied.

Coincidentally, the Master clue enlists the letter O as well. Charades are prone to isolating single letters (O), or letter clusters (IL), as most words when separated won't be as neat as the Mahatma. Take GALLIVANT, say. Broken down, we get GALL + IVAN + T, or G + ALL + IV + ANT, and so on. When playing charades, or building clues, you'll often need to convey a non-word chunk among the larger units. Such a challenge takes guile. Let's look more closely at this special nastiness.

STORM CENTRE – Ximenes vs Araucaria

Shirl O'Brien is an anagram of HORRIBLE SIN, but you won't meet a sweeter crossword compiler. The Brisbane mum of five has made more than 1200 puzzles for that city's *Courier-Mail* under the alias of Southern Cross. Now in her eighties, Shirl has quit the local gig to spend more time with her grandkids, though she still draws a puzzle income, exporting her brand of homespun humour to the United Kingdom. Notably, Shirl belongs to a select group of females making cryptic puzzles at the top level, as well as being a very rare Australian who compiles for an English audience: her work appears once a month or so in the *Guardian*, under the code name of Auster.

'A lovely man called Custos, whose real name was Alec Robins, suggested I go with Auster, which means the southern wind.' Shirl can't help a girlish snigger when she recollects this. 'These days, with my flatulence, that's a good name for me.'

Alec Robins – one letter switch from becoming BINOC-ULARS – was a veteran setter for several British papers, the *Guardian* included. Together with a setter code-named Ximenes (christened after a torturer during the time of the Spanish Inquisition), Custos helped draft the rules of cryptic crosswords. Notably, both Custos and Ximenes, whose real name was Derrick Macnutt, taught classics at prestigious colleges, but maybe that's no coincidence, since a head for strange tongues often implies a good head for puzzles. And so it was, in 1966, that the two teachers took a break from Cicero to collaborate on a bestseller entitled *Ximenes on the Art of Crossword*. (Guess which compiler had the bigger profile.)

While both authors have since moved on to that great conundrum in the sky, the impact of their manifesto still ripples through Cryptopia. Not least in the matter of charades.

'Alec was a purist in that regard,' recalls Shirl. 'For him a phrase like CIVIC CENTRE is not an indication of the letter V, while CENTRE OF GRAVITY was fine. The difference is a matter of grammar.' Mind you, there are times when Shirl still signals a letter like B with the phrase BOTTLE-OPENER rather than OPENING OF BOTTLE, flouting the puritan rule book and feeling a minor pang of guilt. 'I'll look up to heaven and say, "Sorry Alec" because he wouldn't have liked that.'

Bottle-opener, by the lights of Custos and Co, is a horrible sin, in fact, and should never denote the letter B. Just as *Radio-head* is lazy shorthand for R compared with the probity of *Radio's head*, which looks daft on the page. To see where your impulses lie, browse the list below and pick which samples seem a reasonable signpost for the letter R:

start of race
middle of April
end of summer
ringleader
birth centre
never-ending

If you reckon the first three examples are the only fair ones, then you belong in the Ximenean camp. This posse makes up the hardliners, setters and solvers who insist on every clue being thoroughly sound in both grammar and execution, even at the expense of creative tangents or a dose of lateral thinking.

However, if you can live with all six listed samples, chances are you belong in the libertarian camp, the opposite mob. As a solver, I'm guessing, you don't mind facing a clue that seems a little out there, either in its wording or in how the wordplay functions, so long as the Piñata Principle prevails. No matter the mischief, the answer must be gettable, especially in reverse, when solution and clue are held to account.

The golden rule of cryptics was coined by Afrit, a *Listener* compiler of the 1930s whose real name was A. F. Ritchie. Dubbed the Afrit Injunction, the rule reads: *You need not mean what you say, but you must say what you mean.*

Despite the flame war between the two crossword schools, this dictum is central to both approaches, from the exacting Ximenes to the loose-limbed Araucaria, alias John Graham of the *Guardian*. For a sense of the latter, try this charade for size:

Garment of polyester not cotton? (7)

If the answer is SINGLET, can you see why? Because *polyester* (versus *cotton*) has a SINGLE-T. True-blue Ximeneans would be appalled – a rubbery clue, a deviant whim, not a verb in sight – but I reckon it's funny, and inventive, and Araucarian – the other word to describe libertarians. Besides which, the Afrit Injunction has been obeyed.

Athens versus Sparta, Crips versus Bloods – the two camps have been scrapping for decades, despite having so much in common. Naturally, everyone wants their puzzle to be concise and witty. Regardless of your flag – Ximenean or Araucarian – the principles of neat wordplay and sound definition don't alter. You still desire seamless clues with vivid imagery and subtle traps. To return to the classroom for a moment, I think the Ximenean is much like the classics master who demands a clinical translation of Virgil, while the Araucarian heads up the art department, splashing colour on the canvas to mirror the galaxy that Virgil wrote about. Both executions require great skill. Both delude and delight. And as with art, a solver will decide what they like.

So what about 22-Across, our upcoming charade? Does it lean in a Ximenean or Araucarian direction? Let's see:

Nebraskan City Circle gives old lady a laugh (5)

The state abbreviation for Nebraska is NE. Will that be required? The state's capital is Lincoln, and its largest city is Omaha. Are we on track? The answer is yes, regardless of where the clue leads, as good solvers will toss up all those scenarios, keeping attuned to what the clue is murmuring.

Let's stick with the OMAHA theory. All the more since that has five letters, and we already know that O is the answer's opener, thanks to BINOCULARS. Encouraged, let's see if the wordplay backs us up.

To isolate the wordplay, remove the alleged definition – *Nebraskan City* – and see what's left: *Circle gives old lady a laugh*. Good news: *Circle* may suggest an O, leaving us with the tricky sequence of MAHA. Is it M + AHA? What about MA + HA? Read the words carefully. Presuming *gives* to be the linkword, then *old lady* = MA. and *a laugh* (singular) has to be HA. Congratulations, you've just un-pieced the puzzle's first charade.

Although OMAHA, the answer, gave little cause for British Intelligence to celebrate sixty years' ago. If the *old lady* is laughing in our current clue, then the old guard was furious back in 1944.

MULBERRY (BUSH) TELEGRAPH – D-Day Crossword Mystery

GOLD was a fluke, they thought, just like SWORD. And then came JUNO, the Roman goddess of marriage. A few feelers started twitching down at MI5, the military intelligence office. What are the odds, they must have argued. The *Daily*

Telegraph, reduced by wartime to a measly six pages, had kept its crossword. Worryingly, the same puzzle had bleated three code names – GOLD, SWORD and JUNO – each one a classified landing spot for the D-Day invasion planned in a few months' time.

But still, went the reasoning, aren't these compiler chaps into the classics? Gold, sword, Juno: the very stuff of myths and legends. Operation Overlord remained on track – 6 June 1944 – when a fourth clue made the pages:

One of the USA (4)

What the dickens? UTAH had nothing to do with Homer or his sea stories. The word in fact embraced a different maritime yarn, namely the Normandy beach assigned to the 4th US Assault Division, the western flank of the D-Day operation, and that was five weeks off.

Journalism has a saying – once is an occurrence, twice a coincidence, while three times is a trend. Does that make four a conspiracy? High treason?

To make matters worse, these puzzles had a precedent. Two years before, in August 1942, there was the Dieppe Debacle. The planning had taken months: the spy reconnaissance, the stealthy gathering of infantry and airpower. The target was a French port close to the Belgian border. As Chief of Combined Operations, Lord Mountbatten was intent on wresting Dieppe from German hands in order to gain a beachhead in northern Europe. The raid was two days from swooping when up bobbed 18-Down in the bloody *Telegraph* crossword: *French port (6)*. Crosswords of the era happily blended quick clues as well as the evolving genre of cryptic.

But what tormented MI5 was DIEPPE, the answer. The timing was alarming. After the raid, where casualties were high, the government had no choice but to appoint Lord Tweedsmuir (the son of John Buchan, author of *The Thirty-Nine*

Steps) to investigate the culpable compiler – who is a man you've met already. Like Custos and Ximenes, another classicist with chalk dust on his fingers, Leonard Sidney Dawe had pioneered the *Daily Telegraph* crosswords and also ran the Strand School in London. Students dubbed him Moneybags, a reference to his initials (LSD – pounds, shillings, pence). With his severe Prussian haircut, Dawe at first appeared as a most likely Hitler snoop, though Tweedsmuir found nothing to support the impression. As the investigator went on to remark, 'We noticed the crossword contained the word Dieppe and there was an immediate and exhaustive inquiry which also involved MI5. But in the end it was concluded that it was just a remarkable coincidence – a complete fluke.'

Such tolerance evaporated in May 1944. On the eve of Overlord, the *Telegraph* crossword ran a fifth hush-hush location, fresh on the heels of UTAH. On 22 May, just two weeks prior to US General Dwight D. Eisenhower launching the assault, this clue ran:

Red Indian on the Missouri (5)

The Missouri River, for those unfamiliar with American geography, flows through Great Falls and Sioux City, as well as a city called Omaha, a name that honours the area's original people. If Omaha rings a bell for you, imagine the alarm bells sounding in Westminster. Not just a light cruiser in the US Navy, Omaha was also a classified nook in the Normandy coastline. Give this Dawe fellow a damn good grilling, came the communiqué.

By this stage, with the Blitz in recent memory, the Strand School had been evacuated to the safer vales of Surrey. Dawe himself was living with his brother-in-law, Peter Sanders, a senior member of the British Admiralty, causing further jitters. The home was in Leatherhead, which Ximeneans would despise as a signal for L, but let's keep with the action.

In Dawe's own words: 'They turned me inside-out and ... grilled my brother-in-law. They went to Bury St Edmunds, where my colleague Melville Jones was living, and put him through the works. But they eventually decided not to shoot us!'

Again, MI5 decided, the words seemed to be a mind-boggling fluke. Dawe had no inkling of the covert plans. Nor did the flukes stop. Only days from D-Day, a few more military secrets dropped into the grid. Among the answers were MULBERRY (code for a floating harbour off the French coast), NEPTUNE (the initial naval assault) and OVERLORD (seriously).

Historians put the D-Day Crossword Mystery high on the list of all-time great coincidences, but the oddity gained a new chapter in 1984. A former Strand School student, Ronald French, was reading a forty-year anniversary article about the whole episode and felt compelled to contact the paper.

It seems the fishy vocab of Leonard Sidney Dawe was less an accident than a whim of geography. The school, in its Surrey location, was close to an army camp for US and Canadian troops. Just fourteen at the time, Ronald French was mesmerised by the men in khaki, as were dozens of other schoolboys, many of whom played truant to see army life first-hand. And when men talk, boys listen. 'We all knew the operation was called Overlord,' recalled French in a follow-up article by Val Gilbert, the *Telegraph's* puzzle editor. 'Every-one knew the outline invasion plan ... Omaha and Utah were the beaches they were going to – '.

From spoken word to crosswords, the story took one more step. Juggling the chores of teaching and puzzle-making, Dawe regularly challenged his students to create crossword interlocks as an intellectual test, giving the lads graph sheets and pencils to see what they could do. What they did was almost overturn the course of World War II.

Though let's leave the last word to Chief Command, the original think tank that dreamt up such terms as OMAHA and MULBERRY. Nine months after the critical success of D-Day, with the Nazi empire retreating deeper into Germany, the Allied forces conducted a series of secret negotiations in Switzerland. Top-ranking officers on both sides of the conflict were involved, a chance to negotiate a Nazi surrender in a civilised way. Such high stakes made the secrecy of Operation Crossword all the more crucial.

RECIPE PRECIS: CHARADES

Often a lack of signposts can open your eyes to the charade category – especially if the clue carries a word like *and* or other coupling cues, namely *with, beside, by, on, along, next to* or *after*. The slicker charades avoid any so-called joiners, such as *old lady a laugh* yielding O+MA+HA in our Master example. Often a clue's brevity will put charades on the suspect list. And remember, keep your eyes peeled for abbreviations – see the box at the end of the next chapter.

QUIZLING 5.1

Scramble CHARADES to find
Two verbs similarly defined.

QUIZLING 5.2

The last name of this notorious gangster is an item of clothing
plus a single unit – just as his nickname is an item of clothing
plus a single unit (in a casino). Who's the felon in question?

QUIZLING 5.3

Can you 'canonise' your first answer to create your second?
Crook/yet, say = ILL/STILL. Solving six or more is sterling stuff.

buzz/twine
tree/hide
mature/band
OK/layer
eager/seam
girl/boy
girl/girl
move along/walk
move along/walk

CHAPTER 6

A weir worker set … (7)

Wait, before we start, let's check that clue again. W-E-I-R. Is that the right spelling? I mean W-I-E-R just looks wrong. But then again, we have PIER, which is correct. Or is it PEIR? How about we run the spellcheck?

Wish I'd had that impulse four years back. One thing you learn in the puzzle game – never presume. The moment you think you've made a spotless crossword, a blooper will bite your backside. Maybe a charade skips a vital piece, a clue number is out of whack … or maybe you think that WEIR is spelt WIER.

Without trying to duck for cover, I reckon my lapse links back to Old French. That's the language to filter the Latin *pera*, so giving us the modern-day PIER. Meanwhile WEIR, with the vowels transposed, is an Old English word adopted from Middle German. Dumbly, on the eve of publication, I'd taken the two words as owning identical tails, so making the fatal move from PIER to WIER (sic). The late switch was a bid to resonate a longer entry in the grid, namely WARRAGAMBA, the principal dam supplying the sprawl of Sydney.

To clue WARRAGAMBA I'd chosen the charade path, breaking the word into bits: WAR, plus RAG, plus A, and then MBA (a Master of Business Admin). The clue took this shape:

Water supplier fighting newspaper article, gaining business honour (10)

Can you see each Lego block? *Water supplier* is your dam. *Fighting* = WAR. *Newspaper article* = RAG + A (the indefinite *article*), followed by the degree. As tough as the answer may seem, the dam is a household name to most Sydneysiders. A twisted but fair charade, until I spoilt the effect.

The original answer to 21-Down in this 2007 puzzle was PIER, which once owned the charade clue – *Dock food rationing at first.* (Again, *dock* is your definition, *food* is PIE, and *rationing at first* indicates R.) Yet during the proofing, I turned PIER to WIER (thinking of another word for 'dam') and my fate was sealed.

The slip went to press and the uproar began. Emails jammed the *Herald*'s inbox, decrying the standards of public literacy. Lethal injection was thought too kind a punishment. At Crikey.com.au, the Australian e-newspaper, one reader seized upon 'nadir' – a classic crossword-word meaning an orbit's lowest point – to characterise the fiasco. Tellingly, this reader was Richard Walsh, the former publisher of *Oz* magazine.

For those too young to recall the 1970 scandal, *Oz* was charged by Britain's Obscene Publications Squad with conspiracy to corrupt public morals, or more specifically for the act of depicting Rupert Bear with full wedding tackle. The Old Bailey trial enlisted the likes of John Mortimer QC for the defence, with assistance from Australian lawyer Geoffrey Robertson. Yet despite having weathered all that heat, Richard Walsh saw WIER as the nadir of modern journalism; if not the misspelling itself, then how such a booboo was ever allowed to make the page.

I wasn't too happy either. You make a mistake that dumb, the anguish lingers. If this paragraph contains a spelling mistake, then you and I may never notice. Or if we do, the chapter perseveres. But goofing a crossword answer is an applied type of sloppiness. Even now reliving the trauma is undermining some expensive therapy.

But Walsh was right. The proofing phase at the time of the error was shabby. He called it lamentable, whereas I think the better word is fractured.

Just like a charade, the Fairfax newspaper system (which included the *Herald*) was momentarily broken into bits. Before we consider the *worker* in our current clue, let's jump in the time machine and see how puzzle-proofing has worked (or not worked) over the years. But I must warn you, the pong of bromide is strong.

AHAB'S WOODEN LEG – proofing and unpicking clues

When I first made crosswords for the *Herald*, back in 1983, the word 'internet' didn't exist, while 'outsource' was a toddler. Preparing the grid meant using a marker pen to block out the squares and then a felt-tip to etch the numbers. Clues I typed onto postcard-sized triplicate sheets – white on top, then pink, then yellow. Next I folded the bundle into an envelope and addressed it to the puzzle editor.

In those early days Ron Nichols was the man in charge. A veteran journo with a dry wit, Ron typeset the clues on his Visual Display Unit (a Jurassic computer), turning my scribble into a grid as crisp as a chessboard. He'd then send the proof sheet back in the post.

Industrial love letters, the Fairfax proofs could be smelt a few blocks away, suffused by a mix of bromide and chemical resin. Braving the aroma, you'd comb the clues for typos, then phone through any corrections. (Yes, we had phones in 1983.) During our chats, Ron and I would swap notes, seeing if we agreed on nuances, and the amended puzzle was put to bed, ready to appear inside four weeks. If the WIER business represents the nadir of proofreading, then possibly this one-on-one relationship was the zenith. Not that errors didn't occur, but at least editor and setter were wholly answerable for any screw-ups, as it should be.

This rhythm persisted for fifteen years. From 1983 to the late '90s, the mail system kept both parties in contact. Despite the odd glitch, the exchange held strong, the follow-up calls keeping bungles low as well as ensuring a rapport between setters and their continuum of editors. And what a continuum they were. I can't hope to list the *Herald*'s complete sequence, as the puzzle chair has been a swivel seat for years. Though I can tell you that Ron eventually made way for a Kansan named Jack Ames with a penchant for linen suits and William S. Burroughs. After Jack came a pocket-sized rock-chick named Deb, who needed to remove her latest piercing to speak on the phone, and then came the Taylor clan: Rebecca, Naomi and Linus. The current gatekeeper of Puzzle Land is Lynne Cairncross, an ex-journo with a passion for botany and gluten-free chocolate tortes. Yet undoubtedly the queen of editors is Harriet Veitch, the spare-parts player who has filled as many breaches in the crossword roster as she has different roles across the paper.

Critic, columnist, profiler – Harriet has worn many hats in her twenty-three years on the staff. More recently you'll have seen her byline near the back of Section One, as Harriet is now the paper's obituarist, reducing the late and great to eloquent biographies. 'I get to be a nosy parker for a living,' is Harriet's take on the gig, which is very Harriet. Her plummy voice evokes all things proper, and yet the message is often mischievous.

Against other editors, Harriet stands alone for her free-ranging trivia. She embodies the maxim once uttered by Lindsey Browne, the *Herald*'s iconic compiler, which was: 'A good journalist knows a little about everything.' That journo is Harriet, a woman as cosy with Tudor lineage as with identifying which Bee Gee in a photo is which. (If you want her number as phone-a-friend for the next quiz show, stiff cheese – she's booked.) After years setting the TV guide, Harriet has as much of a handle on *Malcolm in the Middle* as she does on Malcolm X.

One day I clued LIPIZZANER as a Spanish horse. But HV was quick to report that even though Lipizzaners are synonymous with the Spanish Riding School, that school is based in Vienna and the breed itself comes from Slovenia. And she was right, damn it, as well as being genial about it.

A trained subeditor too, Harriet is a spelling whizz. Ironic, in fact, given the deadly IE/EI switch in Harriet Veitch's own name. Whenever we trade emails I need to murmur the mantra: *I before E except after C, or V in her case, but after R is OK.*

Regardless of the editor, that was the system. Setter mailed the puzzles; editor posted the typeset proof; corrections were discussed over the phone. When the internet arrived, the only variation was a sidestepped postman. New puzzles came by email, while proofing remained a mail-and-phone affair.

Until 2000, when a different letter arrived. The sender was Rebecca Taylor, the puzzle custodian of the day, and her opening line was ominous: 'From July 31, the *Sydney Morning Herald* crosswords will be following new production procedures.'

In a word, Pagemasters. Filling a niche, doing a lot of slogwork for papers, Pagemasters is an outsource operation that takes care of share listings, cinema sessions, weather, horoscopes and puzzles. Suddenly the tête-à-tête of editor and setter became a *ménage à trois*. Rather than sending Wordwits and crosswords to Fairfax, I sent them to a production bunker in Melbourne, and their staffers mailed me back the proof to check. Before too long the mail component vanished and this tangled triangle existed wholly online, with setter, typesetter and editor remote from each other.

Our mission of course was to squash all bugs before the puzzles appeared in public, and we didn't always succeed. Owing to the disjunction of the new system, the lines of answerability blurred. Where did the buck stop, and whose inbox had the latest version of the buck? Wires often crossed, one party oblivious of the action of the other two. Or a word like WIER was entered, yet not sighted by the editor, the bungle reaching the morning papers. Clearly, where two people could once get a puzzle to the page in good condition, three could not.

At least, not then. We took a while to right the wrongs. Nowadays one regular worker in the outsource bunker is allocated the puzzle hat to ensure continuity.

Now, triggered by the Wier Fiasco, all correspondence entails three parties, and all changes require follow-up attachments. Step by step, the dance is choreographed down to the last comma.

Of course, no matter how tight the system, lapses occur. Somehow Lynne Cairncross and I considered the Library of Alexandria as one of the Seven Ancient Wonders, rather than that city's lighthouse. The boo-boo made historians wonder too.

Even Margaret Farrar, among the first and finest of crossword editors, made a comical lapse during her reign at the *New York Times*. At the helm from 1942 to 1968, Farrar single-handedly checked clues, seldom missing a beat, or a typo. Long John Silver, however, caused a minor splash. The pirate had appeared as an answer recently, Farrar remembered. Loath to have the same name repeated so soon, the editor needed a quick clue for WOODEN LEG. So it was Farrar who opted to ditch Silver for another mariner, making the revised clue read: *Captain Ahab's distinguishing characteristic*. The gaffe was detected by an eight-year-old solver, who wrote to the paper wondering why Ahab now had a wooden leg instead of an ivory one, as in *Moby-Dick*. For her part Farrar was wondering what kind of eight-year-old solved the *New York Times* crossword, let alone read *Moby-Dick*.

ANT MUSIC – cryptic shorthand and multiple meanings

After all this talk of brain-fades, have you fired up your nerve cells? We have a charade to solve, right? Let's put the clue on the table:

A weir worker set ... (7)

A weir is liable to be A + DAM, since weir has few other synonyms, and the letter A can't afford to be redundant. If our theory holds water, what seven-letter word starts with ADAM? Checking a large dictionary, you'll find three. One is a greenish cousin of zinc – ADAMITE – and the other is a surname, ADAMSON, both nominees failing to satisfy the clue. Leaving us with ADAMANT. But if that's the answer – why? If *a weir* is A DAM, then how can *worker* render ANT?

Regular solvers will be wise to plenty of cryptic shorthand. Point, the word, will often mean a compass point, being N, E, S or W. Journalist is ED. Way is RD or ST. Sport can be PE or PT – just like your gym class – or perhaps RU or RL, the two rugby codes. Cricket is another favourite, with team (XI), maiden (M) and duck (O) entering the fray. Any chemical element, any American state, any chess piece can imply its shorter self. In the same vein, every puzzle enthusiast will know that worker, the word, is liable to denote ANT.

Perhaps the logic harks back to Aesop, whose fable of the industrious ant has invaded the Western psyche. Then there's Biology 101, where we learnt that most colonies are subdivided into various castes, from drones to soldiers to workers, just as bees (another option for *worker*) are classified. Yet after years of clueing I can tell you that the most compelling reason for ANT earning such a simple definition gets down to the word's importance. Language is riddled with the little varmints! *We can't escape their constant quantity. Unwanted but incessant, an insouciant word like ant guarantees the setter an elegant and pliant indicator* ... Making ADAMANT our odds-on answer –

Adam Ant, did you say? The post-punk singer with paint on his face? No, not him, tempting as it was to add a dash of glam pop. But then I went cold at the idea. In coming clues you'll be trying to uncover a Renaissance figure, then a novelist from the 1800s, as well as a 1960 movie and a spot of cyber slang. Adding Adam Ant would have been cultural overdose. Besides, I found *Antmusic* irritating.

I opted for a shot of plain vocab instead. But wait a tick – where's the definition? What is *set* doing there? And what about those scary dots in the clue's tail?

Best way to explain the clue's finale is to take a side trip into the dictionary, where SET is the Zelig of lingo, the pinnacle of versatility. The *Oxford English Dictionary* allocates twenty-five pages to this active midget – that's some 60,000 words (give or take) to capture the protean life of 'set'. From Lego set to set the table, from sport to nautical terms, music to slang, from transitive verb to intransitive, set has close to 200 meanings, a synonym for ADAMANT included.

The moral of the story? Take extra care around those little words, and even more so those of an elderly persuasion – such as *out, get, take, do, round* – as these are masters of misdirection. Each owns so many meanings you need to be aware of which nuance is operating. As for those dots that end our charade, Chapter 24 will unveil that mystery. But first we have a pressing appointment with a cheerleader ...

IN SHORT

Charade clues frequently call on abbreviations, since a word like TENACIOUS won't break into neat fragments the way ADAMANT or STUBBORN can. Instead, a setter may try TEN + AC [current] + IOUS [debts]. Below is a mere glimpse of other abbreviations you might encounter across cryptic clues, charades or otherwise.

AB (sailor)
AD (nowadays)
AM (morning)
B (born, bowled)
BA or MA (graduate)
C (caught, cold)
CA (about, circa)
CE, CH or RC (church)
DR or GP or MO (doctor)
E (drug)
ED (journo)
EG (say)
EP or LP (record)
ER (queen)
ET (alien)
F (fellow, loudly)
H (horse, heroin)
IE (that is)

IT (computing)
L (line, learner, left)
M (married, maiden)
MP (politician)
NT or OT (books)
OP (work, opus)
P (quietly, parking)
PE (sport, gym)
PR (publicity, spin)
R (river, right)
RE (about)
RL or RU (football)
SOS (help)
ST (street, way)
T (time, shirt, model, Model T)
U (turn)
X, Y or Z (unknown)

Also watch out for point (E, N, S or W), note (A to G), chess pieces, chemical elements and Roman numerals.

QUIZLING 6.1

Each charade leads to an item of office supply. Enchanting +
assessor = MAGIC MARKER.

lofty + fairer
squeezebox + abrade
dopes + limit
sensed + prediction
fix + fruit drink
main + expert

QUIZLING 6.2

Ironically, what form of fortune-telling can break into a
charade saying: 'cheers bunkum'?

QUIZLING 6.3

My first is in one, but not in two;
My second's in two, but not in three;
My third is in two, but not in one;
My fourth is in three, but not in two;
My fifth is in five, but not in one;
My sixth is in one, but not in five;
My last is in eight, and the puzzle's twist
Is technically the answer doesn't exist.

CHAPTER 7

Early curve superb on cheerleader (7)

Sex sells. Sex sizzles. It diverts and distracts. It titillates and shocks, makes us laugh and leer and catch our breath. Sex is how we got here, and sex is not going away.

Birds do it. Bees do it. And according to Cole Porter, even educated fleas do it. From the torsos printed on cereal boxes to the smoky glances of night-time soaps, sex stalks every waking hour. We hear it in song, read it in scandal. You may even be enjoying the bona fide article on a regular basis, though as Shakespeare is quick to remind us, 'Is it not strange that desire should so many years outlive performance?'

And is it not natural, then, that sex should bob up in crosswords too? After all, we are dealing with the twin realms of double entendre: the cryptic clue and the loaded phrase. Under 'sex' your average thesaurus lists close to 100 words, and that's barely breaking into a sweat. *Score. Do. Shag. Mount.* Each offering so flexible – the perfect toys for a fertile mind.

Done well, sex can add zing to a clue, a dab of raunch, a comic image. The crunch comes down to execution. One false move and innuendo can topple into smut. Like so many things, composing naughty clues is about establishing the right mood. A cheeky connotation is provocative with a small 'p', as opposed to offensive. But that balance is hard to strike, as the setter tries to guess a solver's tastes. In the end, the same clue is as likely to make one reader smirk as cause another to go purple round the gills.

Comedians call it 'working blue', and once you sit through the first gig you'll know in your bones, hopefully your funny bone, whether the performer warrants an encore. Speaking of performance, here's a clue I made a few years back:

Perform on a bedspread (5)

Keeping to the charade recipe, the clue leads to DO + ON + A = DOONA (which is Australian slang for 'duvet'). At drafting stage I'd tried for a tone somewhere between risqué and ribald. Or I should say *my version* of risqué and ribald, as, in the end, the solver will be the judge. The best you can expect as a compiler is that your stuff entertains the majority. Aunt Mavis might throw her paper across the room, or take up arms in the letters page, but for every Mavis in the world there is, one hopes, an Agatha and a John, a Chloe and a Lachlan, getting a grin and coming back next week.

Sex is the humid air we breathe. Just ask Madame Bovary, literature's finest adulteress. Even her letters own a sleazy charade vibe, with MAD (bonkers) + AM (morning, or live) + EB (or BE backwards, hence to live up?) + OVARY. Not there yet, but the lewdness is tantalising.

ADULTERESS too has plenty of legs, puzzle-wise. ADUL is a blend of DUAL, opening the way for an anagram with the right signpost – *dual romp?* With E – *middle of bed?* – covered in *hair* (or TRESS) the climax …

I've already jotted down both of these ideas, the raw makings of future puzzles, which is how we clue-mongers operate. We live for hidden kinks in names and phrases, and should those kinks murmur boudoir business, then that's no bad thing.

Like AMATEUR, a word I clued ten years ago. There it was – A MATE with YOUR other half. True to the French, the whole means lover. With all these overlaps, the clue had to be:

Lover, a sex partner with your other half (7)

No paper is immune. Who'd ever suspect a *Times* compiler could channel the spirit of Mills & Boon when clueing PETROLEUM? But he or she did:

Crude caress with part hesitation (9)

'Oh Fabio, stop it, please, you'll ruin me! Your *caress* (PET) with *part* (ROLE) *hesitation* (UM) is so damnably *crude* (PETROLEUM)!'

In the same vein I once reduced CUBISM to a school of depravity:

Copper faces sexual dilemma in art school (6)

Can you see the poor officer's crisis? There he is – CU, the chemical symbol for *copper* – facing the *dilemma* of BI (bisexual) or SM (sadomasochism). Certainly a bluer clue than average, one that Mavis *and* Chad may both resent, yet the cubist copper, just like the curvy cheerleader in our current clue, touch on an important issue.

How far is too far when it comes to sexual subtext? What clue-approach will see most titters turn into outcry? If erotica, says novelist Isabel Allende, is using a feather, and pornography the whole chicken – then where does plume give way to poultry? And can we get coleslaw with that?

WAYWARD SEX – gender bias and crosswords

Researching racy clues, I recently dug up DUG. The word is archaic for breast, though this didn't stop it from appearing in two separate crosswords. The first was a morsel from *The Times*, a bit of charade shenanigans:

Dug light carrier (3,4)

Here the synonym for *light* is RAY. Thus TEAT + RAY = TEA TRAY. Offensive? Hardly. Certainly no match for Rupert Bear with his meat and two veg.

Further down the slippery slope, one English setter made reference to the Murdoch innovation of 1969, when the media baron propped up drooping *Sun* sales by adding topless girls to Page Three. Did sex sell? It did in 1969. As for the clue in question, its compiler settled on a louche pun, trying to invoke Polynesia with *Dugout location (4,5),* when all along the answer of course was PAGE THREE.

But let's stay for a moment with the Page Three concept, the buxom poppet and her al fresco assets. In many ways this dated custom captures that moment where sex mutates into sexism. I doubt whether Ximenes would escape public wrath these days with his (albeit brilliant) clue for HOUSEWIFE:

I have most of the time to stitch – then I iron (9)

Can you unpick the clue? *Most of the time* is almost all of HOUR. *To stitch* is SEW. *Then I iron* = I + FE (the chemical symbol again). Wrapped into one bundle, the wordplay also serves as the dubious definition, where the housewife is depicted as a dedicated seamstress and laundry-wallah. Scarcely a stereotype you can peddle in the new millennium, though the chauvinism pales in comparison with a storm created in Sydney twenty years ago thanks to an outrage sporting the fingerprints of one Lindsey Browne.

It should be said, in order to set the scene fairly, that Lindsey was in his seventies by the time the clue appeared. Born in 1915, and setting crosswords since 1935, the bloke was the product of a less enlightened era when it comes to sexual equality. He was also an incurable punster, one day daring to the call the HEAVENLY HOST a dreamboat who throws good parties. As cheeky as that sounds, it wasn't LB's cardinal sin. That occurred in the late 1980s, when the issue of domestic violence seized the media. One phrase in particular caught the master's eye, which he tackled in his clue:

Pan-fried delicacies for criminals? (8,5)

I won't torment you. The answer is BATTERED WOMEN, and the backlash was savage. Calls came from victims, social workers and the judiciary, all condemning the clue's perversion. Elspeth Browne, Lindsey's wife, herself a social worker, was gobsmacked. 'Lin,' she said when the *merde* was flying, 'whatever were you thinking?'

Lindsey himself seemed mystified. Her husband, says Elspeth, kept wondering why people couldn't see the 'punny side' of things. It's a crossword clue, after all, he argued, a piece of entertainment, but the *Herald* saw it differently and published an apology.

Ideally, once the dust had settled and a chastened LB had returned to his grids, that day would have marked an end to sexist clues, but no. As recently as 2004 I almost spat out my muesli when a *Herald* colleague – I won't name him – thought the following clue was in good taste:

Chick picked up by vacuum cleaner? (1,3,2,5)

The answer, I realised with mounting dread, was A BIT OF FLUFF, a double-meaning clue and the kind you'd hope we'd left behind with the Model T. To echo Elspeth, 'Mate, what were you thinking?'

But is that the real problem? Are too many middle-aged men in charge of clues? If every setter is a whiskered cad bred on a diet of Biggles and Benny Hill, then no wonder such bigotry prevails. Yet such a notion is as wrong-headed as that of the all-sewing, all-ironing missus. Hugh Stephenson, the puzzle editor at the *Guardian*, recently did a headcount to learn that a third of his contributors are female, including Australia's own Shirl O'Brien. Nearer home, three of the seven Fairfax setters are women. With a twinkle in the eye I tried to highlight this equality trend with a charade:

Excellent to Ms, perhaps? (3–5)

The answer is TOP-CLASS, or TO-PC-LASS, where the lasses of yesteryear are the Mses of today. A superior clue in a similar vein was crafted by Pasquale, the code name of prolific British compiler Don Manley. (You can tell when Manley is at the helm, as his bylines across numerous papers betray a notable Don, namely Quixote, Giovanni, Bradman or Duck.) Here's his clue:

Sexist description thus to upset females (3,5)

This construction is a hybrid, combining the two recipes we've met already – anagram and charade. *Sexist description* is the definition. Upset the six letters in *thus to* and attach *females* (FF) to the tail and HOT STUFF emerges. The clue may be viewed as having your cake and eating it – getting away with a garish term as well as bewailing it – but I'm guessing that the combo of wordplay and social awareness delighted most who solved it.

Unlike the clues of Cyclops, a setter who seems happiest when offending as many punters as possible. His puzzle runs in London's satirical magazine *Private Eye*. The shockproof solver must navigate such anagrams as SEX ON CUE (NO EXCUSE) and A MA'S BUTTER (MASTURBATE), while HELP CASTRATION, HO renders LANCASHIRE HOTPOT.

Filth, in fact, is a cultish subgenre of puzzling. In 2008, over in America, Chronicle Books released a lewd book of brainteasers under the intriguing title of *Where's Dildo?*

Thumb the pages and you'll find Wonderbras shaped into mazes, X-rated riddles and find-a-words teeming with WELL HUNG and WHISKEY DICK.

But the cream of the salacious crop must be the Kama Sutra. Not the original Hindu manual for the bedroom arts, but two enigmatic variations. The first is a jigsaw, with 83 lovemaking positions shattered into a thousand pieces – the ideal honeymoon gift for puzzle nuts.

The second incarnation outsold most novels during my stint at a Melbourne bookstore. A cartoon collection at first glance, the book depicted the heads of two lovers, each wearing a sublime grin. Scattered between them, like a Big Bang galaxy, was the dense array of a dot-to-dot puzzle. Contortion by numbers. Cue cheerleader.

PLEASURE PRINCIPLE – the last charade and the oldest joy

'Winning isn't Everything – It's the Only Thing.' This is a tagline from *Bring It On*, a cheerleading movie that doesn't need to join your bucket list. The film is a dance-off between the sassy San Diego gals and the hip-hopping plagiarists of East Compton. As for who wins, you'll have to ask Tess, my tweenage daughter, as she's the only one in the family to go the distance. But one line stuck with me: 'It's all about making the best moves.'

Cheerleading *and* crosswording. One error and a charade will fall on its face. So bring it on, compiler. Let's step it out:

Early curve superb on cheerleader (7)

Tellingly, *cheerleader* has next to zero synonyms. On top of that, just as *circle* signalled the O in OMAHA, or mid-April suggests R, a word like *cheerleader* is likely to indicate C, the leader of cheer.

Thinking this way, you start to isolate the clue's latter half as the wordplay element – a big leap forward in the solving stakes. The same theory also implies that your seven-letter answer ends in C. And what does the whole answer mean? *Early*? Or *early curve*? Which makes more sense?

Early – exactly.

Honouring the C-theory, and dashing out the letters we've gained from earlier answers, we now have this spread: A _ C _ A _ C. (Does any word fit?)

Only one. And sweetly, this one word also means *early* – ARCHAIC. So let's match the pieces to the words: ARCH (*curve*), AI (*superb* – as in A-1) and then your C for cheer. All right. We've solved 23-Down, our final charade. Give me an A – A! Give me an R – R! Give me … a break.

By the way, beware that A-1 trick. Just like ANT in the last chapter, clued by *worker*, AI is a regular ruse. Any word for excellent can suggest the pairing, while fine often denotes OK. Notice too how the 'one' of A-1 morphs into a capital I when entering the grid, another piece of close magic, where numbers turn to letters before your eyes.

As the setter, the moment I twigged that *arch* and *cheerleader* both embrace curve as a concept I knew I could splice wordplay and definition, lending a bit of match-day sizzle to the overall clue.

Not that ARCHAIC isn't sexy on its lonesome. English has precious few words ending in AIC, and rarities need our love. Sex, in fact, is as archaic as humankind, the mystery that brought us into being, and occasionally the analogy for solving a crossword.

I kid you not. Regardless of style, compilers need to remember that the pleasure principle outweighs all other considerations. Charade or anagram, the moral dilemma plays second fiddle to the joy a smitten solver can find in the challenge.

Take Dunn Miller, for example. A 64-year-old librarian

from California, Ms Miller was irate when the *Atlantic Monthly* decided to withdraw its brilliant cryptic, known as the Puzzler. Constructed by the conjugal duo of Emily Cox and Henry Rathvon, the Puzzler's grid could be shaped to mimic a pinball machine, a goldfish bowl or a pirate map, depending on the month's theme. When asked to describe the puzzle's appeal, Dunn shocked the *New York Times* journo by replying, 'You get the pleasure of solving each clue, so there's the aha moment over and over – it's like having multiple orgasms.'

Some solvers can make a more direct link between word-play and foreplay. Like the letter I received in 2009, days after sharing my puzzle passion on a radio show. The listener was a palindrome called Alamala, and she wasn't backwards in coming forwards:

I am one of a couple of cruciverbalists – that's couple as in two people who snuggle up together over cryptic cross-word puzzles. We're evenly matched and complementary in that we have different areas of specialist interest. The satisfaction of this shared and cooperative intellectual activity brings us closer and excites our bodies via our minds. Usually we manage to finish at one go, but sometimes pen and puzzle are set aside for a more urgent activity. Sadly, I think this aspect of cruciverbalism has been overlooked. Please tell your guest setter he makes people happier in more ways that he might imagine!

QUIZLING 7.1

Charade-wise, what item of clothing is a narrow winning margin beside a shared win of no margin?

BLUE CLUES

Risqué is OK – till you cross the invisible line. How far is the envelope pushed by these five clues? The first two come from *The Times*, with Rufus and Paul (twice) of the *Guardian* bringing up the rear.

Not easy being like Casanova after time = THORNY
Coach possibly organised porn at strip club = PUBLIC
    TRANSPORT
Stimulated to use a rod, perhaps? = AROUSED
As such, female unlikely to bend over = FRIGID
Swimmer giving bottom a good licking = SEA TROUT

QUIZLING 7.2

To reveal today's mystical name, solve the four clues below, reverse your answers and link them together in the same sequence.

Male offspring (3)
Knack (3)
Commercial (2)
Aggregate (3)

QUIZLING 7.3

Keeping with curves, what are the only two foods spelt entirely with curved capital letters?
(No brand names, please.)

CHAPTER 8

Cockney chaos going to stir green (7)

To see him in a tuxedo was to make you look twice – his towering frame, that purple-dark skin, darker than the jacket cinching his torso. Maynard had grace. He used that spoon like an extension of his fingers, scooping up pumpkin wedges with ease, an upper spoon all the while poised to prevent the load from toppling.

'Silver service', Meredith called it. A stiff woman with gelled bob, Meredith sucked olive stones to deaden her smoking urge. But that was her only sloppiness. Everything else was military, her scissor-like gait, her terse instructions – *less chatter, more wine, table four, water check.* Rather than help, she liked to stalk the dining room to ask why the waiters weren't helping enough.

Look like a waiter and you'll be a waiter, she said, but that was bollocks. Catching the tube that afternoon, dressed in tux with patent leather shoes, I felt more the secret agent. Even the stations – Baker Street, Charing Cross – had that movie déjà vu. Yet the minute I walked into the kitchen the aura evaporated as Meredith transfixed me with her eye.

'Tell me you didn't commute in your uniform.'

'I thought it was OK.'

'You're wearing half of bloody London on your jacket.'

This was my first gig with Dunford Catering, a

dog-and-pony operation that hired backpackers with no fixed abode, and no National Insurance numbers. Meredith dabbed my jacket with a damp rag as she trotted out her favourite barb, 'Just because you work in a zoo doesn't mean you belong there.'

When I first heard I'd be waiting tables at Regent's Park Zoo I had monkeys in my mind, gibbons stealing avocado off the tray, but the room was a blank space of ten round tables with a low stage for ceremonies. The only hint of zoology was an idle howl from an open door or the faint smell of dung seeping through the air grilles.

Yet the name alone was great for postcards. *Hi Dad, you'll never guess, I'm dressed up like a penguin in London Zoo.* Aside from its tourist appeal, the zoo also had crossword kudos. Not that I told that to Meredith, the woman squaring my bow tie and telling me that excellence was a benchmark. But later, hearing a phone in the distance, I thought of all those calls in the past, in the early 1920s when crosswords first appeared in British papers. They were 'Quicks' back then, the fad imported from America. Before too long the Brits were as hooked as their Yank cousins. Afternoons all over Britain were spent leafing through dictionaries, trying to find that last elusive word which all too often was an obscure animal.

Brazilian aardvark (5)
Camelopard (5)
Madagascan bee-eater (6)

Who knew the names of such offbeat fauna? Regent's Park Zoo was who, the phone running hot as solvers hoped to fill their final corner, hunting COATI and OKAPI and HOOPOE respectively, until the zoo snapped and banned all puzzle enquiries. That's right, this zoo, Regent's Park, where I tried to balance a stewed pear on a spoon.

'Wait a tick,' came a voice. 'You doin' it all arsey-versey.'

I turned around expecting to see some real-life version of Andy Capp, the cartoon Cockney with the fag on his lip, but standing there was Maynard, all 190 centimetres of him, and my pear went splat as a result. 'No bovver,' he smiled. 'They grow on trees, don't they?'

I rescued the mess while Maynard went looking for two fresh spoons. 'It ain't easy first time, but soon you'll do it wiv yer eyes shut.'

'My benchmark is excellence,' I said.

'Yeah, and my name's fucken Santa Claus.'

Despite seeming the most exotic of the waiting crew, Maynard was the sole Londoner. His parents came from Ghana and had settled down in Wapping on the Thames. We clicked straight away, faster than my spoons at any rate. The guy was a natural mentor, though I was a D-grade student and Meredith was on the warpath. The harder I tried to master silver service, clapping two spoons in a single hand, the more I resembled a lobster on Mogadon.

First course was soup, thank God, a doddle aside from the dinner rolls. For all its advancements in engineering, Great Britain had yet to hear of tongs. Instead I used my spoons to pincer each roll, balancing the bread as the diners watched in a mix of amusement and dread. Meredith was just as nervous, looking on. Her job was to look for weak links and I was it. 'What's the story?' she seethed in the kitchen. 'The agency said you had waiting experience.'

Waiting for trains, I felt like saying, but this was zero hour, and Meredith had 200 mouths to feed, a charity gala with all the nobs of high society. 'As soon as those soups are done, I need you to perform.'

Maynard could see the problem. Just relax, he said. 'The more you 'assle the more you'll screw it up.' Which wasn't the balm I needed but the voice did wonders, the familiar lilt of Family Steptoe in my ear, or maybe I was drawing on the comfort of crosswords, since cryptics rely on the East End habit of H-dropping as a handy device when it comes to trimming words. To Maynard the zoo would be full of 'ippos and 'owler monkeys, whereas Meredith was an 'ag, an 'orror, or she was in my eyes. From the kitchen door you could hear the final slurps. Next on the à la carte was trout from the upland streams of Cumbria, poached and silver-served onto your plate.

'Ow did it go? In a word, 'opeless. The trout was so soft it sagged like wet paper. As soon as I betrayed my accent the diners were more simpatico, knowing a colonial would hardly have the politesse to manoeuvre silverware, but the mood of the table took a dive when I tried to convey one trout to a gentleman's plate, the animal's head falling loose, landing with an intimate thud on his ladyship's pumpkin. Meredith moved in. I was marched to the kitchen, banished to water duties. Predictably, my first evening at Regents Park was also my last, the whole charade coming apart at the seams much like my rental jacket. I said goodbye to Maynard, knowing this Ghana giant had tried his best to save me, and he just beamed back, 'Take it easy, awright – 'appy travels.'

WHITE ON BLACK – race versus racism

Where Cockney heartland begins and ends is a matter of debate but as a rule of thumb the term applies to the working-class hubs of East London. Think Fagin and the Artful Dodger.

The Cockney device can appear in most clue types, turning hedge into edge, harrow into arrow, hairline into airline. See if you can solve these two Cockneyisms:

Cockney control of nightmarish street (3)
Mother of Cockney pet in The Netherlands? (9)

Once you find your inner Eliza Doolittle, you should be able to hear ELM and AMSTERDAM, being reductions of *helm* and *hamster dam*. (Dam – when not a weir – is a pastoral word for mother.)

Note, too, that not every setter will flag the device with the word Cockney but may opt for other ways to suggest this special patch of London. These next two stem from *The Times*:

Snag commonly an irritation (4)
Scoundrel in Albert Square a slippery type (3)

The answers are ITCH and EEL, paring back *hitch* and *heel*. *Commonly*, the adverb, is a dig at the raffish associations of Cockney, the coarse voice of Tom, Dick and 'Arry. Albert Square, meanwhile, is Cockney territory. Other nudges to note are East End, Eastender, Cheapside or Whitechapel – Jack the Ripper's turf.

It's handy to remember that whenever you see the Cockney code, you generally know that the target word begins with H, and that the H will be dropped. Our current clue, for example, opens with the phrase *Cockney chaos*. So what chaos synonym begins with H? That's the canny way to think.

Importantly, the H can only be the initial and nowhere else in the word. *A Cockney chook*, for example, doesn't mean a COOK, nor will *Cockney Irish* equal IRIS. Think of the trout fiasco, where only the head is lost. Setters know this category in general as a deletion clue, which gets its own chapter around the corner, but for now let's return to the idea of race. When, in Puzzleville, is it kosher to refer to a person's ethnicity? Is *kosher*, for instance, a kosher word to use in this regard, or does that demean the Jewish tradition? If Cockney warrants its own subgenre of clues, what other ethnic groups may be enlisted?

Fewer than before, put it that way. Once upon a time, back in the baby boom, a pet trick of several *Herald* compilers went by the dubious banner of Orientalisms, or the Flied Lice Loutine. Here ROCK would turn into LOCK, or RAFTER into LAUGHTER (soundwise), the cheap trick a reference to Asians reputedly struggling to pronounce their Rs.

Like passé sexism, the notion of labelling one group of people has fast lost currency. Now and then Kiwis (people known to say *trek* for *trick*) or Brooklynites (*boyd* for *bird*) will be implicated, but this is tame compared to the racism of the past. Let's take a look at two notable jaw-droppers.

The first comes courtesy of A. F. Ritchie, the post-war maestro and senior Anglican minister. This clue occurs in Afrit's own anthology, *Armchair Crosswords*, published in 1949:

> *What do happen, Mose, if our gals lose deir heads? Oh, den you find de ways out! (8)*

The answer is EGRESSES, as the so-called gals of Mose were deemed to be NEGRESSES. Losing their heads, they become exits, or *ways out*. Blasphemy in this day and age, but Afrit was a setter of his epoch.

Some 30 years after Afrit's book, a second clue tested public mores, this time in the *Herald*. For reasons to become apparent I'll omit the setter's name, a colleague no longer among our number. His clue:

> *Blackman goes walkabout in NSW town (9)*

The indigenous people of Australia have suffered a legion of hateful labels, all of them taboo in modern vernacular. One is ABO, which some English puzzles have only recently eschewed and US setters clue more wisely as *Blood classifications* (namely A, B and O). Another no-no is COON, borrowed from America where it's a shortening of raccoon. Here the town is COONAMBLE, and aptly the *Herald* took decisive action, telling the culprit to take a hike.

The message was clear. Lindsey Browne (or LB) might have peddled *Jap drink* in 1971 (the answer being NIP), but those days were history. Naughtiness and racism were separate modes. Clues could refer to ethnicity – an observation about place or cultural background – but using pejorative names or mocking accents went against the grain.

As do slurs aimed at exotic food, or so you'd hope. Now and then lapses occur. One compiler, the late Bob Smithies, alias Bunthorne, trundled out this clue in 2006:

Ruthless order to setter on Korean diet? = DOG EAT DOG

But what about those 'apless Cockneys, you ask. Seems some racial affronts are more affronting than others. Even Aussies have been spoofed. Most notably, in 2009, American Richard Silvestri built a crossword for the *LA Times* entitled Heard Down Under. The puzzle ribbed the Aussie habit of lengthening vowels (turning Purple Rain into PURPLE RHINE, and brainstorm into BRINE STORM). Did the paper suffer an Aussie jihad? On the contrary, the theme was applauded as a fresh piece of '*entertinement*'.

Measure this against the furore of 1993, when Hasbro, the licence-holders of Scrabble, received a letter of enquiry from Judith Grad of Virginia. According to *Word Freak* by Stefan Fatsis, Grad objected to the racist terms condoned by the game's official wordlist. JEW, she discovered, meant to haggle, and therefore could be played on the board with impunity, as could JEWING or JEWED. NIGGER was also there, along with SPIC, MICK, KIKE and DAGO. Grad alerted Milton Bradley, of Hasbro's game division, prompting Dave Wilson, the company's president, to send a sympathetic reply. He described the listed words as abhorrent, but argued they existed under the rules of the game. Frederick C. Mish, the editor-in-chief of the *Merriam-Webster* dictionary, took a similar view. 'Such slurs are part of the language,' he wrote.

Not happy, Grad enlisted the NAACP (or the National Association for the Advancement of Coloured People) in league with several Jewish alliances to have the terms ousted from the game. Eventually, after nine years, the game's overseers identified 205 words as being vulgar, racist and/or derogatory. Nowadays any tournament has the option of playing or ditching the divisive set, from ABO to YID, and the fury has eased.

Mind you, here in Australia, Jewish campaigners were stirred into action in the late 1980s, thanks to a freakish *Herald* crossword. This time the offence lay in the grid itself.

Current puzzle-checker Lynne Cairncross recalls the episode: 'When I was head of Daily Events, my excellent crossword editor, Deb Shaw, let through a grid with a swastika on it … and so did I when I signed off the page. The compiler, a marvellous, philanthropic fellow, was horrified.'

Squinting, the pattern resembled a Third Reich flag: a regrettable fluke of the squares. Cold comfort to the Jewish readers that contacted the *Herald* on the morning of publication. Just as quickly the mishap's main players apologised, the matter regarded as both vile and accidental. Working so close to the grid, setters and their editors can sometimes fail to see the black for the white.

MAYHEM MAYHEM – tautologies and tautonyms

So, has the ha'penny dropped? You're looking for a word meaning chaos that starts with H, then pretending Maynard is pronouncing it for you. (*'Jeez Dave, your trout 'ead caused one 'elluva 'oop-la.'*) Let's consider 19-Down with this hint in mind:

Cockney chaos going to stir green (7)

Seasoned solvers will know that the front end holds the

wordplay for a couple of reasons. First, the Cockney mention is a giveaway. Second, *Cockney chaos* has no distinct meaning in isolation.

What about *havoc*? That could work. Do you know a word starting with AVOC? I bet you do. One is the avocet, a black-and-white wader which may well reside at London Zoo. The other is avocado, which wasn't on the menu that night.

AVOCADO of course is defined by the clue's end word – *green* – which is not to say the fruit is a vegetable, but a shade of green. The balance of the wordplay rests in the word *stir*, which isn't a kitchen instruction, nor an anagram signpost, but more the muddle I created at Table Three, namely an ADO. The linking phrase – *going to* – captures the notion of transfer, how one half (AVOC) moves closer to the other (ADO).

Just like SPARROW, a bird doubtless free to roam London Zoo, AVOCADO has that rare quality of being two synonyms side by side, at least before a Cockney utters it: *havoc* + *ado*, à la *spar* + *row*.

Such rarities aren't to be confused with orthodox tautologies (such as *end result* and *new discovery*) or zoological tautonyms, being those Regent's Park residents who own such Latin names as *Uncia uncia* (the snow leopard), *Lemmus lemmus* (the Norwegian lemming) or *Cricetus cricetus* (which Sid Vicious, Eliza Doolittle and a handsome waiter called Maynard would know as your common 'amster).

SPELLING TROUBLE

Eccentric spelling turns some names into booby traps. I had to undo an entire grid as a result of bungling Twilight's creator STEPHENIE MEYER, falling for the Stephanie Trap. Beware these other names below:

Addams Family	Muhammad Ali	Jimi Hendrix
Condoleezza Rice	Scarlett Johansson	Axl Rose
Brigitte Bardot	Keystone Kops	Cybill Shepherd
Adrien Brody	Freddy Krueger	Ashlee Simpson
Stieg Larsson	Barbra Streisand	Nicolas Cage
Tobey Maguire	Kristen Stewart	Forest Whitaker
Willem Dafoe	Olive Oyl	Salley Vickers

HALL OF FAME: CHARADES

Quick run ending in wicket (5) [Paul, the *Guardian*]
Many revs make small car go (8) [Hendra, the *Guardian*]
Polish plants and animals (9) [Cincinnus, *FT*]
$100 springs doubled in disreputable garages (4,5) [Henry Hook, US]
Prisoner taking cellmate, perhaps, as wife? (10) [*Times* 8558]
Shades of Clementine, K-K-Katy etc? (10) [Orlando, the *Guardian*]

SOLUTIONS: fleet, ministry, buffaloes, chop shops, conjugally, sunglasses

QUIZLING 8.1

Drop the first or second word's initial H (in 'earty Cockney fashion) and you'll create each clue's answer. Abhor octet, for example, is HATE EIGHT.

Toss aristocrat (4,4)   For an Irish gun? (6,7)

Dump journos (3,5)   Lance? (6,6)

Tougher love? (6,6)   Moorage urge (9,9)

QUIZLING 8.2

What singer answers this charade: fair + fashionable + lumber + tarn?

QUIZLING 8.3

If B + bird = dog (that is, B + EAGLE = BEAGLE), can you figure out the zoology below? No mixing is needed.

W + reptile = insect

F + mammal = mammal

F + bird = bird

B + mammal = fish

T + seabird = seabird

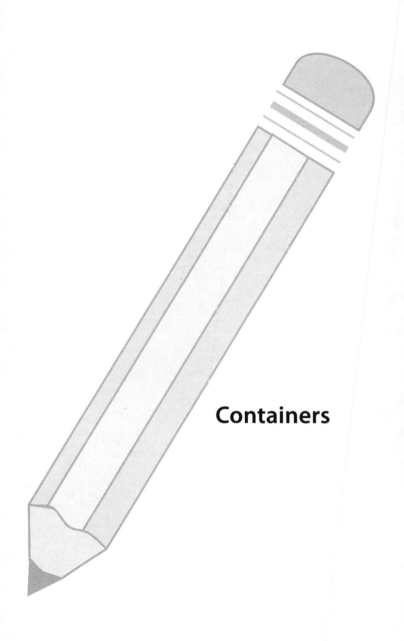

Containers

CHAPTER 9

Sucker pens article for website guide (4,3)

Adam Ramona has paisley skin. He wears knee-high disco boots and purple mascara, and when he walks he prances like a marionette – *clomp, clomp, clomp.*

Usually he hangs out with Mashup and a guy called S1 Gausman. If you want to tell them apart, you'll see that Mashup has the jet-black drainpipes, while Gausman prefers the platform soles. The trio loiter on ACVA Island, a grassy patch dotted with gum trees and a tower built of words.

Tall as the clouds, this tower grows non-stop, changing shape before your eyes. Blue letters, crossing the sky in flocks, approach the island all the time, linking to the tower like molecules to a chain. A lower-case 'e' hooks its tail around a G's open hollow. Each letter turns to green as they rest, nesting like starlings in a growing steeple.

Known as Babelswarm, the tower is the world's highest structure built of language, virtually speaking, and a project fostered by the Australian Centre of Virtual Art – or ACVA, the island's sponsor.

The island itself is closer than you think, locked inside a universe called Second Life, a parallel world where anything is possible. If real life can't accommodate a spire like Babelswarm, then Second Life can. A popular MUVE, or multi-user virtual environment, Second Life is a cosmos unto itself, complete with day and night, launderette and forests, currency and market pressure. Much like Babelswarm, Second Life is shaped and enriched by its residents – or signed-up users.

The world was created by San Francisco think tank Linden Lab. Rather than car-jacking or alien-shooting, Second Life, from its launch in 2003, offered a different kind of gaming. Or is it a game? Among the 70,000 concurrent Residents worldwide – that's *this world* I mean – Second Life represents a chance to push your imagination, to interact with the likes of Mashup and Gausman and all the other avatars.

Off-screen, Mashup is Christopher Dodds. He lives a few blocks from my place in suburban Melbourne. We met at a barbecue, our kids attending the same school. We kicked around the usual topics of suburban males – sport and news – when Christopher asked, 'So what are you into?'

'Words,' I said.

'Yeah?' Chris raised his eyebrows above his sunglasses. 'What do you do with them?'

'Put them in boxes. I mix them up and make clues. What about you?'

'I'm building a tower,' he said.

Not that Christopher – or Mashup – is doing all the making. Every syllable joining the tower comes from the passing crowd – that's the crux of Babelswarm: the structure is built by the online observer. Just like the original Tower of Babel, the monument embodies the hubbub of multiple languages uttered within earshot. As soon as Adam blew his chances in Eden, the paradise of one tongue divided into a hell of many. Poet John Milton imagines Babel as a place of hideous gabble, but as a puzzler looking for new ways to see old words, the blah-blah verges on musical.

Mashup and his virtual mates are composers of a kind. Or decomposers, breaking language down into letters and then rebuilding. Or maybe they're just plain posers – those disco boots, for starters. But the architecture is staggering.

Nine to five, the artist in Dodds earns his keep as a graphic designer. Gausman is Dr Justin Clemens, a lecturer in English at Melbourne University, while the paisley freak in boots is 3-D artist Adam Nash. To build their spire the team relied on a start-up fund they won in 2007, a creative grant from the Australia Council for $20,000, the country's maiden sum dedicated to establishing a virtual artwork.

Is it art? What's art?

Is it a game? You tell me.

A new direction for wordplay? That's a resounding yes.

French thinker Roger Caillois once put games into four boxes. Crosswords, for example, belong in the *Agon* box, where games of competition go. (Your opponent in this case is the puzzle's setter. You strive, you agonise, and hopefully you triumph.) Other games, said Caillois, match the labels of *mimicry* (games of expression, like charades, or *Second Life*), *alea* (games of chance) and *ilinx* (games of giddiness – which include rolling downhill and bungee jumping). I don't know how long Caillois took to draft this natural order, but the universe pretty much turned upside down a decade after he died in 1978, when the world of websites and avatars and MUVEs moved the goalposts forever. Instead of Go Fish or tennis or Space Invaders there's a new habitat alive with risk, thrill, struggle: a meta-game, as eggheads call *Second Life*. Or as Clemens/Gausman prefers, 'The game itself forces you to decide about what sort of game it is.' And that's just a corner of cyberspace, one microcosm inside the new cosmos. In the world of puzzling, the changes have been equally profound. The rise of 'crogs' (or 'crossword blogs') alone has turned the black-and-white art into Technicolor.

FEEDBACK LOOPS – blogosphere and containers

When Michael Sharp started a blog back in 2006 he didn't know what a blog was. Talking to the *New York Times*, he confessed, 'It sounded like something that might be cool to develop in relation to a comics course I was teaching.'

Sharp also teaches noir fiction and seventeenth-century literature at New York's Binghamton University, and, just like S1 Gausman, this hip academic plumped for an alias when braving the new frontier, going with the hardboiled-sounding alias of Rex Parker just in case the online caper floundered. No danger there. After five years, Rex Parker Does the NYT Crossword Puzzle scores 10,000 hits a day, with as many people coming to enjoy the Sharp humour as to peek at an answer. In pre-web days, the major dilemma was pen versus pencil; now, that question is more about brain versus Google. If you need to crack that final clue – do you go surfing? Hundreds do, if Rex's hit rate is any guide. A great many of his first-time callers have stumbled on the site by virtue of a clue-search. Going by traffic patterns, the seekers clearly liked what they found.

Sharp will solve the day's puzzle as it appears online, usually beating delivery of the hard copy. He'll then crank out his clue-by-clue appraisal the next morning before heading out the door to play professor. But this is no dry analysis or grammatical soapboxing – Rex Parker is the love child of quipster Dorothy Parker and a deadpan Raymond Chandler character. Any given puzzle will inspire a welter of images cropped from photo banks and personal collections, adding colour to Rex's critique. A gallery of Cartesian maps, say, will honour the answer MERIDIAN, or links to a Superman fanzine will recognise XRAY VISION.

Yet ironically, back in those first timid weeks, the blog's initial post tried to jinx the project: '*Please do not comment on puzzles the day they are printed. This blog is just a bad idea. Signed, grandpamike.*'

Amy Reynaldo, a Chicago book editor, had encountered this kind of attitude a year before Rex set up shop. Reynaldo once went to the *New York Times* crossword forum, keen to discuss the day's puzzles, only to find others who thought like *grandpamike*. Everywhere she looked a spoiler rule applied, where users were free to debate a clue's merits but forbidden to blab its answer. The edict cramped Reynaldo's style. How can you really rant or rhapsodise, if a puzzle's solution is off-limits? It's like trying to discuss kayaking without using the words water or paddle. Amy's response? She set up Diary of a Crossword Fiend, the first crcg of its kind in the United States, paving the way for Rex and many others to follow.

The sober twin of Rex's delirium, Crossword Fiend is the site for solvers who take puzzling to heart. Reynaldo is an omnivore, solving and discussing puzzles from New York, Los Angeles, Boston and Philadelphia across the week. Crucially too, editors surf Amy's site to see how their puzzles are being received, creating an ongoing feedback loop that keeps all players honest, and the puzzle quality high.

You could say the blog craze is the Tower of Babel in reverse. Before chat rooms, a compiler could only guess how a puzzle was received. Fun or foul, good or bad: a setter could only speculate about what solvers thought. Stray letters would give you hints, but it was random clamour in a lot of ways. *Great clue! Bad clue! Boo, yay*, etc. But thanks to new media, responses are now constant and orchestrated. Much like village greens, crogs are places for solvers to assemble and compare notes, single cut flaws and strengths, declare a verdict. While debate seldcm reaches a consensus, the combined wisdom is there for anyone listening.

In Australia the online trend is accelerating. Two active blogs chew over Fairfax puzzles most days, the first a long-running forum called Deef (or Feedback), the Web annex of the Australian Crosswcrc Club. The second, I discovered, is

The DA Trippers, a site mounted in 2008 by three Melbourne solvers who go by the aliases of AS, RC and TH. (Do I know their real names? No. Are Mashup and Rex Parker any relation? Possibly.)

Holding my own puzzles to the light, the DA brigade debates fairness or ambiguity. Clues are divided into Gold, Confusion and Bullshit. Dropping by either blog I feel like a pastry chef seeing how his latest confection went down – too much glaze? Not enough honey? Did those nougat snails work out?

In the UK there are several standout crogs. One of the earliest is Fifteen Squared. This grand-scale meeting of minds is run by a team of erudite solvers who review under such Net-names as Uncle Yap, Rightback and Holy Ghost. The volume of puzzles it handles is what distinguishes the site. Every week, multiple forums will slide some ten UK puzzles under the microscope, plucked from as many different newspapers.

Smaller in scope, but zestier for images and with a playful tone, is the crog newcomer nestled within the *Guardian* website. The forum was established in August 2011. Its curator is Alan Connor, a self-confessed lover of cribbage and asparagus, who also has a flair for unpacking puzzles. A random week will see all manner of dispatches uploaded, from setter profiles to clue round-ups, or even live web-chats, regularly drawing a legion of responses. The same crog offers mini-tutorials, picking out recipes like anagrams, or charades, and explaining how the formulas operate. Which sounds a lot like my job at hand. So let's inspect the next recipe on our roster. That's right – time to get stuck into containers.

PANDORA'S CONTAINER – nesting names and container clues

Sally Heath is a former editor with the *Age* in Melbourne, as well as being a friend in a condom. You're not following? Nor was Sally when I happened to let slip the condom thing over the phone.

Heath ran the arts pages of the Saturday paper, the A2 supplement that carries reviews, profiles and puzzles. One day she needed my proof notes, and that's when I shot myself in the foot. I couldn't stop my tongue from obeying my brain, as I said, 'You realise your name is a friend in a condom?'

Worryingly, Heath's end of the phone fell quiet. Either the line had dropped out or I'd just alienated the *Age*'s arts boss. 'Your letters,' I added, desperate now. 'They're a perfect container clue: ALLY inside SHEATH, which I'd clue as friend in condom.'

By now in my late forties, I should have stopped saying this sort of stuff aloud, a thought that must have occurred to Sally as the conversation returned to the business in hand. What was she *meant* to say?

'You bastard,' is what Bill Leak said when I pulled a similar stunt on his name. Perhaps Australia's greatest living cartoonist, Leak is also a puzzle addict and happened to be solving the *Herald* crossword one day when his gaze fell a few centimetres to read a Wordwit rhyme:

Despite thousands laughing at him
This cartoonist is sick in grim.
Who is he?

ILL in BLEAK is who, another container, and Bill rang Rebecca Taylor, the puzzle editor, saying he had a message to pass on to Wordwit. Rebecca grabbed a pen. 'Sure, what would you like to say?'

'You bastard.' And Bill hung up.

Momentarily Rebecca and I feared that the cartoonist was genuine, and I rang the *Australian* to douse the flames. I didn't mean to cause offence, I said. 'What offence?' he asked, 'It's what I've always suspected. I'm sick and grim all wrapped into one. Took a bastard like you to show me.'

And now the same bastard wishes to show you something, this time how container clues work. Let's try these two examples. The first is from Virgilius, alias Brian Greer of the *Independent*, while the other stems from my own batch:

Doctor binds a fracture (3)
Greek island confiscates a coin (6)

Doctor is common shorthand for such abbreviations as DR, MD, MO (medical officer), or, as here in the first clue, GP. When GP *binds* A, you create GAP (or *fracture*).

CREATE is your second answer, this time using the idea of seizure. Here we have CRETE (*Greek island*) detaining A, making *coin* (the verb) your definition. Verbs of enveloping are integral to containers. Think grab, swallow, hug, accommodate.

Alternatively, in our CREATE example, rather than make CRETE do all the holding, you can just as easily angle the clue to suggest the A is entering CRETE. (So a variation for CREATE could be: *Make army leader occupy island*.) Containers can function either way – evoking capture, or injection, depending on which action the setter selects.

Prepositions play a big part in the container recipe, words like in or around. Though watch out for *without*, in the word's quainter sense, where furniture can be found within or without the house. In other words, *many without a hog* could give you MAHOGANY. You'll be glad to learn, though, that our current clue is without *without*:

Sucker pens article for website guide (4,3)

Now that we know containers will suggest surrounding, or being surrounded, where is that signal? Look twice at *pens*.

As a reflex, most will think of biros, the impulse encouraged by the surface sense. Just don't forget that hogs are as like to be penned as novels – so what *pens* what? We need a word for sucker to enclose either a word for *article*, or *article for website*, depending on what remaining chunk is the answer's definition.

Sucker can be a vacuum cleaner or the victim of a scam. What else? We need a smaller word to double for *sucker* – PATSY, GULL? What about SAP? If SAP is doing the penning, can you conjure a word for *guide* that starts with S and ends with P?

Ask these sorts of questions when tackling containers. The tactic is called bookending, speculating on the answer's edges to fill out its inner space. Or speculating the other way – imagining what word might own certain innards, and filling out the fringes.

If SAP is the outer shell, then SNOWCAP or SUNTRAP are possible solutions. Though in the domain of bloggers, of forums and avatars, a browser can't cope without a SITE MAP. That's right, SITE MAP – where SAP pens ITEM – and 2-Down is done.

Yet to grasp containers more tightly, we should set our watches to 1500 AD, packing our bags for Renaissance Italy, our next clue's destination.

RECIPE PRECIS: CONTAINERS

The giveaway of most container clues is the hint of holding, or being held. *Wrong to swallow gird's first hint*, for example, is SIGN, with SIN (wrong) to swallow G (grid's first) making SIGN (hint). Here's a loose A to Z of other common container signs:

about, absorb, accept, around, blocks, boring, boxes, bury, captive, carrying, clothing, cover, cut into, disconnect, disrupts, eat, feeding, fencing, grab, hold, in, interrupting, keeping, out, pocket, retained, ring, settle in, stocking, stops, surround, swallow, without

QUIZLING 9.1

Bizarrely, what word meaning empty is a container containing a container?

QUIZLING 9.2

We want two Muppets, please.
Each lodged inside a type of cheese.

QUIZLING 9.3

If LLAMA lies inside *Cinderella Man*, what ten other films enfold the words below? In each case the hidden word bridges at least two other words in the title.

bygone	tyre
braid	wove
Koran	yell
Keith	glee
temper	grit

CHAPTER 10

Women's mag covers one Italian painter (6)

'Oh my god,' says the flight attendant. 'Are you Jimmy Barnes as in the rock star Jimmy Barnes?' Jimmy shrugs. Sure. It's 9 a.m. Not a good time for icons. But the attendant can't let the moment rest. 'Maybe if you sign your boarding pass ...'

That's how I opened my profile on James Dixon Swan – better known as Jimmy Barnes, best known as Barnesy, the former lead singer of Australia's biggest pub-rock combo, Cold Chisel. Touching down in Rockhampton I saw first-hand the glow of fame radiate on to others. Age meant nothing – teens, Gen-Xers, retirees. Everyone wanted their little piece of Barnesy. Here he was in living colour.

Which was my end of the deal – the colour. I'd been writing for ten years for *Sunday Life* magazine, Fairfax's feature supplement. It would be hard to put the stories into one neat pile – my first entailed jumping into a pool with ten lobstermen. This was 1997, the exercise part of a sea-survival course. After that, I dived into pop psychology, chef profiles, health stories, the chemistry of love. Whatever the topic, from biker clubs to gigolos, I added my brand of humour and colour, with a few incidental insights. With two young kids and one large mortgage, freelance writing and puzzle-making kept our heads above water.

OK, so the mag never covered an Italian painter, but I

did get to meet a blind mother of five. And the guy who lost his memory thanks to a tick bite. And Barnesy, of course, when I shadowed him to a coal town called Moura in remote Queensland. I have to tell you, ghoulishly, that six months earlier in May 2007, surgeons had opened the singer's chest to insert a bovine valve into his heart. Plane-hopping, sound-checking, I felt like the post-op observer assigned to see if the implant was a success, or whether the explosive last chorus of Jimmy's hit song 'Khe Sanh' would see the rocker himself explode.

Thankfully, he survived. In many ways, at 51, Jimmy treated his zipper scar as a reminder to live wisely. No smokes, no booze. The only liquid to pass his lips was bottled water to wash down a regimen of co-enzymes. Come show time, the ballads were ballistic. Vein-popping. The miners loved it. Jimmy loved it. He sang two encores and came offstage in a sheen of sweat.

I loitered near the cattle chute backstage, eager to ask how Jimmy was feeling, how the ticker felt, but he fired first, 'So you make crosswords, yeah?'

'Um,' I said. 'Who told you that?'

'Like the cryptic one, yeah? Can never bloody do them, you know.'

'There's a formula,' I said. 'Each clue has a recipe – '

But Barnesy was after a favour. A crazy idea, he said, but maybe I was the guy to ask.

Moura was in October, the comeback concert. My feature ran as November's cover story, and closer to Christmas, a crossword appeared that seemed like any other – unless you were Jane Mahoney, the Thai-Australian wife of Jimmy Barnes.

Fluent in several languages, Jane was an ardent crossword fan. She was also approaching her forty-ninth birthday and the couple intended to fly off to Bali for a romantic getaway with a twist. The twist was the reason Jimmy bolted left and right at Sydney Airport, raiding every newsstand in the departure lounge, ensuring that Jane would have the *Herald* in perpetuity.

The reason was simple. Almost every clue that day, every solution, was a reference to the couple's life: from their first meeting place (CANBERRA) to the city of TOKYO, where Jane fled to escape the rock 'n' roll chaos. The puzzle also swaddled a daughter (ELIZA-JANE), a mate (NEIL FINN of Crowded House), and ARIZONA, where Jimmy hit the wall in 2001, flushing out the drug and booze in a desert detox centre.

A time of equal darkness was captured at 32-Across in the shape of a container clue:

Operating pusher in Sydney fringes? (7)

Despite *pusher* lying in the clue, the reference isn't addiction. Here the word translates as URGER, being one who pushes. The question mark alerts the solver to this unorthodox reading, telling you that one part of the clue has a playful slant. As for *Sydney's fringes*, forget the outer suburbs, and think S and Y, the literal margins. Put URGER in SY and you have one more answer for Ms Mahoney to negotiate.

So that's how SURGERY works, but how does our current clue operate? Could the women's mag be *Sunday Life*? Is the Italian painter Da Vinci, or do we have another code to crack?

GYPROCK AND ROLL – magazines and clue mix

When not writing articles for magazines, I've also helped to enliven their pages with puzzles, and my client base takes in anything from computer zines to *Inside Sport*. The briefest dabble would have to be my stint for *Club Gyprock*, a trade newsletter for fibro-cement workers, not a sector you readily link to crosswords, as my two-issue tenure proved.

That's the way it rolls in Magland. No matter the title, the latest issue is tomorrow's kitty litter. Fame, you could argue, has similar limitations. Jimmy Barnes may be a household name in Australia, but try testing a Cleveland household or a village in Mogadishu. A certain Italian painter may have made the signori swoon in the 1500s, but is he bathing in the same glow half a millennium later? Building a crossword, you need to ask yourself those questions. Dizzy Gillespie is a trumpet-blowing legend, but what about Herb Alpert or Chet Baker? How deep does our consensus of fame extend?

If you had to name as many Italian painters as you could, I'd wager that you wouldn't snare our man in question. That's no crime; he was famous once. But is once enough, if the same artist has slipped into oblivion? Tough as the challenge sounds, at least you have wordplay to help you unmask Signor X:

Women's mag covers one Italian painter (6)

Covers looks like it could be a container signpost. *One* is prone to be I or A, either vowel liable to be covered by a *women's mag*. Hang on, mag. Why not magazine? Your detective skills are sharpening. Thanks to *mag* (versus magazine), you are more than likely after a title in its shortened form. Just as *Tele* is a nickname for the *Telegraph, mag* is your warning to make a matching chop.

We can surmise that the title is five letters long (since only one letter needs to be contained). We can also guess the mag will include an S, owing to SITE MAP's initial. So what women's mag obeys the pattern of __ __ S __ __ ?

While you rummage around, let me confess to a Sein-feld temptation. When clueing 1-Across I'd almost recruited Kramer into the fray, as I relished the collision of Renaissance art and a modern sitcom. But I reneged. Too much, I thought. The solver has enough leaps to make, so I left Cosmo Kramer on the bench and opted for a magazine like *Cosmopolitan*, better known as *Cosmo*.

Art history books will tell you that the Italian Renaissance included two painters with the designation 'Cosimo' – Agnolo di Cosimo (better known as Bronzino) and Piero di Cosimo. Both hang in the Uffizi. Both had a thing for nudes and died in Florence amid a horde of protégés. So which one did I mean here? Cosimo A or Cosimo B? *Non importa*, as the Romans say. Either can double as our 1-Across solution.

Yet fame, we know, can fade like Titian blue. For ten seconds, as I contemplated this puzzle on the drawing board, ADAMANT almost ran as singer ADAM ANT, but I figured New Wave was candyfloss compared to *Perseus Rescuing Andromeda*, the famous painting by one or other Cosimo. Or maybe I wanted to balance the centuries. After so much OUTSOURCING and SITE MAPS, why not an ounce of archaic Italy?

Nonetheless the question remains. How does a famous person differ from an oh-yeah-that-guy-in-the-TV-show person? While Sally Heath has rich potential as a container clue, she does fall short on celebrity.

Jimmy Barnes is another matter. The singer is fair game for puzzling, in Australia at least. To up the temptation, his surname has solid container credentials, being R in BANES, or N in BARES. Jane Mahoney, on the other hand, is even better (HONE in MAY) but her profile can't rival that of her hubby's. So when it comes to names as puzzle fodder, what's the minimal score on the Fame Index? Where does Cosimo end and my Uncle Les, who dabbled in watercolours, begin? And what about the beautiful people themselves? How do they feel being trapped inside the chequered square? We can't ask Cosimo, but we can consult a guy like Shane Morgan.

THE V OF VIP – fame factor and career highlights

Nick Hornby is a well-known writer. *About A Boy* was a hit film, in league with *High Fidelity*, and that's just for kick-off. In puzzle circles, the English writer is A-list, whereas Shane Morgan is off-off-Broadway.

The difference between the two men – one a best-selling writer from Surrey, the other a battling actor from Sydney – was driven home by a puzzle in 2006. Omega is a jumbo grid blending trivia with current affairs. Arrayed below the puzzle is a picture gallery of seven faces, each one tied to a clue. Photo A, say, may be Nicolas Sarkozy, or Imelda Marcos, or SpongeBob SquarePants, and the solver has to ID the portrait to fill in the answer.

Fine when the faces are famous, but imagine Shane Morgan's shock when he opened the paper to see himself as Nick Hornby in Picture E. The gaffe was forgivable when you consider that Morgan was gearing up for a return season of *Nipple Jesus*, the play adapted from a Hornby short story. Somehow the notable author's photo had been replaced with the flyer image of the less notable actor who plays Dave the bouncer in the famous one's play. Mind you, Morgan didn't begrudge the mix-up, as he wrote to the *Herald*:

> I had people calling me saying you look nothing like Nick Hornby. I've only got slightly more hair than him. But it's absolutely fantastic – I'm right between Sandra Bullock and the robot from *Perfect Match*. I'm a couple down from Robert de Niro, so I'm in good company.

Mistaken ID is one sin. Yet a far greater lapse in the eyes of solvers is the use of almost-celebrities. For *Guardian* solvers the final straw was FI GLOVER, a broadcaster on Radio 4. Her name appeared in a puzzle composed by Enigmatist, who couldn't resist the luscious charade of FIG-LOVER. In fact his clue was quite funny if rather long:

On the evidence of her dietary preferences, she should be a
regular broadcaster (2,6)

As a container clue, LOG chopped in FIVER is another lush choice. But wordplay aside, the gripe among *Guardian* readers was Fi's low score on the Star-O-Meter.

The Times avoids this scenario by recruiting only dead people as answers. Tempting as LEVEL CROSSING may seem to the *Times* setter, being LESSING outside VELCRO, the container trick is on ice until the Nobel Prize-winning Doris Lessing, born in 1919, pens her last sentence.

The *Herald* and most US papers have more elastic limits. American puzzles thrive on the now, throwing astronauts alongside Cosmo Kramer. Veteran actor Rip Torn is realistic about the lifeline his curious name has provided puzzlemakers. As two synonyms of varying tense, Rip Torn is also a tidy length, and thus gets a regular airing amid US clues. 'Crossword puzzles,' he once joked in the press. '[They] kept my name alive for years!'

The Australian singer Sarah Blasko is famous in indie circles, a winner of multiple awards and maker of three bestselling albums. But was her profile high enough to warrant a puzzle berth?

I faced that dilemma in 2008, shaping a grid around the Three Little Pigs. Owing to the offbeat theme, and my four long theme-entries – STICKS AND STONES, STANLEY KUBRICK, STRAWBERRY MARKS, plus YOUR PLACE OR MINE – I had limited scope with the cross-running answers. Trapped in one corner, the best entry to promise escape was BLASKO.

I tried alternatives, of course. GLASCO is a town in New York State. GLOSSO is a prefix for tongue. Then there was BLASTO, an obsolete arcade game, or PLASMO, a claymation alien from the planet of Monjotroldeclipdoc (I had to look that up), all of which firmed my preference for Sarah B. If her clue was a container it might have read like this:

Songwriter Sarah to request endless blog coverage (6)

Or ASK in BLO spells BLASKO. The day the puzzle went to press I anticipated the usual whines about overblown fame, but instead I received an email sent by singer and songwriter Darren Hanlon, a mate of Sarah's, who wrote:

> On the very day Sarah became immortalised in cluedom it was my phone that was all abuzz with text messages urging me to buy the paper and do the crossword. Until then I had no idea how extensive this indie-rock cryptic society was.

Though the BLASKO in question had no idea of her inclusion – not yet. Darren's email told the story:

> Sarah was in a meeting and couldn't be contacted for hours and when I finally got through she told me to calm down and I said 'you won't believe this!' We met at a cafe to see it for ourselves … I then explained that although she'd already played the Commonwealth Games opening ceremony, gone platinum, programmed RAGE, shook Cate Blanchett's hand etc. that this was her career pinnacle. She should bask in the moment.

HALL OF FAME: CONTAINERS

Face rival carrying flag (6) [Taupi, the *Guardian*]
Gun sure to grab attention (7) [Paul, the *Guardian*]
Square seen circling square, sort of square (7) [Paul again]
Cook in boiling water (8) [Rover, the *Guardian*]
Stop old leftovers blocking sink (9) [Mass, the *Independent*]
Bone from a fish found in tin? (10) [*Times* 8562]

SOLUTIONS: visage, firearm, sixteen, irrigate, forestall, metacarpal

---

QUIZLING 10.1

What four colours, three within the spectrum's red band, each carry the word CAR inside their letters?

QUIZLING 10.2

MALTA, the nation, can sit inside FOFD to create two adjacent words – formal/tad. What three countries can separately sit inside TOM to create paired words on each occasion?

QUIZLING 10.3

Can you 'isolate' each Scottish island below within an English word? Arran, say, may lie in arrant, though warrant or rearrange are sounder, since they both encircle the island entirely.

Iona	Cara
Tiree	Vaila
Cava	Barra
Unst	Lamba
Islay	Danna

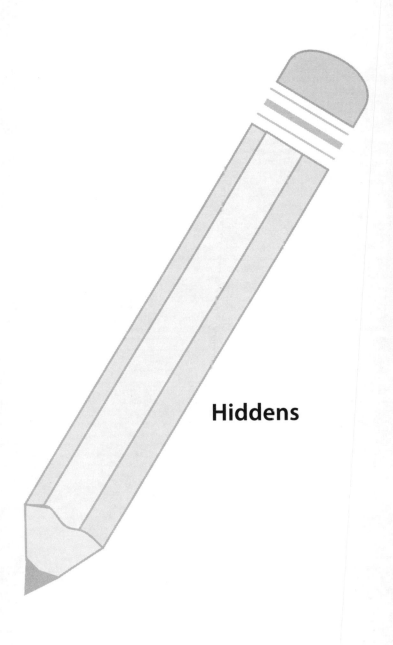

Hiddens

CHAPTER 11

Creepy film absorbed in autopsy chopping (6)

Seven FBI trainees, one observer, one island, nine deaths – or maybe I lost count between the drowning and the beheading. When deaths outnumber the ad breaks, the census tends to falter.

Released in 2002, *Mindhunters* revives the spirit of Agatha Christie, with steel-shafted arrows replacing arsenic and lace. The reason these 'seven little Indians' are stranded on the island in the first place is to solve a mock crime committed by a make-believe scumbag nicknamed the Puppeteer. The weekend is a test of nerve, a simulation that soon turns into the real McCoy.

In the psycho tradition, each death is accompanied by a broken wristwatch to predict the killing time of the next trainee. Of course, no spree is complete without a prime suspect, a role played by LL Cool J, the eighth member of the party; a Philadelphia detective and former navy SEAL, he's been assigned to observe how the junior profilers cope with the strain. Older and wiser than his fellow castaways, Lieutenant Gabe Jensen passes the time by tut-tutting the newbies, or solving crosswords.

So how did the critics cope? One reviewer called the movie a perfect waste of six good watches. From a crossword angle, however, Gabe is good for some solid advice.

When not chewing a pencil, the cop delivers two zingers. The first is just bad-funny (*'Eeny-meeny-miny-mo, who's the next motherfucker to go?'*) while the other is the catchphrase of our next two chapters: *'What is the trap? Where is the trap?'*

For now we enter a maze of traps, where every string of words can hold your answer – or undoing. The hidden clue is a misnomer in some respects, since the answer itself is as plain as day, if only you have the eyes to see it. A trained solver will spot CINEMA sitting in *medicine man*, but the rookie will need more time in the field. Sir Peter Ustinov and Sophia Loren may be old-time stars in your eyes, but to me they cradle RUST and PHIAL.

The first clue I ever solved, as you may recall from the Intro, was a hidden: *Follow in green suede*. Look within and there's ENSUE, a match for *follow*. The recipe dates back to the Jazz Age, when English cryptics were testing the unwritten rules. Back then, the hidden clue required neither brevity nor definition, meaning a setter could waffle at length, stashing the answer en route. Check out this clunker from the *Daily Telegraph* of 1928:

> *'Thou rebel damsel, do me the favour of tying this turban,'*
> *quoth the knight (hidden) (6)*

Alas, with no hint of meaning, the clue carries several eligible stowaways. With six letters in mind, you could snaffle BELDAM (a woman of advanced years), or SELDOM, or BANQUO (the ghost in Macbeth). Which is right? For the record, the answer was SELDOM. For the good of cryptics, the hidden art has since improved, losing its flab, and gaining definition – in both senses.

Once their category is revealed, though, hiddens don't stay hidden for long. Ask any profiler: the brain-strain comes with recognising your suspect. The moment you realise that the killer is the sexy Latina or the crossword dude with the sharp tongue, your chase is over. Okay then, here's the evidence:

Creepy film absorbed in autopsy chopping (6)

To stick with the creep-show concept, let's say that finding the solution to a hidden means looking out for snipers. To save your neck you need to examine the layout carefully. Lurking behind the furniture is a six-letter word that lazy eyes will miss at first sweep. So step warily.

Avoid false leads too. If you're new to the game you may see a word like *chopping* and suspect the anagram formula. Bang, you're dead. Wrong move.

In the same vein, the word *absorbed* could hint at a container clue. Bang, two shots. Dead twice over.

What is the trap? Where is the trap?

Diligence is needed. If you can't isolate the definition, then unpick the letters. Laborious, yes, but you'd rather be methodical than maggot bait. Gullible souls will glance at *Soviet names etc* – thinking of Krushchev or Kiev – and fail to notice VIETNAMESE hunched in ambush. You need that savvy to survive this jungle exercise.

Anagram clues, we know, require a signpost of change. Containers – a signal to protect or inject. Hidden clues are no different, though their pointers are more versatile, with three possible signpost approaches.

First, the idea of fragmentation. (Keep your eyes peeled for signposts such as *some, sample, part* or *slice.*) Here's a sample:

Cheese chunk in apricot tart = RICOTTA

Second, think confinement, akin to one breed of container clue. (For this approach, look out for words like *nurse, bound, holding* or *stocking.*) Like this one:

Monster trapped in filthy drain = HYDRA

Last, the hidden will play with the idea of clustering. (Watch out for words like *sequence, string, train* or *bunch*.) Or something like *slab* (a clump), as here:

Drop dolomite slab = OMIT

With a three-way bet you can see why hiddens are lethal – despite how simple they end up being once you suss out the category. You can spend five minutes staring at a clue, while the whole time the answer's staring back.

So what style of hidden is the Master clue? *Creepy film absorbed in autopsy chopping*. This one clue offers three possible signposts, namely *absorbed, absorbed in*, or just plain *in*. Whichever is the right command, look twice at the less familiar phrases. Which is clunkier: *creepy film* or *autopsy chopping*? Tucked away in the latter is Hitchcock's black-and-white classic, ready to join your black-and-white square.

But wait a minute. PSYCHO may be the answer, the clue works, the letters fit, but what about that cadaver image, all those gory *CSI* vibes? If solvers want blood and guts, then solvers can rent *Mindhunters*, right? This argument underpins a famous rule in Clueville. To go there, we need to set the breakfast table.

SEEMLY MUESLI – public taste and the S-word

What is the form of diarrhoea in which the food is discharged undigested? (8)

Hope you weren't eating. The quick clue above came from a *Sunday Age* crossword published in 2008 and the answer is the medical obscurity known as LIENTERY. Puzzle-solvers are always thirsting to learn new vocab, yet a clue like this confirms that our thirst isn't (sorry) bottomless.

Margaret Farrar, the iconic New York editor, called it the Sunday Breakfast Test. Nobody in their right mind wants to deal with FAECES over porridge. LEUKAEMIA and SODOMY can be added to the list. AUSCHWITZ and AUTOPSY CHOPPING.

Among the personal papers of Merl Reagle, the only cross-word-maker to appear on *The Simpsons* – more of that later – is a message from Margaret Farrar, dated 1966: 'Crosswords are an entertainment. Avoid things like death, disease, war and taxes – the subway solver gets enough of that in the rest of the paper.'

For Will Shortz, Farrar's eventual successor in the New York chair, the diktat still holds good. In a Q&A with puzzle fans back in 2008, Shortz admitted that, *'It's true that URINE has never appeared in a* New York Times *crossword ...'* . Public taste has loosened to some degree, though; a 2009 puzzle revelled in a toilet theme, including such entries as LITTLE JOHN and ROYAL FLUSH.

Going with the flow, I ran with CHAMBER POT in 2007, barely giving the phrase a second thought. Swine flu may be racking Mexico, wars raging in four corners, but invoke the notion of wee-wee or poo-poo in a crossword and you'll invite a furious letter like my CHAMBER POT harangue. The angry note ended in a kind of haiku:

'Shame, shame, shame.
Friday's *Herald* is now being cancelled.
Yours in disgust ...'

This was a blip compared to the day in 2006 when Shortz green-lighted a seven-letter word starting with S. Ooh, what word, you're thinking. Must be SHITFUL or SEXBOMB, or maybe a dosage of grim news like SCABIES or SUICIDE. None of the above. In fact, just to test your breakfast reflexes, I put the S-word in this chapter's opening page. If the word passed your gaze, then you're at one with the major-ity of New Yorkers who saw no reason to complain. But a vociferous few made up for them, decrying the filth of SCUMBAG.

To most Gen-Xers, a scumbag is a scoundrel, which is how Lynne Lempel clued her entry. For older solvers, the slang refers to a used condom, with scum a quainter synonym of semen. Hardly the trinket you want in your Froot Loops, and Shortz was understandably contrite. In the blogosphere, Lempel herself confessed, '*I'm dumbfounded – and also just plain dumb, I guess. I was totally ignorant of its vulgar side.*'

Etymology, of course, can be its own booby trap. ORCHID, did you know, derives its name from the testicle, in the same vein as AVOCADO, a previous answer in the mix. As enough time passes, or the root language fades, the potential for offence recedes.

War, disease, the naughty bits – don't go there. Not at the breakfast table. Advice ignored by our next three clues, all culled from British sources that had best remain nameless. In recipe order, you're looking at anagram, container and hidden:

Incest with boy could be this = OBSCENITY
Bodily fluid left inside granny, perhaps = PLASMA
Some fancy stitches employed in pouch = CYST

Even Alfred Hitchcock, our *Psycho* director, has suffered low digs at the hands of compilers. This insolent pun was made by Crux in the *Financial Times*:

Hitchcock's memorable double feature? = CHIN

Going from blue language to grey cells, and staying with the *Psycho* theme, the moment seems right to visit another taboo. To finish off, let's meet some vigilantes, and appreciate the difference between one person's psycho and another's Froot Loop.

LOOSE SCREWS – SANE and mental health

David Plomley is not a malicious man. This civil engineer is as civil as they come. But not if you ask the good people at SANE. According to this Australian media watchdog, thanks to a crossword in 2008 this DP-person is a prize ratbag.

SANE is an organisation dedicated to the cause of improving the lot of people affected by mental illness. Speaking as someone with a friend who suffers from a personality disorder, I applaud SANE and its equivalent bodies around the world. There's no place for derision or discrimination in the realm of mental illness. David Plomley struck that truth head-on when opting for insanity as a crossword theme.

In 2010, DP ran such entries as *troppo, crackers, a screw loose.* But the fun wasn't appreciated by SANE's media sweep. On their website, the compiler was rebuked under the banner of Crass Crossword, the outrage added to a so-called Stigma File, with office bearers later expressing the group's disappointment to the editor.

You can only wonder whether similar groups in the UK made an equal stink when these two anagram clues popped up in the British press:

> *Can't use bananas for fruitcake* = NUTCASE
> *Loonies entrust doctors* = NUTTERS

Separate from the Sunday Breakfast Test, this is the issue of playing loose with a serious matter, in the same way that PSYCHO (both word and movie) can be overused to the point where fewer people can properly grasp the term. On the SANE website: *'Media reports frequently confuse "psychosis" (which refers to psychotic mental illness) and "psychopath" (which relates to extreme violence and anti-social behaviour, not mental illness).'* My advice to setters: if you have a splendid clue for BONKERS (and the mind does boggle), I'd suggest

BENDERS, BANGERS or BONNETS could fit the grid as snugly.

That said, not every solver will want your guts for garters over a mental-health allusion. Or so I must presume if one *Herald* letter is any guide. My crossword that week must have been extra-twisted, inspiring a solver to submit his thoughts: '*Having contemplated DA's cryptic crossword of last Friday, I am yet again uncertain whether he is a genius or a schizophrenic.*'

RECIPE PRECIS: HIDDENS

The hidden signal infers inclusion, or a smuggled entity, though the most frequent signal is *some*. (See other possibles below.) As an added hint, the fodder holding your hidden answer can often betray itself by an air of strangeness, like *Chicago gold* storing agog or *select rice*, electric.

accommodating, amid, among, bear, contribute to, harbour, inside, integral to, keep, lodgers, nurse, part, partly, protects, sandwich, stowaway, tenants, within

---

REVERSE HIDDENS

As with most other clue types, such as charades and containers, the reversal element can spice the recipe. (We look at pure reversal clues in Chapter 25.) Here are two reverse hiddens from my own kitbag. Notice the dual signposts of inclusion as well as backspin:

Some footnotes wrote up western sidekick = TONTO
Catch retro Op Art near lodging = ENTRAP

QUIZLING 11.1

What classic musical holds the word IN four times in its title?

QUIZLING 11.2

Hidden in the sound-grab below are two whole names from the one pursuit. Namely?

'When it comes to Tassie salmon, I case less than 50 kilos,' utters the fishmonger. 'Mind you, I expect albacore fillets, which rise vertically in sales over the winter, to increase tenfold in volume.'

QUIZLING 11.3

If SLANG hides within TEEN'S LANGUAGE, can you compose a terse definition of each word or name below that also embodies the consecutive letters of each example? BALSAM (6,6), say, could lead to HERBAL SAMPLE.

CALLAS (7,4)   TALC (5,8)
CREDO (6,5)   EVIL (4,4)
STORM (7,2,7)   IMMERSING (8,7)

CHAPTER 12

Partial set closer?! (3.)

'My smmr hols wr a CWOT. B4, we used 2go2 NY 2C my bro, his GF & thr 3 :-o kids FTF. ILNY, its a gr8 plc.'

That's how a London teen began her English essay in 2003. No further details of the school or girl's ID were provided, which makes most journos suspect an urban myth. But the snippet was posted (and translated) on the BBC website, only to be picked up by other news services across the globe.

For text newbies, here's a translation: 'My summer holidays were a complete waste of time. Before, we used to go to New York to see my brother, his girlfriend and their three screaming kids face to face. I love New York. It's a great place.'

Great yarn too, no matter the veracity, since anyone over thirty seems to fear the rise of text-speak. John Humphrys, a British broadcaster, compares texters to so many Genghis Khans. 'They are destroying [our language]: pillaging our punctuation, savaging our sentences, raping our vocabulary.'

John Sutherland, a London professor of Modern English Lit, has observed that text derives from 'tissue' in Latin, making textese like 'writing on Kleenex. One blow, then throw. Snot-talk ...'.

Luddites turn to the same old rhetoric. Since when did BAG mean busting a gut, they ask. Or JAM mean just a minute? Texting, they despair, is 2M2H (too much to handle).

BSF – but seriously folks – English has a history of mutation. For an ancient corpus the dear old girl is remarkably limber. Textese is not another language, but proof of our language's adaptability. Contriving a cluster like L8RG8R for 'later gator' is not the end of the world, but dizzying invention, and IABF.

Steady on – what does IABF mean exactly? I'm A Big Fan, of course. LHID, you say. Like Hell It Does. And here we have the crux of txt. LME: Let Me Explain.

Ironically, all this talk of reduction is exaggerated. Skimming txt glossaries you'll come upon logograms (clusters using symbols and letters – like L8RG8R), acronyms (LOL) and initialisms (like OMG, where the abbreviation – for Oh My God – doesn't offer a pronounceable entity). Weirder entries include NALOPKT ('not a lot of people know that') and BOSMKL ('bending over, smacking my knee, laughing'), which seem cool yet have as much chance of reaching the next decade as a typewriter.

The key to survival is handiness. Txt will see the clumsier stuff die out and the neater novelties flourish. LOL is a lock-in, now listed in the *Oxford Dictionary*. But the minute that BOSMKL requires a footnote, or loses sizzle, it's toast.

English may seem ravaged by all this thumb-talk, but the mother tongue has long been riddled with abbreviations and spelling deviations. Starting this chapter, your hackles may have risen when reading of the girl's 'smmr hols', but was your fury matched by my mention of the BBC, journos or ID? Less likely, I'm thinking. So how do you cope with the diminutive terms exam and pram, vet and fridge? And if you're still taking a puritan stance, have you ever fallen for the moral filth of RSVP or BYO? Anglo speakers have been crafty since the year dot, quick to find new means of moulding language. If pianoforte is unwieldy, then let's agree on piano, and the band plays on.

Or maybe your anguish is less about shrinkage and more to do with the poverty of a texter's vocab. Sorry, vocabulary. If so, chillax. A study mounted by Coventry Uni in 2006 discovered that a texting talent reveals a positive link to literacy among young learners. In Melbourne, a kindred study in the same year found SMS can also boost the language skills of less literate students. In other words, U need to have a solid grasp of English in order 2 play with it.

Noah Webster, the editor of America's first comprehensive dictionary, in 1825, was a texter before his time. His driving goal was to make spelling logical. In a stroke, Webster turned DIALOGUE into DIALOG and MOULD into MOLD, etc. (OK, so Noah didn't get his wish with TUNG for TONGUE, or SOOP for SOUP, but he tried.)

Telegrams were delivering equal havoc around the time of Webster's death in 1843. (It's only natural that as soon as word tally became a matter of dollars, the message tended to shrink.) Resourceful Scrooges jammed their words together – like *tomorrownight* – or boiled them down – like *sd* for said – to minimise the bottom line.

In many ways, last century's telegrams are this century's text messages – and language will weather both storms. Before too long we'll see which 'textonyms' deserve to survive and which will RIP.

Crossword-makers play a minor part too, choosing the abbreviations to warrant a place in a clue. *Mag* in our last container seemed a fair card to play, just as our current answer, another abbreviation, is familiar to everyone. You can tell the answer is a shrunken term by the numbering (3.), the full stop flagging the reduction. Would it help if I said the answer's already appeared in this chapter, minus the optional full stop? Or maybe we should first sound out what the clue's other punctuation is doing. In short, WTF is '?!' all about?!

SHORT IS SWEET – ? & ! and &lit clues

Twitter. Haiku. Slogan. Txt. The common thread is brevity, distilling a message to its gist. You'll recall those prototype clues from our last chapter, the tall tales of damsels and knights. Each sample owned over ten words, a modern mouthful. With shades of the old-time cable sender, the current cluesetter works on the principle that short is sweet.

The longest clue in the whole Master Puzzle has just nine words, while nine others own four words or fewer. Such numbers highlight a cryptic law – *be succinct*. Which isn't the same as *be bleeding obvious*. Where telegraphers slashed words to save pennies, they did so at the risk of ambiguity. We compilers embrace a similar discipline, cutting the waffle, yet all the while *pursuing* ambiguity.

If I say *autopsy chopping* and you think anagram, rather than a hidey-hole for PSYCHO, then my job is done. Gemini in the *Guardian* composed a stylish hidden in early 2008, writing:

Worth reading – gripping yarn (6)

Four words only and the surface sense sublime. Misleading too, as I spent an age mentally browsing airport novels, wondering which blockbuster was the answer. None was. Gripping, of course, is the hidden signpost, and THREAD the hidden answer.

So what about 17-Down? The one with *?!* for an ending? What's that all about? Let's take it one mark at a time.

Remember, a chapter back, how we found a question mark tailing the CHIN clue: *Hitchcock's memorable double feature?*

In this clue the punctuation signals a fresh perspective. Forget films – focus on flab. Often a question mark equates to the vaudevillian wink, a pun alert directed at the audience. Take this clue for HERB GARDEN: *Place to make a mint?*

Question marks can also suggest a playfulness in the definition, asking the solver to give that element greater leeway. Here's an example:

British celebs George and Peter made hot cakes? (11)

The celebs in question for this charade recipe are stars of the 1960s, namely George Best and Peter Sellers, or BEST + SELLERS = *hot cakes.*

Consult any dictionary and you won't find *bestseller* defined as *hot cake.* Here the question mark acts as a kind of idiom-alarm. Punctuation underlines the setter's licence.

Exclamation marks, on the other hand, declare a different mischief. And here we get our first peek at the '&lit' clue, an odd label for a rare achievement. The term was coined by Ximenes, drafter of the first cryptic rule book, and applies to any clue where the wordplay not only suggests the answers but also *defines* the answer, literally. Here's an exquisite &lit from US master Henry Hook:

Insane Roman! (4)

Despite its brevity, this is a hidden &lit where the camouflage doubles as definition. Look in *-sane Roman* and you'll uncover NERO, the *insane Roman.* Dovetailing the signpost – *in* – with the hidden fodder – *sane Roman* – is inspired, an embedded style of signposting. The exclamation mark is etiquette, warning solvers of the trickery. Whenever you see an exclamation mark, especially tagging a terse clue, consider the likelihood that words serve both demands of the cryptic clue, wordplay and definition all rolled into one. Not always, of course – but the chance is there. Here's another &lit hidden, drawn from my own archive:

He's smart in a mischievous vein! (6,4)

Vein here alludes to a sequence of letters, such as a vein of gold. Chip away the excess and you'll hit MARTIN AMIS, the smart and mischievous writer.

As top of the cryptic pyramid, &lits deserve their own chapter at least. But right now it's more important to make the quick intro, and warn you against treating &lit as a recipe unto itself. The tag is better viewed as an ideal, with any recipe capable of being involved. In this chapter we have the hidden &lit. A glance at the Master's unsolved clues, and seeing three more exclamation marks in waiting, suggests we have more &lit recipes looming – perhaps. With that treat in mind let's return to the clue at hand:

Partial set closer?! (3.)

Partial is a nimble word, meaning both biased and incomplete: the perfect guise for a hidden signpost. *Partial payment*, the phrase, could hint at MEN, lying inside *payment*, just as GIST may result from *partial magistrates*. So what part do we need to extract to solve 17-Down, the linchpin holding the pattern together? To find the answer, you'll need nerve and know-how, etc.

Because ETC is exactly that – a *partial set closer*. An abbreviation of the longer Latin phrase, the word is partial for being shortened, just as you're likely to borrow the term as a rambling *set closer*. And there it is, ETC, enveloped by its own definition, with *partial* wearing two cryptic hats: signpost and accomplice in the answer's definition.

Txters could well admire the clue's brevity, while the answer itself is the king of space-savers. In this expanding universe of abbreviation, ETC is da bomb, that shortened phrase made to keep any list from exceeding its measure. In the spirit of ETC, let's quit this chapter early.

EXTERNAL HIDDENS

We've met orthodox hiddens, and reverse hiddens. The third member of the clan is the external hidden, where the answer lies on the edges of the fodder phrase – much in the vein of a *MAD* magazine's fold-in. Hardly common, but still a formula you may encounter. Below are two from my own archive. Notice how both rely on a signpost (*fringes, bordering on*) that encourages you to look on the edges of things:

Glad social fringes are moving slowly = GLACIAL
Reserve bordering on Timorese validity? = TIMIDITY

HALL OF FAME: HIDDEN

Some want it left? Right! (5) [Neo, *FT*]
Shy bride holds cross (6) [Henry Hook, US]
Some medicines supplied for cold (7) [Henry Hook again]
One more helping of tea (not herbal) (7) [Flimsy, *FT*]
Sign used by vendors everywhere (7) [*Times* 8531]
Rubric 'abracadabra' revealing old curiosities (4–1–4) [Brendan, *Guardian*]

SOLUTIONS: title, hybrid, iciness, another, endorse, bric-a-brac

QUIZLING 12.1

And on the subject of texting, what two eight-letter words of the opposite meaning share the text combo 7–3-5–3-2–8-3–3?

QUIZLING 12.2

In cryptic terms, what major ice-cream chain can be said to have a hidden AGENDA?

QUIZLING 12.3

If 2/1 = seduce,
7/3 = contest,
9/2 = clear,
does 3/4 = gold, knot or coral?

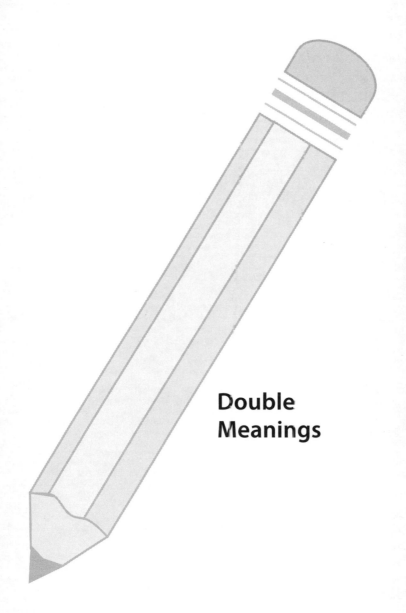

**Double
Meanings**

CHAPTER 13

Giant flower shop online (6)

For a good part of 1988 I knew warfare backwards. Over spring, I caught the train to Canberra a few times and spent my weekend cooped up in the Australian War Museum, poring over medals and photos, xeroxing telegrams.

My job description was Fact-checker and Caption Writer for a series entitled *Australians at War*. Stretching from Gallipoli to Vietnam, the books were a Time-Life project packaged by John Ferguson, a publishing house occupying a reborn terrace on Foveaux Street, near Sydney's Central Station.

John had published *Marzipan Plan*, my first novel, back in 1986. I'm not sure why. Fiction was hardly his forte. *Marzipan* sold modest numbers and somehow made the national shortlist for the Miles Franklin Award. Six months later a film offer appeared, and fell over.

Moral of the story? You can't build an empire on almond paste. Fresh off campus, I deemed myself a novelist when really I was a puzzle-maker with a bent for storytelling. Read the small print on my BA Communications and you'll guess that majors in journalism, creative writing and Samuel Beckett were hardly geared to pull an executive salary. After a brush with drama teaching, my sole income for most of that period came from crosswords, which kicked off in 1983 at the *Herald*, followed by the daily Wordwit puzzle a few years later. That was it. No mortgage, no car, but enough to finance a meander round Europe, then later South America. Thanks to wordplay I'd become a professional bum, inventing puzzles at the Gare du Nord, revising clues on Amazon ferries, writing short stories in Patagonia. Three wild years, only to return to Sydney with no career, no address, no money, a sputtering relationship, a deepening recession and a single novel about a mirror maze. At 28 I needed a real job.

'What do you know about war?' asked John.

'Which war?'

'Take your pick. We need someone who can write.'

Real experts wrote the manuscripts, yet often the text needed a delousing for jargon. Lay readers might know an F18 from a B52, yet not everyone will be able to distinguish an AK47 from its spot-welded cousin, the AK74. So I went to Canberra; I haunted the armoury; I spoke to top brass at Duntroon Academy. And in between captions I gossiped.

At least that was the accusation from the team's production manager. A true believer in books and efficiency, Tracy O'Shaughnessy had no truck for idle chatter, especially when the Battle of Long Tan was two days overdue. 'Are those captions ready yet?' she asked, not warmly either, and I told her some guff about clarifying artilleries, and she looked straight through me like the former radiographer she was.

We couldn't stand each other. I treated John Ferguson Ltd as a playground, a place to exchange one-liners with Julian, a closet librettist. Or I'd flirt with the barista downstairs, or relive great novels with Lesley, the associate publisher who also shared the alcove. Make jokes, not war. My work ethic, after years of sleeping in Latin fleapits, was too *mañana* for Tracy's blood. She regularly stomped to my desk with a range of scowls to ask after my copy, which invariably was missing in action.

'Never knew the Nazis were Irish,' I whispered to Julian.

'Eva O'Braun,' he said to me, and we chuckled into our coffees.

On reflection I have no idea what position Julian actually held in the office except to sit beside me and better my gags.

Anyhow, Saigon fell and the Paris Peace Accords were signed, meaning I was demobbed to a life of crosswords. That's when Lesley the book-lover asked a favour. Her farm in the Hunter Valley needed a caretaker. 'Ever used creosote before?' she asked.

'There's always a first time.'

So November was a month of low-key farm work, painting a fence near Wollombi and spraying Zero on blackberry thickets. Two weeks later, Lesley and Tracy arrived, both women on their way to Armidale, four hours further north. Lesley was off to see her daughter, a boarder at the Armidale School, while Tracy was aiming to see her boyfriend, who worked at the same town's hospital. Tellingly, this overnight stay was the first time that Tracy and I had coexisted outside the office, not a deadline in sight, and we found ourselves talking freely. We argued why saffron was overrated, or how 'fun run' was an oxymoron. My own legs were giving me murder thanks to a day of mountain biking. My skin was burnt, and welted with insect bites. While Lesley was engrossed in a long-distance call, Tracy volunteered to scour my calves for ticks, lassoing their heads with a cotton strand and pulling the varmints out.

Next morning the travellers left and I returned to my creosote duties. By December I was back in Sydney, house-minding for a friend in Dulwich Hill. Making puzzles and writing – what other life could I expect? Clearly, if I wanted a view of the harbour I'd need to invent something like Post-it notes or kidnap a dowager's chihuahua for ransom.

Around this time the Time-Life gang threw a party, a chance to reunite with my fellow militants. The office was lined with tinsel, the inner courtyard a makeshift bodega. Again, as on the farm night, Tracy and I could chat without the clock ticking. She admitted that her romantic weekend in Armidale was no great shakes. Perhaps the relationship wasn't working, she said. Not an invitation, as such, but a ray of light if I had any plans to know her better. What about a cliff walk, I asked her. 'From Bondi to the cemetery and back again?'

Metaphysical, sure, but the girl took the bait. This was 1988, before the same track was crowded with chin-up bars and bike racks. The weather toyed with Tracy's long brown hair. The heat kept climbing, growing into a Sydney thunderstorm, and by the loop's end I suggested a thing called Eggs Perico.

Despite its fancy name, the meal was just Venezuelan for scrambled eggs. As a chef I'm a reasonable crosswordmaker, though the lunch was set to uncover a deeper truth. The house at Dulwich Hill was a mess. Tracy did her best to ignore the kitchen's junk while I broke eggs and warmed the pan. That's when she noticed the graph paper on the table.

'What's this?'

'A crossword.'

'I know it's a crossword, but what it's doing here?'

'That's how I make them.'

Irish in complexion, Tracy is pale for starters, but sitting at the table the girl went ghostly. 'What's wrong?' I asked.

She tapped the graph and said, 'This.'

The butter was burning. I was missing the significance. Then she read a clue aloud, 1-Across, 'Heavy metal fan a leading Snag.'

'What about it?'

'That's the Armidale clue. You wrote this?'

No, I felt like saying. I just do the Down clues and some black-and-white fairies visit overnight to add the Acrosses.

Of course I wrote the bloody thing. That was my job. Yet the puzzle side of life had never surfaced in our conversations. The weird thing being, the clue for HEAD BANGER (where a leading 'snag', or sausage, may be dubbed a head-banger), was the very clue to make Tracy chuckle over a month ago, 400 kilometres away, seeking a moment of warmth in a glacial weekend with the boyfriend. As it happened, HEAD BANGER was the whimsy that made her smile, and so did the man with ticks in his legs who was just then melting butter, and suddenly those two men were one and the same, standing in front of her.

I'm tempted to call the moment eerie but that word's overdone in crosswords. She couldn't believe the boy on the kiwi farm was the boy inside the crossword, the same boy who had made her laugh while trying to get some breathing space from the Armidale boy in a long weekend that felt too long. 'I love cryptics,' she said, and the rest of our lives felt almost straightforward in comparison. In the space of one puzzle, *Australians At War* became a couple of Australians in love, anointed by coincidence and the giggle-value of a random clue. To be honest I can't recall how the Eggs Perico worked out, but I'm grateful for another recipe, a slangy double meaning my future wife worked out, a clue that made her smile all those years ago.

CHICKEN INCIDENT – homonyms and heteronyms

Often, when I think of double meanings, I recall that strange head-banger moment in a Sydney kitchen, or remember another story – about a boy called Luke. He was nine, a sweet kid whose dad was an old friend

The meal was BBQ chicken. Luke was the eldest of four, chomping on a drumstick when his dad asked, 'So what did you do at school today?'

'Homonyms,' said the boy.

'What are they?' asked Maggie, his sister.

'Like bark and bark,' said Luke. 'You know, how tree has a bark and a dog has a bark, but they're different.'

The table was inspired. These sounded fun. Jo, the mum, held up her wine and said, 'Like stem on a glass and stem on a flower.'

Stuart rocked his hand. 'They're kind of related, aren't they? Maybe stem on a plant and stem the flow.'

'Or chicken,' said Luke, pointing to his plate. 'There's chicken on the farm and the chicken you eat.'

The room fell quiet. Stuart coughed and said, 'They're the same thing, mate.'

Luke's face dropped. He stared at the drumstick and then his mum, who nodded. The boy left the table. That was ten years ago. He's been a vegetarian ever since.

Language is duplicitous. We take the word *rock* as a solid place, only to discover it's a verb, meaning wobble. We've already seen how *set* has 200 meanings, and that's one cranny in the dictionary. In a *split second* you'll realise that *split* and *second* both wear other masks, in other places, as does every synonym of the same term: *flash, tick, mo, wink, shake, instant, twinkling*. Older words, like *set* and *second*, commonly own several meanings, gaining layers as English evolves. Look at *cob*, which can be three different animals (a male swan, a squat horse or a black-backed gull) on top of being a cylinder of corn, a clay mix for building, a lump of coal.

This single (song) book (reserve) has type (kind) and pages (servants) and chapters (franchises) and letters (mail). This sentence (stretch) has (laughs) a subject (servant), an article (story), an object (complain) and a raft (float) of brackets (supports).

Returning to the clue that made Tracy grin – *Heavy metal fan a leading Snag* – we have the definition as opener, where a *heavy metal fan* is slangily known as a HEAD BANGER. Next comes a pair of alternative definitions, re-slanting the solution's two parts. *Leading* is HEAD, and *snag* the nickname for a sausage, or BANGER. SNAG of course is also the acronym for Sensitive New Age Guy, explaining the capital letter in the clue, a bid to have the solver imagine the modern male as a Motörhead tragic rather than a sausage.

Double meaning clues are good places to begin a crossword. For starters, their brevity can often expose their category. Take these snack-size samples:

Career ladder = RUN
Fit exec = SUIT
Less inclined to sweet-talk = FLATTER

The recipe tends to be short due to the wordplay element being no more than a second synonym of the answer. Not that all double-meaning clues are brief. As you can see, the clue for FLATTER is standard length and the same applies to HEAD BANGER. And likewise 9-Down, our latest clue:

Giant flower shop online (6)

As always, the dilemma comes down to the split. Do we isolate *Giant*, or *Giant flower*, or maybe the more absurd idea of *Giant flower shop*? Or maybe the answer lies in the cyberspace angle.

Can you name any online flower shops? Google can – more than 5,000,000 of them – with no dominant name jumping out. Thankfully, says you. What sort of puzzle expects its solver to know some e-florist? Fear not. Crosswords can't afford to dabble in small-b brands – the human or the corporate kind. Proper nouns must be reachable through wordplay and a sound general knowledge. Should either be unfair, then the compiler isn't keeping their side of the bargain. Hence my choice of a Web retailer with perhaps the highest profile – the online giant that is AMAZON.

Whoa there. A brand name? Am I getting bankrolled by private interests to make this Master(card) Puzzle? Before I face that charge, let's tidy up 9-Down, our maiden clue in this category.

Amazon can help you buy books on botany, or bucketfuls of fresh flowers, or a magic wand that hides a cloth flower in its tip, but Amazon is no *flower shop online*, let alone a giant one. Instead it's simply a *shop online*. Meaning the clue's other half – *Giant flower* – is the answer's second definition. So how does *giant flower* equal Amazon?

After the Chicken Incident, the week young Luke turned vegetarian, he may well have tackled heteronyms at school – words like polish and Polish that resemble each other but vary in pronunciation. Puzzle-makers love them almost as much as we cherish double meanings. Does *does*, for example, mean deer or a form of the verb to do? Is row a paddle or a spat? Is flower a blossom or something that flows? In our 'current' clue, the 'flowy' idea applies, the Amazon river the biggest 'flow-er' on the planet, just as shower can be drizzle or an exhibitionist.

As for those payola accusations, I'm guilty to a point. Smack in the heart of the Master Puzzle is the taint of trade-marks, a registered company holding court in a central clue. What was the kickback? Do I own shares in Amazon Inc.? Why sully a perfect pastime with talk of dot-com merchants or the whiff of corporate interests? Read on to realise you've branded me all wrong.

CLUES R US – brand names and copyright

Slumped in your Jacuzzi, sipping Kahlua from a Thermos, you are living the decadent life of trademarks. But fat cats and fashionistas aren't the only suckers for labels. The deeper we enter this millennium the more brands enter our conversation.

Jacuzzi was named after the Jacuzzi brothers, who dabbled in bubbles. Kahlua was a Mexican distiller, since bought out by Pernod, another brand. As is Thermos, coined by a Scottish chemist, James Dewar.

Excluding guns and publishing houses, this chapter alone has borrowed a clutch of brands already, from Google to Xerox, Post-it notes to Zero. The minute you Hoover the Lino, ride an Escalator, open Facebook, you're inviting brands into your life. Velcro, the fastener stuck inside LEVEL CROSSING is a trademark, and so is the Zipper, its alternative. Name your game – Frisbee, Yo-yo, Trampoline, Hula Hoop. Yep, all brands. Nowadays we can hardly move without colliding into a ™ (or a word that started life as one).

Puzzles aren't exempt. Besides, as soon as you see that NINTENDO is INTEND in NO, what compiler in his right mind can resist?

I recently made a puzzle with a chocolate theme, filling the grid with 15 well-known products, from Cherry Ripe to Kit Kat. Several of the clues called on double meanings:

Faint chocolate = FLAKE
Chocolate piece of cake? = PICNIC
Bar laughter = SNICKERS

Curiously, despite all the trademarks on display, the only solver to complain was a Lake Macquarie woman who demanded I avoid such high-sugar temptations in the future as she was trying to shed her Christmas excess. 'Having my puzzles come with calories,' she wrote, was giving her no chance.

You'd do well to find any compiler who dodges trademarks altogether, whether it's an overt reference to an online bookstore or accidental lapses like *kerosene* and *lanolin, gunk* or *heroin*. In all my years of crosswording, turning RENAULT into NEUTRAL, or seeing AEROBIC as a 'chocolate pen', I've never drawn any major flak from solvers or stakeholders – except once.

The year was 1991, the same year Tracy and I wed in Melbourne. The letter came via lawyers representing the Sony Corporation. The matter regarded 'Clue 19-Across of the *Sydney Morning Herald* cryptic, 5th ult.' Midway down the page I found this lyrical burst of legalese: 'WALKMAN ® is an Australian registered trademark No A351776 in class 9.' This was followed by more poetics: 'Preserving the value of a trademark is both in the public interest, as a trademark is both the public's guarantee of quality and reliability, and in the interest of the industry generally. It is particularly important in Sony's very brand-conscious industry.'

Forthwith I promised to eschew and desist from any use of Walkman® in future puzzles, but of course this amounted to a Band-Aid solution.

RECIPE PRECIS: DOUBLE MEANINGS

Generally the skinniest clues on the page, double meanings don't need a signpost. Instead, you get a double dose of definitions. While some examples (like FLATTER in this chapter) can carry several words, most are brief. Even when triple meanings come into play, like the *FT*'s Cincinnus who gave us MANDARIN – *Tongue is orange, and that's official* – the result is typically lean.

QUIZLING 13.1

What two golf shots – plus a slang word for golfer – are also computer terms?

QUIZLING 13.2

What pizza ingredient, mainsail section, Alpine projectile, trumpet blast and two generic flowers become approximate synonyms when treated as verbs? Remarkably, half the words rhyme with each other.

QUIZLING 13.3

Explain how BUTTON, elevated
Equates to PIPE, relegated.

CHAPTER 14

Decrease anaemia remedy?(4)

We know about question marks. If one appears, then word-play or definition is likely to be curly too. Away from cross-words, the meaning of the word BEACON is as clear as the object it describes. Yet taking the lateral route, the same light-house can mutate into a jail sentence – your chance to BE A CON.

Keeping with CON, could CONTEST be a trick question – in other words a quiz designed to deceive? Or CONQUEST, a bid to escape? Or CONFORM, a rap sheet? Every time I see a flashy salesman preaching the virtues of a time-share condo, I revel in CONDO nursing two words for swindle. So let's get lateral, and go direct to the next Master clue:

Decrease anaemia remedy?(4)

Where's the trap? Look closely at *decrease*, as this is the more flexible word. By that I mean it has the best chance of step-ping outside its standard meaning. Just like CON, DE is a versatile prefix, taking on multiple guises, including removal (as in *debark* or *dethrone*), reversal (*decompose, deactivate*) or departure (*detrain, decamp*). We all know DEMOTE means to move down, yet can't the same word mean to cleanse of dust particles? Can't DESPOT play a similar game? Keeping the momentum, a longer list might read like this:

decay: annihilate atoll
decider: oust booze (see deport)
define: quash a penalty
delight: darken
device: purify

When the farmer's wife attacked three blind mice, was she *detailing*? Canadian author Margaret Atwood, in one of her short stories, wonders if *remember* is the opposite of *dismember* – the rejoining of severed limbs. Lateral flexibility lies in countless words. Yet to expect a solver to see a word like *depot* and automatically imagine the removal of hemp plants is clearly demanding too much. Far more likely, a clue will deliver its strangeness from the opposite direction, an incentive to see the answer afresh. Paul of the *Guardian* does so with BEACON:

Do time and make light of it?

Or, returning to DEPOT, could the clue read:

Remove marijuana from terminal?

Again, a question mark alerts you to a twist in perspective. Though with our Master clue, the word you need to re-see is sitting on the page – *decrease*. A similar trap was set in the clue for AMAZON, the treachery resting in *flower*, a heteronym. Yet this time round we face a trap based on lateral meaning.

If CREASE means to rumple, then is DECREASE to smooth or iron? Wait a minute. Isn't IRON a means of fighting anaemia? Without getting too Dr House, I know that iron is produced by haemoglobin in the blood and stored in places like the liver and marrow. If your haemoglobin decreases, then your system soon craves iron. This kind of tangent alone makes me love crosswords. Sudoku may tune your logic, yet no other puzzle can take you to Brazil in one clue, the liver the next, with Alfred Hitchcock in between. On top of that is the benefit of getting your brain to embrace the idea that LIVER, the body's purifier, can also refer to a human being in general – or one who lives.

Premium compilers make you see common words as if for the first time. The best clues play between familiar words and their unfamiliar qualities. GORED, for instance, not only describes the matador's fate but also what happens to his clothes when injured. President OBAMA must be freezing, since the man equates to zero degrees, or O+BA+MA.

Different from puns, a word's lateral version is a new interpretation of how to read what you see. Even the word LATERALLY can suggest a fifth-set comeback, or late rally.

The visual equivalent of this offbeat thinking is the Magic Eye puzzle. You know those squares of funkadelic wallpaper printed in magazines? Stare at the pattern long enough and a 3-D *Titanic* will rise from the blur, or a space shuttle, whatever image is encoded below the surface. Of course, for some of us, that pay-off doesn't occur. You may gawk for minutes and get nothing but eye strain. But give it time, loosen the brain, and you may be delighted by the hologram beaming back.

Lateral thinking demands the same faith. True, you may not realise that IMPLORE refers to FAIRY TALES, or imagine ALIMONY and EXCLAIM could share their meaning, but give the game time, and one day the *Titanic* will rise.

This 'magic eye' is a vital tool for cryptic solving. It's like the chess player who sees the board so many moves ahead of the present moment. You see the reality in tandem with the game's potential. Lateral thinking, in a word sense, is the deeper strategy lying below a crossword's mechanics.

Just don't expect to be Bobby Fischer in your first few puzzles, or first few years. But the more devoted you are, the more intuitive you become. The key is training your eye *away* from crosswords too. Small things – like seeing TESS in DELICATESSEN, or noticing that Fe, the symbol for iron, ends KNIFE, a metal tool – are steps in the right direction. Let the mind meander and it will become readier for battle.

But let's return to IRON, and why this word lies in the Master Puzzle. Back in 2008, writing an essay for *Meanjin* quarterly, I tried to capture the day-to-day mania that goes with puzzle-making. The word I chose as a demonstration tool was IRON.

ALCHEMICAL REACTIONS – rare gleams in common words

Iron has been corrugated, galvanised, pumped, wrought. The stuff has been around for ages. Yet put the word on paper, and IRON tells a new story. Apply heat and the letters make curious patterns. What you see below is a symptom of the craze I own for a headspace, a cry for help perhaps. Anyway, here goes:

Mixing IRON with its symbol Fe, I spell ON FIRE.

Applying more flame, I note how IRON in reverse reveals NORI, a seaweed source of iron

NORI can also be read as NOR I – and not iodine? And not me? So who then? The answer: I, RON.

Meantime NOIR means black in French, though iron the mineral is red in the raw, while NOIR the genre sees Harry Lime on the silver screen.

Pluralise IRON and out steps the actor, Jeremy. Mix the past participle – IRONED – and DE NIRO makes a cameo.

Still with cinema, IRON MAN – the movie – opens with a mixture of MINOR, the legal opposite of MAN.

Weirder still, IRON MAN renders FE/MALE, a truer
opposite of the macho hero, and an irony in any
language.

Soundwise, IRON mimics ION, its own constituent.

Just as IRON is central to ENVIRONMENT, both on
the page and on the ground. And not overlooking
IGNORING, a word that holds our metal backwards.

Globally, IRON is one country code (RO for Romania)
nesting in India's IN.

Rolling IRON backwards in the alphabet, sliding every
letter back three places, uncovers the word FOLK.

So how did folk respond to this essay at the time? With
pity, for the most part, and who can blame them? Anagrams
aren't enough. Verbs, nouns, names, titles: I crave to uncover
the dictionary's secrets. As soon as a new word enters the
language – bling-bling or the irukandji jellyfish – I want to
explore the new pattern. English of course has a limit on how
many newcomers it can handle, meaning we lateral think-
ers need to stare longer at household words, trying to find a
novel vein in their composition.

At one level, the art of crossword-making compares to a
kind of alchemy, turning the everyday iron of human expression into gold. One setter who takes this challenge to heart
is John Young, alias Shed in the *Guardian*. Note the glister
he lent these common words, each with the double meaning
formula:

Perverted aptitude = BENT
One who pinches child = NIPPER
Threaten to go out with the disemboweller = GUTTER

With Shed, the alchemy analogy is even sounder. When

not shaping clues, Young has devoted several years to encoding online conversions of ancient manuscripts, including the doodlings of Sir Isaac Newton. The gig inspired a treatise in 1998 entitled *Faith, Alchemy and Natural Philosophy*. Seems that mysticism is never too far away from the art of crossword-making, that occult knack of making IRON dazzle in a dozen different ways, most of them laterally.

WOULD SIR LIKE PAPPADAMS? – vowel dumps and alternative spellings

All this fuss over *decrease* and we've barely glanced at the Master clue's other morsel. *Anaemia* stands out for owning far more vowels than consonants, joining other oddities like *amoebae*, *nouveau* and *evacuee*. Scrabble players dub them vowel dumps, not a lyrical name, but useful to know when nursing the Hawaiian alphabet in your rack.

Hawaiians, by the way, have a vowel fixation. You won't find a word from their culture where two consonants are side by side. One glance at Oahu, or *aloha*, or *ukulele* will tell you as much. This last word, curiously, shares a link with *anaemia*.

Sir Arthur Evans, the man to discover the Palace of Minos on the island of Crete, was an archaeologist. Indiana Jones, on the other hand, is an archeologist. Notice the difference – AE versus the plain E. This spelling debate has been raging for eons, which were once known as aeons, since the word derives from Ancient Greek.

Already in this chapter I've sprung haemoglobin on you, which Indy would spell without an A. Americans, in fact, began the pruning, turning paediatricians into pediatricians and selling the *Encyclopedia Britannica* door-to-door. Anaemia suffered a similar fate, becoming anemia in the USA, while squabbles continue in Great Britain.

As part of a clue, and not the solution, anaemia is an

acceptable risk. Bang in front of you, the grey area will be recognised by solvers of either camp. (*Grey* on the other hand is emphatically *gray* in America.) Such local variations haunted Clint Eastwood in the 1993 movie *In the Line of Fire*. As Special Agent Frank Horrigan, our man is out to thwart an assassin intent on killing the President. The cut-throat race is finally making headway when up bobs the word UKULELE.

Or that's how Frank spells it. Agent Chavez, his contact, reckons it's UKELELE. The spelling is crucial, as the right combination is the seven-button number for the San Diego office, which Frank needs to reach before a bullet finds its mark. The dilemma captures the risks inherent in borrowing words from other tongues.

Chiefly an oral culture, Polynesia gave us ukulele via speech, and we *haole* types have been second-guessing its spelling ever since. While most of us have settled on Frank's version, the *Oxford Dictionary* is still hedging its bets, offering the alternatives of *ukelele, ukalele* and *eukaleli*.

Even when the source language has a written tradition, translation can still give rise to dispute. Open any tandoori menu and your choices can range from *pappadam* (*papadam? puppadam? poppadum?*) to *chapatti* (*chapati? chupatti?*).

Another foreign dish, filched from Persia, holds the record for culinary options, with the *Macquarie Dictionary* listing *pilaf, pilau, pulao* and *pilaw*. In the territory of proper names, that of ex-Libyan ruler Muammar al-Kaddafi is only for the brave to run in a puzzle. The issue isn't politics, but a spelling debate. In fact some readers may recall *The West Wing* opened its majestic run with a crossword spat in the 1999 pilot episode. Here's a snippet:

> Chief of Staff Leo McGarry: Seventeen across is wrong.
> It's just wrong. Can you believe that, Ruth?
> Staffer Ruth: You should call them.
> Leo: I will call them. [long tracking shot through the

West Wing] Margaret! Please call the editor of the *New York Times* crossword and tell him that Khaddafi is spelt with an 'h' and two 'd's and isn't a seven-letter word for anything.

Eventually Leo is connected. What follows is a glimpse of the passion nursed by so many crossword solvers, as well as the perils of playing with alternative spellings:

Leo: Seventeen across. Yes. Seventeen across is wrong. You're spelling his name wrong. What's my name? My name doesn't matter! I'm just an ordinary citizen who relies on the *Times* crossword for stimulation. And I'm telling you that I met the man twice and I've recommended a pre-emptive Exocet missile strike against his air force so I think I know how to –

Click. The phone goes dead.

LATERAL COUPLES

Decrease, we've seen, may well mean iron, just as warbling may refer to a medal (war-bling). Flex your brain and see if you can spot the lateral links between these 15 couples:

B-team/subside	firefly/sack race
border security/hemlock	glee club/joystick
callbox/title fight	letterheads/Y-fronts
canned beef/toxin	ninepin/square leg
coma/understate	pay phone/wagering
demon drink/impale	reallot/zillion
dunces/thickset	substandard/torpedo
doe/party drug	travel permit/triplet

HALL OF FAME: DOUBLE MEANINGS

Close walrus relative (4) [Paul, *Guardian*]
Break silence (4) [Dogberry, *FT*]
Trendy a while ago, like vinyl records? (6) [Fawley, *Guardian*]
I order fish (7) [*Times* 8558]
LSD, but not pot, is in this drug box (5,4) [*Times* 8097]
Still together (2,3,4,4) [Orlando, *Guardian*]

SOLUTIONS: seal, rest, groovy, grouper, upper case, at the same time

QUIZLING 14.1

This device, designed to stretch out your dough, is a word for wealthy beside a means of accessing cash. Weirdly, no part in all this is connected to money. What's the device?

QUIZLING 14.2

Cleave means to separate as well as to bind together. Also starting with C, what's a simpler word that owns the same two contradictory meanings?

QUIZLING 14.3

If *Generous sort* = KIND, can you solve these other double meaning clues? Mixing the six initials of the correct answers will solve the double clue, *Fix brush*.

Look noble (4)   Moved camp (8)
Condition jockey (5)   Consider host (9)
Cattle drive (5)   Summit custom (10)

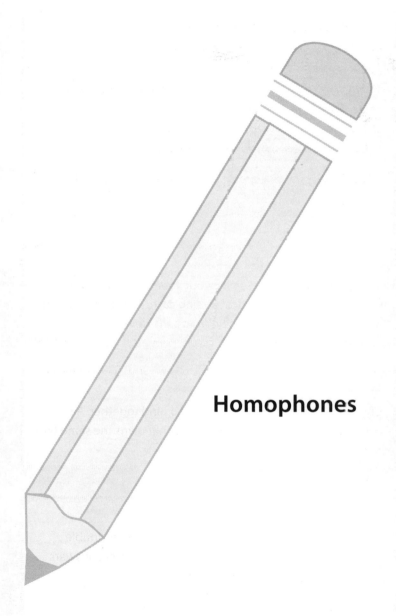

Homophones

CHAPTER 15

As mentioned, weather to get hotter? (5)

Chair/Resign/Felt

Say the words aloud. Does a certain comedian crop up? Not working for you? Then try the trio of *Eye/Sarcasm/Off*.

Can you hear Isaac Asimov? Better than Jerry Seinfeld in the first example? Sketchy, I know, but say these clusters quickly and I'm sure the casual eavesdropper will hear Jerry and Isaac loud and clear. I hope. Since there's always that doubt in the world of sound. Compare a *Seinfeld* episode (where *bomb* sounds like *balm*, or *cumin* comes out *koomin*) with *Wallace and Gromit* (which prefers short-a *grass* and a very long-u in *alluring*) to realise English is fickle.

Nowhere is that truth clearer than in the homophone category. Until now, clue styles have dealt in letters, or tested meanings (straight and lateral), yet that kind of comfort deserts us in the realm of sound.

I remember entering an audio debate in 1983 with a solver named John Le Gotha over the question of PAWPAW. The impetus was a Wordwit puzzle. Solvers had to find a word of twin halves (such as *dodo* or *beri-beri*) where either syllable sounded the same as three other words. PAWPAW did the trick, I thought, as each half mimicked *poor, pore* or *paw*. Yet John Le Gotha heard things differently.

PAW + PAW, he wrote, may equal two PAWS on the page, but as soon as you marry those halves that lavish *awww* sound gets clipped closer to a pair of *oars*. Measure this corruption, Le Gotha went on, against the purity of AYE-AYE, either the sailor's consent or the possum-like lemur of Madagascar, whose twin parts likewise own three homophones – *eye*, *I* and *ay* (the poetic word for alas) – yet preserve their sound quality once coupled.

Small beer, but these issues loom large in the world of homophones, where one person's ado will never be another's adieu. I've always considered Ovid, the Roman poet, as matching a Cockney version of hovered, though that whimsy was scorned in 2009 when I ran this homophone clue:

Latin poet and Cockney hung around in recital (4)

Latin poet, of course, is OVID. In the wordplay half, *hung around* points to HOVERED, and Cockney we know signals the h's stripping. *Recital*, the final word, is a homophone signpost, your cue to utter the wordplay's outcome to reveal the answer. I'll talk more about signposts and homophone rules in the coming section, but let's get back to that Latin poet, as the argument matters.

To many solvers, their OVID went closer to mimicking *off-id* (not *of-id*), same poet, different emphasis, meaning half the public had no idea what a Cockney was doing with an old Roman in the first place.

OVID and PAWPAW typify the delicacy of sound. In 2008 I spent a good week squabbling with the crossword editor, Lynne Cairncross, over a BLOW-UP DOLL. The clue in dispute read this way:

Swell welfare invoice a comfort for the prurient loner
  (4–2,4)

With BLOW-UP DOLL as answer, I'd always presumed the issue would be about tastelessness. I was wrong. Taste played second fiddle to sound.

Teasing out the clue, we're looking at a hybrid, where a double meaning (*Swell* for BLOW UP) meets homophone (*welfare* – or dole – matching the sound of DOLL). Lynne was less convinced. DOLL in her ears did not echo *dole*. 'I don't pronounce it the same way,' she wrote, in her first email. 'My husband doesn't either.'

But I do – that was the hitch. DOLL and DOLE. Say them together, swap them around, utter them in random order and you're all but chanting a singular sound over and over.

For proof, I wrote DOLL and DOLE on two separate cards and tested their pronunciation with students at the college where I teach. I even spelt D-O-L-L down the phone to Mum to see if her bias was mine.

Such a speech test recalls the infamous Parsley Massacre of 1937 in which soldiers serving the Dominican tyrant Rafael Trujillo used sprigs of parsley in order to identify Haitians among the population living in the border area. 'What's this?' they asked. Should the response be *perejil* , with the fricative j of pedigree Spanish intact, then the speaker was safe. However, if the j was soft, the speaker was shot. Ultimately, some 30,000 speakers were executed, owing to a j's phonetic qualities.

Lynne and I recognised that our stand-off centred on a shibboleth. The Bible's idea of a password, a shibboleth refers to a term that distinguishes two clans. It stems from the Book of Judges, where the Hebrews of Gilead detected incognito Ephraimites thanks to their inability to pronounce the Hebrew word for flooded stream, or *shibboleth*. Stumble and you were smote.

Asimov, that sci-fi writer who sounds like *Eye/Sarcasm/Off*, refers to a shibboleth in the chemist community. Write

UNIONISED on a slip of paper, he said, and dozens will pronounce the word the obvious way. But show the slip to a chemist, and he or she will utter the word as un-ionised, betraying their vocation. In the same way, two execs may glance at RESIGN, the pessimist pronouncing the synonym of quit, while the optimist stresses the first syllable, intoning a command to renew his contract.

Lynne and I did not resign over Doll-gate. The poll results were a mishmash and rhyming dictionaries had a bob each way. In the end we agreed to disagree. Lynne laughed, 'I can't believe I've spent two days talking about the sound of a blow-up doll!'

'Wait,' I said. 'That sounded the same as dole.'

'Let's move on,' said Lynne.

GETTING WARMER – homophone signposts

In the game of charades, an ear-tug signals a rhyme. LIFE, say, may be too vast to portray through mime, so a quick pull of the lobe could lead to the portrayal of KNIFE. This tactic tells your guesser that the target word is a rhyme of what they're seeing.

In cryptic crosswords that ear-tug compares to a homophone signpost – a word declaring the sonic dimension. Run your eye (and ear) over these four examples:

Heard sweet animal = MOOSE
Moved material, say = SWAYED
Ten years of rotten report = DECADE
Indulges Chinese vegetarians on the radio? (7)

Heard is high on the list of signposts, along with all its variations – *we hear, in hearing, overheard, hearsay* and so on. Asked another way, the first clue could be posed as a riddle, 'What animal sounds like a sweet?' MOOSE echoes MOUSSE, so the beast is snared.

Ditto for SWAYED, a mimicry of SUEDE, or *material*. Notice how the audio signpost only applies to the wordplay, and so needs to stand beside that element, much like anagram signposts need to adjoin the fodder.

DECADE, the third example, relies on *report* as the ear-tug. Voice the word DECAYED (or *rotten*) – *report* it – and *ten years* emerge, or DECADE. Or do they? When I tackled this clue in a *Telegraph* collection, my ear wasn't convinced. More of the sex-doll scandal, in a way. Homophones are subtle creatures, which leads us to Chinese vegetarians.

Read it again: *Indulges Chinese vegetarians on the radio*. Where to start? Let's break it down. Rarer homophone clues will call on cuter hearing aids, so to speak – such as *so to speak*, or slyer signposts like *pronounced, vocal, outspoken* and *utter*.

Another left-field signpost concerns airwaves. Take extra care with any mention of *broadcasting* (a nod to either anagram or homophone), *registered* and *announced*. Of course radio is the other eccentric signal, which the final sample uses.

Can you name *Chinese vegetarians* that sound like a word for *indulges*? Come to think of it, can you name a Chinese vegetarian full stop? Well, here the question mark joins the game; the definition is liable to be looser. Why *Chinese* in the first place? Why not *vegetarians* and leave it at that?

Testing another tangent, how many synonyms for *indulges* can you list? MOLLYCODDLES is too long. So what about SPOILS? RELAXES? PAMPERS?

Wait, if not PAMPERS, what about PANDERS? Suddenly those *Chinese vegos* make sense, the PANDAS of the airwaves leading to the PANDERS in the grid. Time to indulge in the Master clue:

As mentioned, weather to get hotter? (5)

Kindly, we have the audio signpost coming first. *As mentioned* is a classic phrase suggesting sound. So what's another word for weather? Does this mean weather in general, or what a forecast dishes out? Or there may be a third option, with weather meaning to endure.

Once more the question mark invites caution, as the definition could be devious. *To get hotter* may apply to increased fury or spice or raunch or a dozen other tacks – the *weather* even. Let's see what letters the grid can offer.

C is the answer's initial, thanks to COSIMO at 1-Across. This alone puts CLIMATE back in the gun, the only candidate so far to match that detail. CLIMATE sounds like CLIMB IT, which is almost there. What if we shrink the word to CLIME and test the homophone of CLIMB? Can climb mean *to get hotter*? It does where weather is involved, the column of mercury climbing the tube, and giving you the confidence to enter 1-Down.

Though before you do, double-check if it's CLIME or CLIMB. Which word is *mentioned* in order to create the other? A quick check will tell you that CLIME is spoken to render the other, so CLIMB goes in the grid. Yet before we tackle the next two homophones, a word about the weather.

SMALL VOICE OF PROTEST – partisan clues

Despite the movie's name, *Mercury Rising* is not about global warming but a code inside a crossword. The film stars *brew-swillers*, the aural equal of Bruce Willis, an FBI agent trying to protect an autistic kid called Simon from an evil bureaucrat called *knickerless-could-row*, that is Nicholas Kudrow, played by Alec Baldwin.

Simon, we discover, is the only living American who can break the National Security Agency's code called Mercury. As a bragging exercise, the code-makers bury their new cipher in a puzzle, asking any successful solver to call the agency's number. Simon obliges, enraging the cryptographers. Their only solution? To kill this pre-teen savant, as he poses a threat to federal security.

Life-or-death politics may seem misplaced in a crossword, but some compilers embrace the edgier subjects. Damn it, we love them. CLIMB could inspire a dozen different clues, from charade (C + LIMB) to hidden (*acrobatic limbo*), yet the homophone option felt tailor-made for making a geothermal statement. Stepping through what recipes we've already met, let's take a look at a few more political 'statements' in the guise of clues. Sleuth (alias Philip Marlow) composed this one for the *Financial Times*:

Role in law spun – typical of Blair = ORWELLIAN

This wicked anagram aimed at the day's prime minister recognises that Orwell's real name was Eric Blair. Then we have a brazen container clue, this time from the *Guardian's* Arachne:

President who is snide about English-speaking nation = SARK(OZ)Y

Or a hybrid, pairing anagram with charade, appearing in the same puzzle:

Our men going off to join American legion = NUMERO+US

Or a hidden, such as this *Times* gem:

Chancellor conceals big fiddle = CELLO

And finally two of my own, a double meaning and a homophone, both with a drop of satirical acid:

Scrub US president = BUSH
Monkey with outspoken craft in the Howard years? = TAMPA

This last answer alludes to a Norwegian cargo ship that saved several hundred Afghan refugees from the Indian Ocean in 2001. Effectively, the vessel became a seaborne prison as the Australian government wavered about what to do with the castaways. The result was a makeshift policy dispatching the Afghans to a compound in Nauru until more red tape could be fetched. The name of this policy – PACIFIC SOLUTION – has 15 letters, the ideal crossword length, and the central plank in my partisan theme. To clue the entry I took my chance to score a political point via anagram:

Howard's cop-out worsening pitiful occasion!

RECIPE PRECIS: HOMOPHONES

Listen up. Sound is all in the homophone clan, hence the signposts below (some more subtle than others) opt for audio. In the next two chapters we'll hear about double homophones, and how the formula can fall into hybrid clues, but for now, cock your ear to these warning calls:

announced, apparently, articulate, as they say, auditor, broadcast, by the sound of it, caught, echo, given voice, hear, in audition, in auditorium, in canal, in conversation, in speech, invoice, noisily, on the airwaves, on the radio, orally, outspoken, picked up, pronouncement, register, related, reported, say so, sound, spoken, they tell us, utter, vocal, we hear

QUIZLING 15.1

If urn-yells mimics Ernie Els, can you arrange each cluster below to sound out six more famous names?

pacy, fins, care
nerve, shark, villa
jaw, yet, jelly
riff, nicks, furphy
luck, rubble, sand
honour, corers, kino

QUIZLING 15.2

What beverage owns a homophone that describes what you'll do if you drink too much of the same beverage?

QUIZLING 15.3

Two words. One means approval, the other opposition. And amazingly, when both words are changed into their homophones, the result is a new pair of opposites. What are the four words?

CHAPTER 16

Soundly ushered back and docketed (9)

In late December 1913, Arthur Wynne stared at the emptiness. With no snippet off the wires, no retail ad, the *New York World* subeditor cursed the space on the Amusements page, wondering how he'd ever fill it. Deadline was looming. So desperation struck – he invented the crossword.

Or Word-Cross, as Wynne called it. Diamond in shape, with a hollowed centre, the diagram comprised 72 squares with small numbers inscribed on all the outer and inner extremes. *'Fill in the small squares with words which agree with the following definitions,'* he wrote below the diagram. To give solvers a fighting chance the grid also sported the hand-drawn letters of FUN in the upper quadrant.

This took place in the same year in which the zipper was invented, the era of Henry Ford's assembly line and of Yorkshire's stainless steel. Down under, the first sod of Canberra was turned. The new world was evolving, but was it ready for its first crossword? Or word-cross – or wait, was this puzzle truly the first?

Even today, arguments simmer over whether Wynne's work can lay claim to being the prototype. *The Guinness Book of World Records* affords the honour to an English children's magazine named *St Nicholas* that ran a solid word-diamond in 1875. Its mystery compiler was 'Hyperion', named after the Titan god of light, yet their creation lacked squares or clue numbering.

In fact, Wynne himself grew up in Liverpool, cracking puzzles in *St Nicholas* with his grandfather. Word squares – or magic squares – were regular features: prim waffle patterns where every word appeared the same both across and down. Yet none mirrored the modern crossword, complete with diverse answers, tabled clues and inscribed numbers.

To enhance his innovation, Wynne made his clues pretty basic. *Opposed to less*, for example, was MORE. *A talon* was a CLAW, while DRAW was *What artists learn to do*. Longer entries were equally generous with *A written acknowledgement* being RECEIPT, and REVERIE *A day dream*. Really the only devils were *A Russian river* (NEVA), *A fist* (NEIF) and NARD – *An aromatic plant*. At the time, leaving for vacation, Arthur had no inkling his stopgap remedy would spark a frenzy across the eastern seaboard, and later the world.

Sequels followed quickly. Wynne's paper ran a second word-cross before the year was out, as well as a bank of readers' creations into January. Word-crosses, by that stage, had switched into being cross-words, possibly due to an editorial slip, the hyphen soon lapsing in tandem with the pastime's rising fever.

At the craze's height, the New York Library limited consultation time for dictionaries. The B&O commuter trains between Maryland and Ohio stocked reference books to assist the passengers' puzzle-solving. Broadway musicals saluted the novelty with songs, including the classic 'Crossword Mamma, You Puzzle Me (But Papa's Gonna Figure You Out').

Chequered patterns seized Greenwich Village boutiques. Puzzle talk emerged in sermons, classrooms and even divorce proceedings. (Plaintiff Mary Zaba of Chicago mournfully described herself as a crossword widow, suing her husband for neglect. She won, her contrite fellow agreeing to reduce his daily fix to three grids.)

Nonetheless there remained one more space to fill – the bookshelf. A woman known as Aunt Wixie was chatting with her nephew, Richard Simon, in 1924. She wondered why she couldn't find any crossword book for her daughter to solve. Later that week, Simon scouted the stores to confirm the market gap. He got in touch with his old mate, Max, from Columbia. Under the banner of Plaza Publishing, the two young men bought puzzles from across the newsstand at $25 a pop, binding them into one volume with a pencil attached. The resulting sales surpassed 300,000, providing the seed capital for the publishing empire we've come to know as Simon & Schuster.

About this time, British papers tested the format on their own readers. The first UK crossword, it's believed, appeared in 1922 in *Pearson's Magazine*, the cradle of such distinguished writers as George Bernard Shaw and H. G. Wells. The puzzle's slow migration across the Atlantic might be explained by the attitude displayed in an article that appeared in *The Times* around this period. Entitled 'AN ENSLAVED AMERICA', the piece accused the crossword of 'making devastating inroads on the working hours of every rank of society'. Five million man-hours, estimated the writer, were squandered daily. The Land of the Free, England feared, was so no longer.

Before too long, however, the fever soon crippled Old Blighty too. By the late 1920s, most magazines and papers carried the black-and-white menace, though *The Times* itself – just like the *New York Times* – resisted the fad till nearer World War II when bleak news needed some kind of nostrum. The *Sydney Morning Herald* followed suit, the first crossword appearing in 1934, adorning the women's supplement.

Beyond America, and spicing Wynne's original recipe, came the cryptic element, though the move from definition to wordplay was organic, a slow experiment between the setter and the solving public.

Prime mover in that regard was Oxford poet and translator Edward Powys Mathers, who found a niche in *The Observer* from 1926 onward. His maiden cryptic appeared in January of that year, a puzzle called Feelers, with a weevil-shaped grid and tentative instructions to match: 'This, the first problem, is, as it were, a putting out of feelers from setter to solver, and from solver to setter. A beginning has been made ....'

And a positive impression. The British appetite was primed for cryptic. One reason for this must rest in a strong tradition of parlour games, with Queen Victoria herself an addict of wordplay and acrostics. Then there's *Alice in Wonderland*, the secular gospel of British childhood, a fantasia rife with letter-play. A third theory is straight-out envy. If a former colony can invent a new verbal form, then Britain felt honour bound to reinvent it.

Whichever the case, Mathers is seen by most as the man to marry the American interlock with wry Anglo clues, choosing the alias of Torquemada after a prominent torturer during the time of the Spanish Inquisition. (A generation later, inheriting the same gig, Derrick Macnutt selected the fellow torturer Ximenes in honour of the genre's forefather.) The coming decades would see the art form evolve, with quotation clues and naked anagrams changing into slimmer specimens that Ximenes went on to codify.

Yet cunning as these early setters were, surely the oldest crossword debt must be repaid to Arthur Wynne. Rather than cower in the face of a blank page, Wynne decided to criss-cross words and clue them. In a small way our latest Master clue – *Soundly ushered back and docketed* – rejoices in Arthur's act of desperation.

DIAMONDS ARE FOREVER – Wynne's fix and wiggle words

Pity a man like Leonhard Euler, the Swiss number-cruncher whose doodles now serve as the bedrock for the sudoku empire, 200 years later. Or Arthur Wynne, the man to omit a © among those seventy-two other letters he wove into his diamond. Soundwise, you have to say, Mr Wynne missed a win. If only he'd been a little shrewder, his family might now be making money hand over NEIF.

Which leads me to the other reason I sympathise with Wynne. Even a century ago, NEIF was a dodgy word, a Shakespeare term for fist. Speaking as a fellow setter, NEIF represents a clumsy escape from a tight corner. In hindsight a minor tweak could have put NEIL or NAIF into vertical column N-8 – but no. Arthur opted for Scots via Old Norse, a word that was quaint and dialectic even to his peers.

Even the best of us do it – running one dubious entry that stands apart from the grid's more familiar fill. Last year I succumbed to LOST CAT in one puzzle, and OPEN TEAM in another, two lacklustre phrases added in the name of preserving a high number of themed answers. The lapse can only be forgiven if the remainder of the puzzle is pleasingly dense. Often a shocker like LOST CAT can be the difference between ten themed entries, and a whopping fifteen or so. Which option do you choose?

The great Araucaria yielded to TREK CART in 2004 to allow the grid to carry a lengthy quote. In America, among the tighter grids that Wynne ordained, the claustrophobia is relieved by such wiggle words as roman numerals, acronyms, third basemen and phrase chunks such as OF A, or IS TO. No argument from me – Americans are crisscross wizards, with US software the rising leader in this regard. More to the point, the odd peccadillo is pulp by month's end, and a solver forgives that rare cop-out if the overall mix is rewarding. Yet poor old Arthur went for NEVA – that Russian river – plus a few other fishy terms, including TANE (an archaic piece of Scottish dialect clued as *One*), and now his diamond is forever.

Anyhow, that's the bad news. Better news relates to the current clue we're solving. When first listing words to include in the Master Puzzle, I was keen to share an entry that Arthur himself had selected back in 1913. But it seems I was overlooking the words of LB: 'After the first dozen entries, the crossword takes over.' And so it proved with this puzzle.

Don't worry. It's not a LOST CAT – but it is a compromise. After BINOCULARS and IRON and several other terms had grabbed their berths early, I had little choice but to modify my ambition, captured in our second homophone:

Soundly ushered back and docketed (9)

Tuning your ear, you'll recognise *soundly* as the aural signal. So what is being sounded? Neither *ushered* nor *ushered back* offers abundant synonyms. At times this shortfall (remember the *Chinese vegetarians*?) can be helpful, making a shortlist of options even shorter. Yet here the scarcity of possible synonyms can also make you agonise.

Past tense, *ushered* is another word for LED, or GUIDED or DIRECTED. But what about the *back* part? If you're led back to a place, are you being re-led? Re-steered? Could that be the drift? If a moviegoer has left her seat halfway through the film, is she then re-seated by the usher? Say that again. RECEIPTED. That's what I thought you said!

Wynne himself had used RECEIPT, but that didn't fit, so the -ED is the compromise. In that regard, most dictionaries accept receipt as a verb, but what about the word's cadence? Do RECEIPTED and RESEATED own matching emphases? Tell you what, why not inflate a blow-up doll and thrash out the issue with her? I'm more concerned with a deeper crossword peril, a curse I call Accidental Voodoo, and a clue-word like 'docketed' is a prime example. Time to move from Arthur Wynne and focus on a parking fine I received outside my local noodle bar.

FROM DIAMOND TO CRYSTAL – omen clues and Accidental Voodoo

I churn out a metric tonne of words and clues every year so it's only natural – or supernatural – that some of my selections will be published with eerie timing.

Like that parking ticket. Admittedly the sign said *No Standing*, and the noodle bar wasn't an emergency, but when I re-seated myself in the Subaru and noticed the yellow slip under the wiper I felt peeved and jinxed at the same time.

Part of me blames RECEIPTED. Pitiful, I know, but maybe if I'd chosen another Wynne word, or tried a second recipe, then I'd never have ended up buying a curry laksa for the equivalent of $195. RECIPE, in fact, can be found in RECEIPTED, followed by TED – a bear. Was that a safer bet? Abolish all talk of dockets and tickets, so ditching the chance for bad juju to intervene …

I realise how loco this sounds, but there have been occasions in my thirty years of puzzle-making where I've felt eerily responsible for a series of unfortunate events.

Roh Moo-hyun, for one, the former president of South Korea, is not a name you hear every day. Yet in May 2008 I went with ROH for an answer in a Omega puzzle. Back then I saw no harm in recruiting the gentleman, his first name at least. South Korea is an Australian neighbour after all, and Omegas revel in current affairs. Sadly, the decision backfired three days after the puzzle ran to press, a headline screaming: 'KOREANS MOURN ROH AFTER SUICIDE PLUNGE'. You could understand my goose bumps.

A similar grim coincidence involved Bea Arthur, the

Golden Girl, who died the week another Omega appeared, prompting the Pagemasters gang to send a list of other VIPs they were eager to curse. For a while I gained the mantle of Dr Doom. Even a generic word like AVALANCHE, in August of the same year, coincided with an ice cornice detaching in the Kosciuszko National Park, entombing a snowboarder.

Ghoulish, flippant – I run the risk of being called either, I know. Or worse – New Age. But when the hex descends I feel like a voodoo priest, summoning heartbreak on all those named.

Being rational for a moment, I realise that one ROH MOO-HYUN outweighs a hundred BONOs, BRAD PITTs and TONY BLAIRs – a thousand names who pass through a puzzle with karmic immunity. Yet when the creepy echo occurs, you can't help but overhear it.

Like the day I saw a verbal quirk in the name of champion surfer Layne Beachley. I ran the whim in a Wordwit to appear beside the features section. Unfortunately, Beachley happened to be the cover girl that week, and not for the happiest of reasons. In a story called SHOCK WAVE, she bravely discussed the story of her own adoption for the first time. Suddenly the anguish was on public record – 27 September – the day Beachley shared her harrowing past, as well as learning that her surname can be mixed with L to make BELLYACHE.

Staying with the ocean theme, I clued TSUNAMI on the eve of the 2008 Samoan disaster. And then I opted for LETTERMAN on the week of the TV host's blackmail revelations.

All compilers are prone to such chilly flukes. Ann Tait, a stalwart setter at the *Daily Telegraph*, had the fright of her life in 1990 when her clue for BLUE MURDER (*Outcry caused by Tory assassination*) appeared two days after the IRA murdered Conservative MP Ian Gow in a car bomb.

Yet in 2006, thank God, one omen clue was saved from appearing. The answer was ZOO, one letter short of ZOOM,

I noticed, so inspiring your first glimpse at the deletion formula:

Steve Irwin's property career cut short (3)

An archaic meaning of 'career' is to speed, or ZOOM. And *cut short* makes it ZOO, an enterprise the Irwin family own in Queensland. Spookily, the clue was set to go in the same week that a stingray crossed Steve's path. Suddenly the wording looked ghoulish, malign. But a last-minute change ensured that the Irwin reference was avoided, as a harmless ZOO clue, a charade involving a Zulu leader and two ducks.

Yet as grisly as the Irwin clue could have been, the eeriest example of crossword voodoo was a triple whammy in 2003. I was solving the *Times* on the day a book was being launched, a true crime story I'd written with Senior Constable Joe D'Alo of Victorian Police. An insider's account of a murder case, *One Down, One Missing* shadows the investigation of two police officers shot during stake-out duties in 1998. Controversial for several reasons, not least due to Joe's inside status and the consequent threat of suspension, the launch attracted a fair amount of publicity.

We'd tried to keep the book under wraps for as long as possible, but the secret was out and the TV crews were swarming. Before the event, dodging any media, I took time out in a city café, seeking solace in a crossword. These were the clues I read:

Police officers two similar men replaced =
    SUPERS+ED+ED
Suspended? Previously one would be kept in = ON(I)CE
Unprecedented release just becoming known =
    RECORD-BREAKING

Trying not to flinch, I folded the paper shut, checked the napkin dispenser for listening devices and left.

QUIZLING 16.1

If a sterile noble is a BARREN BARON, can you go forth and identify these other homophonic pairs?

Jacuzzi brawl (3,4)
Plant fruit (4,5)
Act Christian-like (4,4)
Reader's past (4,4)
Spun globe (7,5)
Main rule (9,9)
Muscle-weary? (7,8)
Top tantrum (4,5)
Tomato? (5,6)

QUIZLING 16.2

What nine-lettered word is a mixture of a number beside its consecutive number, sounded -out?

QUIZLING 16.3

The homophones of what two vegetables are synonyms?

CHAPTER 17

Nation hunting craft in Italian canal, say (9)

I still see the dread on my young daughter's face when I told her we were going to the top of Centrepoint Tower, a 300-metre spire in Sydney. Her fear, I presumed, was acrophobic. But for Tess the nightmare related to bugs. Who in their right mind would choose to visit Centipede Tower?

Linguists know these slips as egg-corns, the 'fruit' of mis-heard words and phrases, named after a child's own versions of the true word, *acorns*. In the 'temple lobe' of the egg-cor-ner's brain, babies sleep in the feeble position, while grandpa may suffer old-timer's disease. Real estate signs are often good for egg-corns, with placards claiming sheik addresses or laundry shoots. A favourite of mine was a lost cat notice pinned to a notice board. The missing moggy was 'Ginger and white with blue flee collar'.

Away from egg-corns and homophone fluffs, there's the other mess of human mishearing, or misunderstanding, the one in which boxer Mike Tyson, after so much bad press, longed to 'fade into Bolivian'. Here the founding culprit is Mrs Malaprop, a character in Richard Sheridan's play *The Rivals*. Thanks to this dame's clumsy tongue, any ill-suited word or phrase goes by the name of malapropism, borrowing from the French word for ill-suited or inappropriate.

A college friend collects these boo-boos like normal people

hoard stamps or beer coasters. Her list is impressive, from social piranha to buggering belief. For Rose, a trip to India comprised weeks of scouring menus in the hope of such treasures as cinema rolls and meshed potato. Both sound like dishes you can expect on *Kath & Kim*, the Australian sitcom featuring two alfalfa females using pacific terms in effluent society.

I didn't know whether to laugh or take offence when a caustic letter from a solver in 1992 claimed that one of my crossword clues, involving the unsavoury homophone of the Jewish HORA, was anti-semantic.

Language learning in its early phases is all about the ear. A toddler has only sketchy notions of letters, no less vague than semantics, and yet seems to cope by parroting what parents or siblings say. A small child doesn't care how you spell YOGHURT, or about the word's Turkish history, just so long as blurting 'yo-kit' or 'yoke-cut' works on Mum.

Second-guessing pop lyrics enlivens the experience for us literate beings. If we think Madonna is pining for 'Louise the Bra-Eater' (instead of 'La Isla Bonita') or the Cuban chant of 'Guantanamera' is all about a 'One-ton tomato', then who really cares? So long as we get to sing along with the radio, the imagined words make as much sense as those in the next tune. A vast amount of early language comes from soaking up sounds and repeating an approximation of what we heard. Until being shamed of course, or corrected, or we go to check the sleeve notes.

I felt like a kid reborn when working on a cargo ship back in 1986, learning Spanish from a deckhand named Javier. A craggy Galician in his early fifties, Javier was born with a crocheted cap on his scalp and a Lucky Strike lodged to his lip. Between puffs, he taught me Spanish. Most nights, from 2000 to 2400 hours, we'd stand on night watch, Javier making small talk and yours truly playing mimic. From Sydney to Oslo, we developed our chat from 'The sea is big' to 'The moon is beautiful' to '*Hecho crucigrammas*' (or 'I make crosswords').

Spanish and crosswords in fact were my antidotes to the rigours of a long trip. The work was tough, compared to mixing letters. I had to clean the engine room from stem to stern, my body clock unsprung by three months of racing the sun. When I wasn't scrubbing valves or painting bilge pumps I was trying to relax with a word puzzle – solving or making one – or reading fat books like *Moby-Dick* and Gogol novels, or else standing on the bridge in the beautiful moonlight, growing bilingual under a watchman's eye.

Javier had vaguely heard of *crucigrammas*, but cryptics were another dimension. Keeping things simple, a hostage to the present tense and my own callow vocab, I tried in vain to enlighten the bloke, telling him about '*trucos*' (tricks) and '*mal direcciones*', but the sailor wagged his head and laughed. He dug around in his overalls and lit another Lucky Strike. '*Despacio*,' he said, something of a mantra with Javier – *Slowly*. You can't hope to master a language in a hurry, just as cryptic crosswords demand your care and perseverance, whether you're manipulating letters or voicing experimental sounds.

PUZZLE OVER SECOND SOUND – double homophones

CROW lacks a true homophone, as does SHADE, but put them together and CROCHETED materialises. Does that mean the word when spoken equals black – the one and only crow-shade?

BOW has a homophone in BEAU, just as TIE owns THAI. Together, of course, the pair makes BOWTIE. Yet when the syllables switch positions, the same piece of apparel turns into TAE BO, the aerobic fad of the 1990s. Effectively a clue for this observation could read:

Exercise regime switching formal wear, say (3,2)

Code red, people. We're about to confront the double homophone, where CRUSADE turns into CREW'S AID (a map? a compass?) or TROUSSEAU can be reversed to seem SO TRUE. Suddenly Bear Grylls can be bare grills, and the solver feels left in the wilds. But don't fret. The double homophone is a rare bird, asking for your audio range to extend beyond the first sound bite. Here are two samples from *The Times*:

Tree said to be less healthy on heath = SYCAMORE
     (*'sicker + moor'*)
Puzzle over second sound = ACROSTIC (*'across + tick'*)

Can you see the double billing in both? The signposts vary – *said, sound* – but the trick is consistent. No different in fact than the subterfuge lurking in our current clue, with one added twist.

Let me explain. MAP, as we've just discussed, is an all-encompassing suggestion for CRUSADE ('hearing' the double homophone as *crew's aid* rather than *crews + aid*). In the same vein BLACK could be the ambient definition of CROCHETED. Entering a similar zone, our Master clue asks you to pair two sounds together, treating the coupling as an entity. Let's take a look:

Nation hunting craft in Italian canal, say (9)

Helpfully, we know from the grid that the answer ends in A. Secondly, given that the audio signal appears as the tail, we can speculate that our answer is defined by the opening word, *Nation*. In support of that idea, the extended phrases of *Nation hunting*, or *Nation hunting craft*, make little sense in isolation. One glimpse, and we've established three things:

We're after a nation; it ends with A; homophones are implicated.

Often, when two wordplay elements combine, or the word-play cleaves to the definition, a linkword is used. Common joiners are words like *with* or *on* or *and,* the sort of words that fly below the radar, not just describing the wordplay's action, but also refining the clue's surface sense.

Sometimes, to glue the pieces with a little more flair, the link can be a verb such as making or seeing. (For example, *Jim too drunk to make cocktail* = MOJITO.) *Hunting,* however, as appears in our current clue, is off-limits: too conspicuous, and it cannot be justified to describe any wordplay operation. Which means the word is a vital piece of wordplay, either in its own right or helping to qualify the *craft* we're seeking.

The cargo ship that gave me Spanish was not a hunting craft. All she did was roll-on-roll-off Japanese cars and carry steel boxes filled with cane furniture from Malaysia. Along the way the crew enjoyed its share of drama, from stowaways in Panama to a crewman getting arrested for disorderly behaviour in New Orleans. In the north Pacific we lurched hard left to dodge a basking whale. The monster may not have been white, but I still felt like Ahab with his missing limb, cursing the behemoth as I tumbled in my cabin.

As well as being true, the whale story is also your clue-within-a-clue. But if that's not working for you, then let's explore Italian canals.

Most puzzle setters will presume the solver has a lay knowledge of geography. When it comes to Venice, say, no fair-minded compiler would expect his solvers to know *Canale de Fabbri,* or *Canale di Fuseri,* or any other capillary I've yanked off Google Maps. As general knowledge goes, the Grand Canal is pretty much the long and short of it. Anything else is too parochial, too specialist.

Whales? Venice? Or said another way: Venice? Whales?

Since the clue asks for *hunting craft,* and not its prey, then WHALER is the word we need to try, assuming SEALER,

EELER and PRAWNER are out. So then, treating the two sounds as a single unit, could the *Pequod* of the Adriatic be a VENICE WHALER? Say it isn't so. But it is, we hear. Say it again. Fill it in. You've solved your last – and toughest – homophone, a double no less.

CRUCIGRAMMAS – non-English cryptics and Javier

Before doing Cargo-ship Spanish, I did five years of Latin at high school, reciting the Roman hip hop of *amo, amas, ama*. Mates and career counsellors would tut-tut on a regular basis. 'What are you doing a dead language for?' To which I'd retort *carpe diem*, which roughly translates as 'I don't really know'.

Short of options, I did German too, less dead in comparison, though from an Australian perspective, especially a white-bread, pre-Web 1970s perspective, Deutschland was no less remote than the Circus Maximus. Ancient history or the northern hemisphere: both felt a million miles away, making the offer of a cargo ship, at the age of twenty-five, a chance to break out of a vacuum.

Hopping off in Oslo, tramping south, I found it bewildering to meet Bavarians who actually knew the phrase *Guten tag*. Not only that, they answered back. I felt like asking, 'Did you study with Miss Baker too?'

I'd been to Italy before, defecting from the rugby tour when barely out of pimple cream, but even on my second visit, catching up with family, I still felt confounded that Latin didn't hold much currency in the fallen empire of Claudius.

Dazed from the overnight train, I staggered about the Stazione de Roma Termini wondering why none of the citizens knew what *ipso facto* meant. What was the problem? 'Didn't you invent the bloody language?' I quizzed the cab driver, in Latin, who shrugged. He took my money and left me on the corner of Via Bari and Via Catanzaro, where I went to find my *matertera* – which meant aunt – but not in Italian.

Mum's younger sister, Auntie Glen, had done what I was doing a generation earlier. Back then, also in her twenties, the Roseville girl had fled suburbia to end up in the Eternal City with a wedding rock and a tall Alitalia pilot named Cesare. Once we'd exchanged the usual double kisses, Glen gave me a wad of lire and told me to lose the beard. 'Here,' she said, *'per favore*, go find a barber.'

'A *tonsor*,' I corrected her.

She pointed to Piazza Bologna. 'A *barbiere*.'

Curiously, Auntie Glen shared the puzzle itch as well. When not creating subtitles for American movies, she worked out these dense Italian word squares in *Settimana Enigmistica*, a magazine full of wordplay and rebus puzzles – even a splash of Latin. Back in Australia, growing up with Jessie, my grandmother, Glen had likewise learnt to tackle cryptics, but the genre had yet to find a niche in Rome. Instead she got her fix from haphazard dispatches of *Herald* puzzles – some of them mine – sent by Australian friends. The smell of gum leaves, the drone of lawnmowers and LB's anagrams were Glen's three reminders of her *patria*.

So where was the Italian cryptic, I wondered. Or the Dutch version? The French? How come Javier the Spanish watchman had no idea of what I did for a crust, assuming I was choosing the right words for my explanation?

The closest I came to finding a foreign-language cryptic was Frankfurt, where that city's paper ran a crossword with a few elongated clues. Yet on closer reading these went closer to puns, rather than abiding by the Cryptic Code of Conduct.

Subsequent research has only confirmed my hunch. *The Hindu Times* has a lively cryptic made by local setters, as do other outposts of the British Empire. Seems English is custom-made for duplicity. Like the black hole of space, pulling in fragments of any passing dialect, English has the ideal fusion of influences, with its erratic spelling, its promiscuous roots, the multiple shades of sound and meaning – where MOLE can be a mammal, a skin blemish, a breakwater, a spy or (when spoken with two syllables) a chilli-laced chocolate sauce from Mexico. And that's one word – serving as five – in a language of almost a million.

Anyhow, back in Rome, I'd written half a novel for want of anything else to do. Then Lynda my Aussie girlfriend arrived as a welcome interruption. We hit the road, meandered along the Côte d'Azur and ended up in Spain. It was there in Madrid, just off the city's main plaza, that we found a flat to rent. She scored a job at the United Nations, typing up reports about the nuclear aftermaths of Pacific atolls, while I played rugby for Madrid University, existing on a false student visa that claimed I was studying architecture.

I constructed crosswords instead, and continued the habit of gathering new Spanish words, striving for fluency, yet so much of my vocab harked back to the ship. I felt trapped inside a Conrad novel, the Spanish version, where all I seemed to know were sea conditions and maritime slang.

Did those six months – living as a Spaniard-lite – impact on my puzzle-making? Yes on both levels – the flexibility that comes with a bilingual brain, and the small jewels I found hiding in a new treasury of words. TESORO, for example, the Spanish word for *treasure*, is also a blend of SORTEO – their word for *lottery*. Our word ORDEALS is their anagram for DOLARES, or *money*. Their RECETA (*recipe*) is our CREATE.

If I'd stayed any longer in Spain, if the visa scam hadn't backfired and we hadn't been banished inside seven months, I might still be an expat like Auntie Glen, bringing cryptic crosswords to the señores and señoras. As it was, I played for the Uni Quince (or *fifteen*). When I wasn't stumbling on such marvels as UNO + CATORCE (1 + 14) being a blend of CUATRO + ONCE (4 + 11), I was crash-tackling Basques or getting hammered in return. Towards the end of the season, playing in San Sebastian, I got my chance to learn the hypnotic power of the voice, which seems a fitting way to finish our homophone section.

Javier had described his native village so well that I'd already visited the place in my mind: the deli on the corner with giant wheels of cheese, the stone church, the Virgin and the martyr statues guarding the plaza. I ate salted cod in the bar I'd already imagined, and drank the sailor's favourite beer, Estrella. But when I sauntered over to the domino tables, asking after Javier, I knew there was trouble by the shadow on the men's faces. They didn't wish to speak too much. Instead they gave directions to his home. A further clue was Maria, his wife, dressed in black, and the look of dread in her eyes when I started speaking.

'*Hola,*' I started. '*Me llamo David. Soy de Australia. Trabajé con su marido sobre el barco* ...'

'*Venga,*' she yelled, calling to others inside the house, and suddenly the doorway was jammed with three or four faces, a boy in his late teens, and two young women roughly my age, all of them wearing that same startled expression. '*Habla,*' they said. Speak.

Javier, I soon gathered, their father, Maria's husband, was dead. His heart had collapsed somewhere in Africa on the reverse run to Sydney, and I pictured those Lucky Strike cartons he stacked like bricks in his cabin. I tried to say sorry, to express my grief, to say what a patient mentor he had been, but the family hungered for something else. Talk about anything, they said – your country, your football, your *crucigrammas* if you must – so they could close their eyes and listen to the cadence of Javier's voice.

HALL OF FAME: HOMOPHONES

Heard question about identity of Cockney killer? (3) [Times 8376]
On the radio, get bigger hits (6) [Times 8552]
Bound to believe in pronouncement (7) [Orlando, Guardian]
Articulate frontier resident (7) [Patrick Berry, US]
Girl following nose, we hear (7) [Puck, Guardian]
A jousting contest said to be brief (8) [Times 8271]

SOLUTIONS: Uzi, whacks, trussed, boarder, Nanette, attorney

QUIZLING 17.1

There's a European country that opens its name with another part of Europe. Curiously, the rest of the country's name sounds like that other part's typical weather. Where on earth are we talking about?

QUIZLING 17.2

Homophones – such as PRIZE and PRISE – typically share more than a few letters. Yet what five separate homophone pairs reveal not a single letter shared by either partner? Award yourself a prize for naming three pairs at least.

QUIZLING 17.3

Remarkably, this three-letter word has a five-letter homophone, which can then move its end letter to the front to spell a synonym of the original word. Name this unique trio.

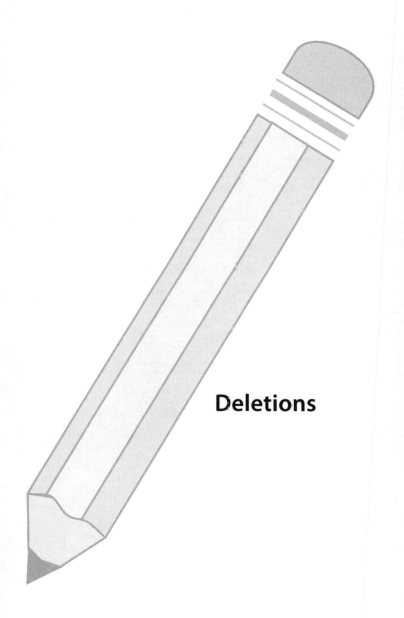

Deletions

CHAPTER 18

Outlaw fled outlaw to repeat (5)

Roger Anderson went to school during the 1940s. Writing to the *Sydney Morning Herald*, Roger recalled a Scripture tutor teaching the class a moral piece of wordplay. If it doesn't make you see the light, then at least you'll see how the deletion formula works:

> A habit is a hard thing to get rid of. Take away the H, and you've still got a bit. Take away the A, and the bit's still there. Take away the B, and you've still got it. Take away the I [point to self], and you've got it down to a t.

That's the principle – less is the key. When BLAIR loses face, so to speak, the former British leader becomes LAIR, a beast's home. (Bizarre when you consider another PM – EDEN – does the very same thing.)

Deletions encourage striking, though not the sort that PMs despise. More a nip-and-tuck operation, turning DISCORDANCE into DISCO DANCE, or FACTS and TRUTH (reverting to Scripture class) into the Bible books ACTS and RUTH.

Perhaps my favourite deletion trick involves writer PHILIP PULLMAN, a fluke with its own scripture echo. Author of *The Golden Compass*, among other adventure stories, Pullman has been viewed by some Church bodies as impugning Christianity through his novel, *The Good Man Jesus and the*

Scoundrel Christ. The rap seems only fitting, given the man's deletion credentials. Get his name – PHILIP PULLMAN – and delete every letter that appears twice or more. With no mixing needed, the aftermath is HUMAN.

Time to turn our focus to 26-Down, our lone deletion clue. In the grid you'll notice that every possible cross-letter has already been secured, giving us the oddity of D _ T _ O.

What fits? Regardless of the recipe, or even knowing what category applies, it pays to think that way. Each cross-letter in place, why not anticipate the answer, and *then* consult the clue, seeing if your theory holds good? Is DETRO a word? What about DITTO?

In crossword parlance, any single-use square is nicknamed an 'unch', or unchecked square. American crosswords have none, since every square is used twice. In cryptics, however, thanks to the waffle pattern, the unches abound.

My advice, therefore, is to make hunches about the unches. Amazing how often you can intuit a solution via the letter sequence. Let's say you're chasing a nine- letter word with this pattern:

_ _ D _ _ _ _ _ A

What fits? Assuming it's a single word we can rule out MODERN ERA or LADY DIANA. Maybe nothing springs to mind. That's fine. The exercise is always worthwhile, a pre-clue means of priming the brain.

In this case, with an A-ending, we could be hunting a proper noun – possibly a country or place name. Verbs are off the agenda. Could it be a fancy plural? Thinking this way, you're poised to pounce, with the clue your final piece of impetus.

Maybe HYDRANGEA is the answer. Then again, if the clue fails to mention plants or bloomers, you're probably amiss. No harm in guessing. Or maybe you'll encounter this clue:

London park shortened walk beside a flower (9)

Even if you don't fully grasp the wordplay, you now have a HYDRANGEA hunch. And you'd be right too, but why? There's the flower, but how does the rest work? Just like Steve Irwin's ZOO, this clue belongs in the deletion category, or at least a deletion/charade hybrid. Here's how it works:

HYDE is the *London park*. The signpost to delete is *shortened*, asking you to drop the name's closing letter. The rest is pure charade, where *walk* (RANGE) + A adds up to *flower*.

Deletion clues are often used as part of something larger. Segmenting any word, charade-style, you'll often make an offcut or two – not whole words but scraps and clusters of letters. We've already seen how a single letter can be signified by subtle means (remember an R can be *nerve centre*, or *right*, or *war's end*). In the same vein, when splitting answers into smaller fragments, deletion is a handy tool.

Typically, a single letter is removed, most often from the front or back. Starting with the head – or its lopping – you scout for signposts like *behead* or *topless* or the other useful markers at the end of this chapter.

When it comes to tail-snipping, watch for commands like *almost* or *endless*. In Cryptopia, if a word *lacks finish* you crop its closing letter. Then again, if FRANK *doffs his cap*, he's RANK. Treat these actions as literal, and beware the more furtive signposts like *dock* and *clip* (often parading as nouns).

And just to keep you alert, a deletion clue may ask you to snip both ends. This double action can come with signals like *shelled, skinned, losing extremes*. A *shelled* PRAWN, in other words, is RAW. A skinned COYOTE is OYOT, which could fill TA to make TOYOTA. That's how deletions can come into play.

Alternatively, a PRAWN's shell would be PN, and the word's meat, so to speak, is what needs deleting. That brand of shenanigans lurks in these two clues of mine:

Clear edges facilitating folding = CREASING
   (CR+EASING)
Aquatic animal trapped by extremely ravenous rats =
   ROTTERS (OTTER in RS)

When it comes to culling, the other piece up for removal is the centre. If an APPLE is cored, it turns into APLE. (As a rule, the fragments to be removed are minimal. A setter won't expect you to carve out a larger 'heart' or an extended 'tail' – unless the clue specifies that liberty.) For this type of surgery, keep awake to such signposts as *disheartened* or *gutless*.

The final trick is when a deletion clue targets a specific letter, or letters, to be removed, rather than suggesting any particular location. So *drug-free year* is YAR (losing the 'E' of ecstasy), or a pointless LESSON could be LO (as you lose all the word's compass points), just as *timeless Stuttgart* is SUGAR.

Now you can see why such an applied recipe is spared for the book's second half. The art is so versatile that only a cryptic Jedi will master it. I swear, if I'd told you this formula 100 pages ago, you'd have freaked. But now I hope you can appreciate the elegance of this next deletion, a clue from Flimsy in the *Financial Times*:

Budget Speech beginning to be ignored (6)

Speech is not a homophone flag, but a definition of ORATION. Ignore that word's *beginning* and you'll end up with RATION, meaning to budget. Cheeky? Yes. Compact? Ditto. Which leads us back to the Master clue:

Outlaw fled outlaw to repeat (5)

Okay, so the answer is DITTO, but why? This is the benefit of a smart guess, just as HYDRANGEA allowed us to step through Hyde Park trickery. Here *repeat* is the definition, while the adjacent word *to* accounts for your answer's tail, TO. So how does DIT, the other chunk, arise from *outlaw fled outlaw*?

Fled must be the deletion signpost, where one piece abandons another – but which escapes what? As a hint, don't forget that *outlaw* can also be a verb, despite the clue presenting the same word as a noun. Given that DIT must play a role, what synonym for *outlaw* holds DIT?

BANDIT. Good. Then what is fleeing? Logically it must be BAN, which is *outlaw* as a verb. When BAN flees BANDIT, you're left with DIT. Plus TO = DITTO.

Bravo. You've cracked your first deletion. Though a word of warning. Apart from charade, the other common accomplice in the deletion category is the anagram, where a clue can ask you to amputate and then perform the makeover. Here's a neat example from Phssthpok, another *Financial Times* setter. (The alias salutes a galactic pilgrim created by sci-fi writer Larry Niven.) See how you cope with this:

Playing sudoku almost earns prestige (5)

If I told you the answer begins with K, and owns D for its heart, would that help? Can you get any hunches form the unches? One word to obey that pattern is KUDOS, which means *prestige*. Following the wordplay then, *playing* looks like the anagram signpost. *Sudoku almost*, or SUDOK, is your fodder, while *earns* is a classy linkword, as your anagram play earns KUDOS.

Not that sudoku enjoyed much kudos in June 2008. As scandals go, the strife in Sydney's District Court must rate among the darkest day for newspaper puzzles, and certainly the most infamous. That said, puzzles and outlaws have colluded to a considerable extent down the years, on both sides of the moral ledger.

THE GAME'S UP – legal proceedings and puzzle novels

Judge Peter Zahra had no choice. Despite the millions ploughed into legal fees, the sixty days of court time, the stream of witnesses, His Worship discharged the jury and aborted the trial.

The culprit was a puzzle. One juror had photocopied a bunch of sudoku, handing them round to help pass the hours spent listening to legal argument. Three months into the proceedings, one accused saw a woman in the jury box juggling numbers in a smaller box. When other grids were observed, the defence counsel applied for a discharge. The judge obliged. The matter in hand was a complex trial, involving drug factories and firearm possession. No juror was the wiser for pencilling numbers during proceedings. The hearing was scratched and the alleged outlaws quit the dock.

Criminals are bound to earn a further reprieve, thanks to puzzles. Michael B. Lewis, a psychologist at Cardiff University, put sixty people through a simple cognitive test, first giving them a range of common pastimes, including Sudoku and both styles of crosswords – the quick and cryptic – as well as random passages of a Dan Brown thriller. Lewis then engaged his guinea pigs in a memory game, asking them to glimpse fourteen faces for a period of three seconds each. Next, after five minutes of distraction, be it crosswords or sudoku or Dan Brown's opus, the subjects were shown a larger batch of faces, twenty-eight this time, with the earlier faces scattered through the deck. The challenge was to pick the faces previously seen. The results went on to raise a few eyebrows.

While a secret sudoku habit may ditch a trial at the Sydney District Court, a cryptic crossword apparently has the power to unhinge an entire investigation. Too many anagrams, Lewis asserts, can handicap a witness who later surveys a police line-up. Too many double meanings, and crucial details start to blur. Put bluntly, Lewis says, 'Eyewitnesses should not do cryptic crosswords before an identity parade.'

The skill is known as 'face processing', referring to how we differentiate subtle details in the features of strangers and new acquaintances. According to this Welsh experiment, all other tested pursuits did little to jeopardise a brain's ability to recall faces. Cryptics, meanwhile, are music to the perp's ear. Expose a witness to a few deletions and he's liable to finger Mickey Mouse for the Great Train Robbery.

In defence, it must be said that crosswords can boast one criminal scalp. The 1980 trial involved a man called Brian Keenan, no relation to his namesake, the writer. Scotland Yard accused Keenan of being an IRA operative, which he denied. He told the court he'd never been to a certain London address, a refuge associated with a known bombing cell, but that story came unstuck when detectives recovered a *Daily Mail* from the premises. Inside was a crossword partially solved in Keenan's own hand. Across and down – open and shut.

Elsewhere a crossword played a vital role in a probate hearing in 1999. One year shy of her 100th birthday, Anetta Duel died intestate in her East Sussex home. Or so it seemed. Leonard Andrean, a nephew, had the task of tidying up his aunt's belongings, stumbling on a page torn loose from the *Daily Telegraph*.

'Our aunt was mentally active until she died,' he said, which seems an obvious thing to say, but the crossword hobby was also a lifeline for the family. Above the clues, Leonard noticed a handwritten message: *Don't throw this sheet away please.*

Closer inspection revealed a scrawl on the puzzle's margins, a makeshift will in the same spidery hand: *I leave all my money and possessions to Len and I hope he will be happy as long as he lives. God bless you, Aunt Netty. Goodbye.*

A frail signature was attached. Yet being adrift from its newspaper, this last testament needed a date to be deemed official. Thus Val Gilbert was summoned, the *Tele*'s puzzle editor, whose filing system fixed Crossword 22515 in the calendar, and Len duly inherited his aunt's earthly goods.

Still with matters legal, Inspector Morse has a strong crossword link, largely through his creator, Colin Dexter, a man who juggled crime writing with puzzle setting for the *Listener*. Now in his eighties, Dexter is the genius behind the Codex alias, as well as the author of some dozen mysteries featuring Morse and Sergeant Lewis. (Both names derive from Puzzleland, with Jeremy Morse and Dorothy Lewis being Dexter's constant rivals in the *Listener*'s clue-writing contests.) If you read deeper into the Morse books, several other puzzle surnames bob up, including such setters as Jonathan Crowther (aka Azed) and Don Manley (Quixote, Bradman or Duck), both as suspicious types.

Around the early 1980s, the puzzle craze erupted into crossword novels. Detective cases in the main, most cases hinged on grids that readers had to solve in league with the shamus. Titles to note are *A Six-Word Letter for Death* (by Patricia Moyes) and *Murder Across and Down* (Herbert Resnicow – with the puzzles set by maestro Henry Hook). There's also a series composed by US spouses Cordelia Biddle and Steve Zettler under their collective pseudonym of Nero Blanc. Cases include *Corpus de Crossword* and *Death on the Diagonal*, with the cutest tagline on offer belonging to *Two Down*, where 'Up, down or across – SOS spells danger …'.

A timely reminder that the clues to come won't be getting any easier. Death isn't waiting around the corner, but concussion certainly. Are you prepared? Down the alley lurk the rarer recipes, including puns and reversals, codes and rebuses – no relation to the Scottish detective. So if you ain't hardboiled, start running.

RECIPE PRECIS: DELETIONS

Deletion signposts tell you what needs losing. If a first letter is to be dropped, then look for *leaderless, doesn't start, lose face* or *fail to open*. If the last letter needs to go, then *curtail, detail, Manx* (those cats with no tails), *nearly, trim* or *incomplete* are candidates. *Gutless* and *heartless* suggest you slash the centre, while *peeled, shelled* or *skinned* call for the dumping of the outer two letters. In contrast, words like *borders, fringes* or *extremely* can indicate that the two peripheral letters are kept, with everything else scratched out. (Extremely WISE, in clue-speak, can mean WE.) When larger chunks go, like MI in MISLED to make SLED, then fair clues will specify which portion (or its size) that needs removing.

HALL OF FAME: DELETIONS

Caligula for one lost his heart to a horse (4) [Times 8309]
Jumped up, not using head – crash! (5) [Crux, FT]
Half Basque, half French? Cool (6) [Bonxie, Guardian]
Figure went during tragedy when outraged (6) [Times 8097]
First of autumn leaves turning putrid (7) [Henry Hook, US]
Mention having cup of tea skimmed (9) [Paul, Guardian]

SOLUTIONS: roan, prang, quench, twenty, rotting, reference

QUIZLING 18.1

We're thinking of a word
Meaning connect, but
When prefixed by a vowel,
The new word means cut.

QUIZLING 18.2

Reading left to right, taking a letter per word, can you spell
three related words? Your six leftover letters can be jumbled
to spell a fourth member of the same set.

CASH   COIR   CARE   RANG   WADE   BAIT

QUIZLING 18.3

What word meaning chicken
Can lose its head
To spell a second bird
Instead?

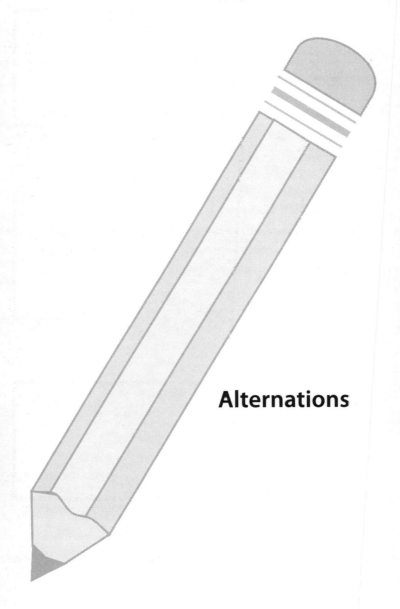

Alternations

CHAPTER 19

After boomers it regularly goes next! (3–1)

'Guess what, Mom?' says Lisa Simpson. 'I'm a cruciverbalist!'

'Oh Lisa – another religion? You know you'll just drop the whole thing at college when you get a Jewish boyfriend.'

A short trip to Springfield Library would have eased Marge's nerves. Lisa's new obsession was secular. Mind you, cruciverbalism does ask for meditation, and inspires a degree of worship and close text study.

Lisa had her epiphany in Season 20, going from lemonade seller to crossword champion in one episode. Bitten by the bug, she dreams in black and white. Hopscotch grids mutate into letters. Before long she enrols in the Crossword City Tournament, where Lisa meets a sharky real estate agent called Gil Gunderson. Despite her talents, Lisa loses, mainly after hearing that Homer has wagered all his dough on Gil. The girl is furious. She renounces her surname and storms off the podium.

To repair the damage, Homer hires the two biggest names in US cruciverbalism – Will Shortz and Merl Reagle – and gets them to phrase an apology. Woven into a puzzle of course, with a hidden message. Viewers only get a glimpse of Reagle's grid, though the same puzzle ran in the *New York Times* a week after the episode, on 16 November 2008. For Shortz, the *Times* puzzle editor, the synchronicity sealed the deal. When Tim Long, a producer of *The Simpsons* and the episode's chief writer, asked Shortz if he wanted to join the storyline, the editor was flattered. 'But I added it'd be really cool if the crossword on the show could also appear in *The Times* on the same day. He liked that idea. And that's when Merl got involved.'

A toon tragic from the crib, Merl had to pinch himself. 'For me, to be such a total nut for animation since I was a kid, I never even dreamed … it's like a dream I never had coming true.'

Lisa's puzzle was no doddle. The eight celebs chosen as the key entries had all been distorted by Reagle's wordplay. (*Passionate tennis star*, for example, is MONICA ZEALOUS, while LINDSAY LOW-HAND has *no face cards*.) Hiding obliquely inside the solution is Homer's apology: DUMB DAD SORRY FOR HIS BET. Lisa spots the message, hugs her dad and all is swell in Springfield again. Cut to credits.

Yet this is not the first message hiding in the *New York Times*, nor the only one inspired by a father's affection for his daughter. Winding the clock back sixty years we find the clean and swooping lines of Al Hirschfeld, the lifelong master of caricature work.

Al plays the Homer role in this story, and the part of Lisa is fulfilled by Nina, the artist's only child, born in 1945.

Hirschfeld enjoyed a dazzling career. At the top of his game, his work generated exhibitions, movie posters, lithographs. But his true signature became the stylish means of hiding NINA – the name – into his work.

The fall of a drape, glassware: the name could appear anywhere within the portrait. Over a span of fifty years, Al became adept at tucking NINA's letters into hemlines and hairdos, jewellery and table settings. But fans grew so fixated on playing seek-a-word that Hirschfeld feared his art was being overlooked. So he dumped the gimmick, only for an uproar to erupt.

The other reason that Hirschfeld quit the habit was linked to a military rumour. With Vietnam shaping into a full-scale conflict, defence academies were teaching pilots to look for 'Ninas' on the ground, their slang for hidden targets to be bombed. Hirschfeld found this idea repugnant. His adoring public spoke the louder, however, and after a brief pause, the word-game was restored.

Years on, in 1991, the US Postal Service asked the 88-year-old Al to illustrate the century's great comedians for a series of stamps. The artist agreed so long as the NINA message could be embedded. Al knew the storm he'd inherit if he thwarted his followers. Philatelists still claim that this series was the first and only occasion on which American stamps have carried a secret message.

Possibly so, though the practice has spread in the crossword realm, with setters planting messages inside their work. And the subterfuge's name? A Nina, of course.

In typical Hirschfeld fashion, the smuggled word or name lacks any indicator to declare its presence. Merl Reagle met that challenge in his *Simpsons* gig, since the diagonal message was there for a girl like Lisa to find. No shaded squares. No signposts. Just a secret seam in the cloth.

That said, Reagle tackled the task with trademark pizzazz. Keeping to the rules of restraint, Merl opted for another route to whisper the extra layer. Not the grid this time, but the clues, using the initial letters to intimate the diagonal Nina. From 1-Across to 109-Down, in Homeric style, those initials spelt DEAR LISA, YOU MAKE ME SO HAPPY, REALLY, REALLY, REALLY HAPPY. SORRY, HE TOLD ME I NEEDED A HUNDRED-FORTY-FOUR LETTERS …WHAT WAS MY POINT AGAIN? OH RIGHT – BOUVIER OR SIMPSON, I CHERISH YOU.

NINAS AGOGO – hidden entries and alternate clues

As a solver I love a good Nina, though I don't always see them. Solvers in general seldom take time to seek any covert entry. Ninas in fact are commonly unveiled in chat rooms by those clever enough to spot them. An *Independent* setter named Mordred, for instance, whose real name is Derek Knight, once stood STALACTITE and STALAGMITE in parallel unches. Even sneakier, the first Nina hung down, the second thrust upward, imitating the limestone masses.

John Henderson, who crafts puzzles for the *Guardian* under the guise of Enigmatist, pulled off a neat stunt in May 2009. The answer to the central axis was WAITING FOR GODOT, flanked by parallel Ninas revealing VLADIMIR and ESTRAGON, the two tramps who did just that.

But if prizes are being handed out for ingenious interlocks, the Americans enjoy a stranglehold. Visually and verbally, the *New York Times* and its fallen cousin, the *New York Sun*, have dished out some dazzlers this millennium. Although these are not authentic Ninas, as they take the form of a set of instructions, or the clues themselves will flag the trick, it still takes nothing from the execution.

In August 2008, Kevin G. Der presented New York Timers with a dotted line around the crossword's border. Solvers were bamboozled for a while, before realising that the pivotal answers to the grid – entitled Come Fly With Me – told you how to convert the crossword into a paper aeroplane.

Elizabeth Gorski, the queen of the visual surprise, has arranged her squares to emulate Frosty the Snowman, the Empire State Building and the vortex spiral of the Guggenheim Museum, each time with theme words as the vital axes and visible Ninas inbuilt.

Patrick Blindauer, another giant of the clandestine art, has made his patterns mimic rope ladders, dollar bills and the *Frogger* video game, to name but three. Rather than bury a

Nina, in the English vein, the American puzzle may carry a key entry which transforms the puzzle once the clues are solved. At the height of one summer, for example, Blindauer had his solver turn the final grid into a blazing sun, getting you to colour in every I, the resultant sketch a central circle with six jutting rays. The entry lying at the operation's hub said it best: SHADE YOUR EYES.

But now let's turn our gaze to the Master clue, as the formula has a Nina quality. Just as shrewd solvers will notice messages lying in unches, the alternate recipe requires you to look between the spaces. Here we go:

After boomers it regularly goes next! (3–1)

Exclamation marks, you may recall, often indicate the &lit style, that rare case of wordplay serving as the definition. (Think of a clue like *Awfully enraged!* for ANGERED and you'll start to get the picture.) Or cast your mind back to ETC, the hidden &lit that read: *Partial set closer!* So how do we read the current wordplay? Right now our surest friend is the word *regularly*.

Like few other words, *regularly* is a reliable signpost for alternation. If not *regularly*, then its synonyms, as seen in these two clues here:

Twitch regularly?! (3)
What's this? Oddly coloured (4)

The first stems from Monk, an *Independent* setter. The dual punctuation warns you of a skewed perspective, as well as the &lit dimension. The answer is TIC, since the regular letters of *twitch*, counting just the odds, spell TIC, a *twitch* synonym.

Oddness is sustained in Orlando's jewel from the *Guardian*. Reading the odd letters of coloured will give you CLUE, which this piece of work decidedly is.

Time to revisit the current clue:

After boomers it regularly goes next! (3–1)

So much easier with an instruction manual, yes? The enumeration of (3–1) is also a major leg-up. As soon as we turn the alternate signpost onto *goes next*, the phrase GEN-X appears, the generation to follow the baby boomers.

Alternation clues are scarcer than mainstream recipes since longer words don't readily splay into new combinations. When they do, however, like GOAT in IGNORANT or the ARSES planted in BARRISTERS, the matter warrants sharing.

More common is the case where an alternation task makes up part of a longer answer. Rather than uncover CLUE in COLOURED, for example, a denser clue may ask you to ransack a word's alternate letters and mix them, or place them beside another word in the charade mode, such as this clue I ran in 2006:

A second membrane's regularly seen as simple life-form
  = A + MO (second) + EBAE (membrane's regular letters)

A tough clue, but a clear demonstration of how Alternate thinking can permeate a clue. Don't worry, though. The AMOEBAE specimen lies at the harder end of the crossword range. That said, all the signposts are intact, and every piece is detachable as long as you have the nerve to isolate them.

Deep as we are in the book, it's helpful to restate W. H. Auden's truth. Peculiar as cryptic clues may seem to outsiders, their nature is precise. Compared to their quick cousins, cryptics are generous, despite all the neural acrobatics. Though occasionally, a clue can be too generous. Now and then the pairing of wordplay and definition can point to several solutions, even if intended to indicate just one. This alternate chapter, then, seems the right moment to meet those cryptic rarities that offer alternative answers.

A BOB EACH WAY – ambiguous clues

Double meaning clues are the prime culprits. If all you get are two definitions, without any added wordplay, then occasionally a dilemma occurs. Smaller words in particular own a wardrobe of different masks, as the next ambiguous duo shows:

> *Drug blow* = CRACK or SMACK?
> *Runs lots of steps* = FLIGHTS or LADDERS (think of a
>   run in a pair of tights)?

Rarer still are ambiguous examples of other formulas, such as the next three clues, involving anagram, homophone and charade respectively. The first two stem from the American cryptic duo Emily Cox and Henry Rathvon. The other hails from Mercury of the *Guardian*. Take a look:

> *Number there is wrong* = THREE or ETHER (thinking
>   of a numbing agent)?
> *Seabird heard change of direction* = TERN or SKUA (turn
>   or skewer)?
> *Problem parking by reservoir* = DAM+P or SUM+P?

Auden would turn in his grave. Where's that famous precision? I ran into ambiguity when publishing this next clue in November 2008:

> *Cast with or without one? (5)*

The recipe is deletion, where the answer is SHIED, a quaint term for *cast*, shown in a phrase like coconut shy. As the clue observes, SHIED means *cast* – just as SHED (SHIED *without one*) also means cast. The clue was designed to celebrate that peculiarity, with a single answer, I thought.

Wrong. An email arrived that same afternoon, alerting me to the word THROW, which also obeys the clue. No it doesn't, I first reacted. THROW doesn't even own an I to lose, so how could it play the game?

Easily, the email pointed out, for when *with or* sheds one, this new combo of WTHRO can be cast into an equally satisfying answer. The accidental anagram is freakier for the clue having *cast* as definition, a verb that needs no changing from past to present tense, so reinforcing the alternative view.

I'd presumed the fluke complete when a second email lobbed. Another point of view, from another solver. Couldn't the answer be SLING, this solver asked.

SLING? How? Well, went the email, the writer of which was an intern at a Sydney hospital who saw the wounded every week, 'a sling is still a sling whether or not a plaster cast is within it'. By that stage I was ready to jump from a great height. The only deterrent was the idea of being admitted to a particular ER wing of a Sydney hospital, where the argument would likely resume on a corridor trolley.

RECIPE PRECIS: ALTERNATIONS

The vital word in most alternation clues is *regularly*, or any term suggesting every second letter such as *intermittent, periodic, evenly* or *defying odds*. Depending on nuance, these letters may need to be dumped or retained, so spelling the solution. Just as common is where the alternation formula plays a small part in a larger piece of wordplay, where the principle is the same.

HALL OF FAME: ALTERNATIONS

Perplexed as odds dropped in Olympic event (4) [Times 7940]
Railways subject to regular cuts, unfortunately (4) [Times 8649]
Good years regularly yielding flowing water (4) [Times 8374]
Drew as lots alternately? (5) [Phssthpok, FT]
Regulars in store aid new business (5) [Sleuth, FT]
Horse, seal, chimp evenly rendered in retro by cubist (7) [DA]

SOLUTIONS: épée, alas, Oder, dealt, trade, Picasso

QUIZLING 19.1

CUT hides in the alternate letters of COURT (or ACQUIT), depending on whether you opt for odd or even letters. Now cutting to objects that cut, can you find two words (including a remarkably appropriate word) that alternately hide the swords FOIL and SABRE?

QUIZLING 19.2

Slash every even letter from the alphabet, and you'll discover that all five vowels, plus the Y, are among the survivors. Using no letter twice, what's the longest word you can make out of this group?

QUIZLING 19.3

This American actress spells a word for automobile with her first name's odd letters, while her surname can be scrambled into a more particular style of the same vehicle. Name her.

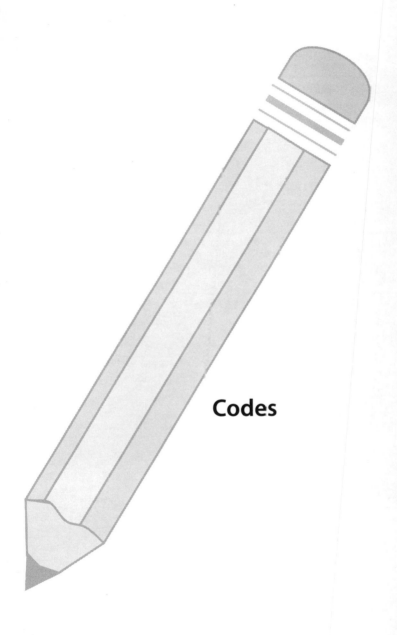

Codes

CHAPTER 20

Koran avidly studied by Arab holy leaders here! (6)

Got up.
Had a shave.
Did Times crossword.
Had another shave.

Roger McGough, the Liverpool poet behind this doggerel, was only half-joking, I'd say. Solving a cryptic can make an hour vanish, and still you haven't fixed that last corner. The good news? The better you get, the breezier the endgame. The bad? If one setter gets too easy, you move up the ladder and tackle the harder one – and there goes the morning again.

In the early 1920s, when the crossword craze hit England, a ghost-story writer called M. R. James took pride in the fact that he could undo *The Times* while boiling an egg for breakfast. 'And he did not like a hard-boiled egg,' joked Adrian Bell – that paper's first setter.

Twenty years on, a London club called the Eccentrics set a challenge to all *Telegraph* solvers. The club's chairman, W. A. J. Gavin, promised to donate £100 to the Minesweepers Fund if anyone could crack the puzzle in under twelve minutes.

There was a catch, of course. The feat had to be done under strict conditions. Hence a posse of twenty-five hopefuls dropped in to Fleet Street on a Saturday in January, including an accounting clerk named Stanley Sedgwick.

The room was set out in exam fashion, as Stanley described, with tables lined up in rows. Supervisors occupied a podium. Rules were explained and the crosswords unveiled. First to finish was Vere Chance from Kent in a touch over six minutes, but a spelling blunder disqualified him. Four others blitzed the puzzle, the winner managing close to eight minutes – and scoring a cigarette lighter. As for Stanley, he hit the wall at the last clue, the answer to which goes unrecorded.

What we do know, however, thanks to an interview Sedgwick granted the *Daily Telegraph* in 1998, is the skulduggery that came after this contest and perhaps revealed the true reason for the event being staged.

'Imagine my surprise,' said Stanley, 'when several weeks later I received a letter marked *"Confidential"* inviting me ... to make an appointment to see Col. Nichols of the General Staff who "would very much like to see you on a matter of national importance".'

Nichols headed MI8, the defence department in charge of a shadowy facility named Station X. In other memos the location was labelled BP, or Bletchley Park, located an hour north-west of London. Assembled there in secret were some of the foremost English minds of the time, including Alan Turing, the father of the computer. The team's task was to intercept and unravel German codes. But as the war escalated, and staff numbers wavered, fresh blood was needed. 'Chaps with twisted brains like mine,' as Sedgwick recalls. After a spell at spy school in Bedford, the best and brightest were then dispatched to Station X.

Tony Carson (TC), a Wiltshire lad, was among them, and he met two recruitment officers on campus one morning. As *Sydney Morning Herald* journalist Harriet Veitch puts it, 'These defence types were handing out crosswords, asking people to solve them as quickly as possible, when Tony came up and said that he did crosswords as a hobby.'

'What's your best time?' quizzed the officer.

'Solving, you mean, or making them?'

'I'm sorry. You mean you *make* crosswords?'

'Yes,' said Tony.

'Cryptic?'

'Yes.'

The rest was a blur, Harriet laughs, as Tony was hoisted off his feet and marched to a room for immediate enlistment. TC's brief was cracking Italian codes, while other word-types and number whizzes did similar work at Bletchley. (The film *Enigma* captures the spirit of the time and place.) Thanks to the code-breakers, British Command secured key data about the Battle of the Atlantic, Rommel's campaign in Africa and of course D-Day, where the *Daily Tele* had something of a karmic debt to pay. Prime Minister Winston Churchill described the decoding team as 'the geese that laid the golden egg but never cackled'.

Tony Carson carried those words through life. In the few times I met TC, a graceful *Herald* compiler who began his role in 1986, he seldom discussed his 'contribution to the war effort'. Code-breaking was a chapter in a book pretty much closed. I do know that his Italian assignment soon became a crash course in Japanese, and TC was relocated to Brisbane as part of General Macarthur's Intelligence Unit. He also took part in the Allied landing in Borneo, and when he wasn't foiling Emperor Tojo he turned his mind to crosswords.

After the war, when he moved to Perth with a young family, Tony had a go at farming (just like the first *Times* setter, Adrian Bell), before getting involved in health review and joining the board of Sydney Hospital. He made a variety of cryptics for the *Listener* back in the UK, under the alias of Swan, in honour of Perth's river, and later plied his trade at the *Herald*, where we first met in a Chinese restaurant.

Our editor, Harriet, selected the venue due to its chequered decor. We met at the table, the full roster of Fairfax compilers, and almost needed to introduce ourselves, despite being long-time colleagues. A monkish pursuit, crossword-making is not the path to take if you aspire to the sociability of office life.

We talked about favourite clues, the screw-ups and inspirations. TC was urbane and handsome, with a nonchalant warmth. His voice still retained a Wiltshire lilt. Perhaps in his mid-sixties then, a spring chicken compared to our patriarch LB, Tony would live for only another five years, succumbing to illness in 1994. But that night was a blithe get-together, a blue moon on the crossword calendar, and Harriet started speculating on the collective noun. If lions have a pride, what is a group of cruciverbalists? A distraction? A mesh? A crypt?

DP, or David Plomley, the civic engineer and Wednesday's stalwart, came up with abomination.

'Scan a kebab clue,' said LB, and we all presumed he'd lost his mind.

'What kebab?' I asked.

'Black bean sauce,' said Tony, studying the same menu and solving the anagram. The habits of code-breaking die hard.

Though every solver needs that Bletchley reflex. If random kebabs and German sea reports make no sense, then persevere. By definition, all codes, all cryptics, must crack eventually.

CRETAN TRANCE – ciphers and acronyms

Sir Arthur Evans was pottering about the ruins of Crete in the early 1900s when he came upon a series of clay tablets, each one bearing a list of strange letters. Neither Greek nor any other language Evans knew, the symbols earned the name of Linear B, and presented one of the great decoding challenges of the day.

Michael Ventris, an English architect who spoke six languages as well as reading classical Greek and Latin, became intrigued by the tablets. To him they represented ancient inventories. But listing what? To deepen the riddle, Linear B comprised strings of coupled symbols rather than whole words, yet after two years of scrutiny Ventris noticed recurring patterns. Four in particular. Could they be gods, or keywords, or perhaps the major towns of Crete? He followed this last hunch, replacing the most frequent cluster with AMNISOS, the island's port, and slowly the enigma gave way. Linear B in fact was found to be an ancient form of Greek, a revelation that caused much of Mediterranean history to be rewritten.

More recently, as computers dominate decoding, we've started to glimpse into the wonders of genetic codes and cosmological data. Across IT, codes have become a new way of speaking, as well as building walls against viruses and hackers. From trog days to blog days, humans have found a need to repack the message. Or hide the message, in the case of cryptic crosswords. Here's our current enigma:

Koran avidly studied by Arab holy leaders here! (6)

As in the Cretan tablets, the answer seems to rest in foreign geography. The surface meaning murmurs a place in the Islamic world. *Here*, reads the final word. But where?

To pinpoint the right location, let's test-run a second clue, much as Ventris contrasted Greek with Linear B. Written by Armonie of the *Financial Times*, this sample shares a key element with the Master clue, which only shrewd cryptographers will detect:

Fool starts to imagine death is only temporary (5)

Look carefully. Compare the two. Before reading the next

paragraph, can you figure out what aspect the two clues share?

The gist is starting, or being in front, as both signposts suggest: *leaders* and *starts*. Are the cogs now churning?

As you know, acronyms are words or names made up of initials, such as scuba (self-contained underwater breathing apparatus) or kippers (kids in parents' pockets eroding retirement super). Sometimes overlapping is involved, whereby 'Canadian oil, low acid' creates canola, or South Western Townships yields the South African enclave of Soweto, but the pure kind relies on initials.

Acronyms, or Abbreviated Coded Renditions Of Names Yielding Meaning, inspire the code category of cryptics, though in more subtle guises. Typically, upper-case initials – like COLT (City Of London Telecom) or ANZAC (Australian and New Zealand Army Corps) – signal a standard acronym. Yet in clue mode, the idea is camouflage, which is why acronyms in the wider world become acrostics in a cryptic setting.

When Arthur Wynne woke the world to crosswords, the next puzzle craze to follow was a reborn version of acrostics. The strongest fad in this regard remains the scattered quote, where a line of verse, a quip or wisdom is broken down into its letters and reassembled into a list of words – a colossal anagram in effect. These words are then arranged in such a way that their initials will spell the quote's origins. Imagine that Ralph Waldo Emerson, say, is the source. Then the wordlist's initials might spell RWEMERSONESSAYONNA-TURE. Little by little, as clues are solved, the gained letters are sprinkled into the diagram by order of coordinates, and Emerson's quote on nature is eventually revealed.

You won't be shocked, then, to hear that our two code clues, the Armonie example and the current Master clue, maintain the acrostic tradition:

Fool starts to imagine death is only temporary (5)
Koran avidly studied by Arab holy leaders here! (6)

Now can you see the acrostic answers? Think initially. In the first clue the phrase *starts tc* alerts you to the next sequence of initials, spelling IDIOT, or *fool*. Meanwhile the Master example uses *leaders* as its nudge. Read the preceding six *leaders* and you unveil KASBAH. The exclamation mark, as we know, is the cryptic way of declaring that the wordplay fulfils a double role. Here the definition, the Arabic quarter of a city, is also a prime location to see the *Koran avidly studied*.

Though don't think that code clues always hinge on initials. True, the most popular strain play in this space, but variations exist. Some, you'll see, involve garden gnomes.

PENAL CODE – code variations and schoolboy stunts

The Boat That Rocked, released as *Pirate Radio* in the US, is a clever name for a comedy, at least from a cryptographer's point of view, since the second letters of each word combine to spell HOHO.

And just like HOHO, not every crossword code you meet will operate with initials. Take this bunch, all drawn from my own archive:

Doc, for one, added two vaccine grams after seconds =
    DWARF (second letters)
Fretted guitar harmony, like Everclear medley by thirds =
    IRKED (third letters)
Laggards in prank keen to throw trash into Law Faculty =
    KNOW-HOW (last – or 'lagging' – letters)

Other clues may refer to the hearts of words, or ask you to count across a certain word, rather than the clue itself, such as every third letter of JOCULARITY spelling CAT. And going to crazier lengths, there was one code thirty years ago that asked readers to isolate every thirteenth letter. I should explain.

My last year of high school was 1979, the same year in which a plaster gnome was kidnapped from an English garden. The crime made the press due to the abductors sending post-cards from around Europe. As if written by the gnome, every message expressed the joy of freedom and a growing self-awareness. A bit like leaving high school, I suppose.

Maybe that's why some of my mates committed a copycat crime, stealing pixies from surrounding suburbs and planting them around the senior campus. We had a dancing gnome, a fishing gnome and a laughing gnome, though the principal wasn't so jubilant. For reasons unknown he summoned me into his office to discuss the hostage situation.

'You have a soft spot for the little people?' he asked.

'Sorry?'

'The gnomes and whatnot.'

'Not really,' I said. 'My sisters liked Enid Blyton when they were younger, Big Ears and so forth.'

'What about the garden variety?'

'My nana has a few frogs in her birdbath. She lives in Normanhurst.'

The conversation was going nowhere, so the boss went for the throat. 'Did you write the code in the school magazine or didn't you?!'

'Oh,' I blushed. 'Yes.'

As literary editor of the mag, I'd favoured a more refined cipher than your basic acrostic. The booby trap sat in the editorial. The key phrase marking the subterfuge was *speaking in a superstitious way*.

Somehow I'd hoped that students would pick up the hint, isolating every thirteenth letter to find the message. Though most students needed telling. The gag did the rounds of the grapevine, and so reached the staffroom as well.

For the record, the encoded phrase was an affectionate insult aimed at the mag's overseeing teacher. DUDLEY IS A GARDEN GNOME, it read, AND SMOKES DOPE TWICE DAILY. Clearly gnomes were the zeitgeist. As soon as I fessed the code the principal didn't care whether I'd stolen the gnomes or not – my punishment was restoring each sprite to its rightful garden, liaising with local police, and fulfilling a fairy godfather sort of role.

At the far end of the gnomic scale, California Governor Arnold Schwarzenegger chose a simpler code to rankle authorities in 2009. Or did he? In essence the Governor's letter explained to the State Assembly why he was reject-ing a portside project, yet in code the same communiqué said something else. Down the left margin, in acrostic style, the eight initials spelt I FUCK YOU. *Yours sincerely, Arnold Schwarzenegger.*

Freakish, said an office spokesperson, Aaron McLear, who also noted SOAP and POET had flukily occurred in the margins of previous letters. Loving a challenge, the statis-tics department of Berkeley went on to calculate the odds of the expletive occurring by accident, bearing in mind the fre-quency of U and K as common English openers, and came up with one in 8,031,810,176. Monkeys have a better chance of banging out a sequel to Arnie's blockbuster, *True Lies.*

RECIPE PRECIS: CODE

Codes are fairly rare, and can catch you napping for the same reason. If you see words like *leaders* or *initially*, then your answer may be staring right back. Ditto for the rarer formulas, where the second, middle or end letters are recruited.

HALL OF FAME: CODE

Journey starts in the red, ends in the black (4) [Times 8955]
Sir as heard in Bangalore primarily? (5) [Times 8366]
First of December every year our tax return fiddled (5) [Times 8647]
Tips on friendship do as nice Christmas presents (5) [Times 8597]
Cement, in part, lasts during any cheap renovations, you claim (6) [DA]
Revolutionary House of Commons history is mentioned in new Hansard, initially (2,3,4) [Times 8252]

SOLUTIONS: trek, sahib, toyed, poses, gypsum, Ho Chi Minh

QUIZLING 20.1

Who are the only two US presidents whose surnames can be spelt exclusively using the letters that end the surnames of any other US president?

QUIZLING 20.2

While Johnny Depp never appeared in HAIR, he did bob up in a 1993 movie whose title spells HAIR with the second letter of each word. No tangling needed, can you comb his backlist to find the film?

QUIZLING 20.3

All seven numbers below are animals. How many can fly?
(You may find a calculator will shed some light.)

300
338
733
900
5181
35009
90439034

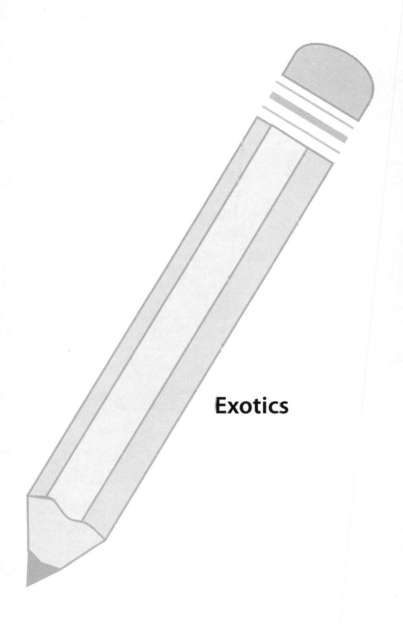

Exotics

CHAPTER 21

Pizza centre behind which French grill?(4)

Fresh from codes, you'll be glancing at a phrase like *pizza centre* and nursing the possibility of Z, the centre of pizza. Check the grid, and the idea will firm on seeing the Z of VEN-EZUELA. So where does that take us? We need a four-letter word, ending in Z, meaning what?

If *pizza centre* gives us the Z, then this part of the clue is the wordplay. Jumping to the other end, therefore, we can isolate *grill* as the likely definition. Or maybe *French grill* is up for the task, but that makes as much sense as *pizza centre*, in terms of a definition. Safer to single out *grill* as the answer's meaning. Hence a straight clue might read *Grill (4)*, with three dashes and a Z.

RAZZ in some quarters can mean to tease or criticise, a shrinking of the word raspberry. As a noun, RAZZ equates to badinage or a reprimand. But grill? The link looks flimsy. Besides, does RAZ – with one Z – mean anything in French? *Non*.

QUI, on the other hand, is how Parisians say who, or whom, or that, or which. *Behind which French*, says the clue. Place Z behind QUI (*which French*) and there's your match for grill. But wait, is that really fair? Since when does a solver need to be bilingual? You don't. But a *petite* bit of knowledge comes in handy.

I don't speak French, but like most people can claim *eau* and *le* and all the other Gallic staples. You may be a fluent French-speaker, but that's not vital in order to be a solver – just a plus. On paper, my grasp of German and Italian is modest, and I can speak a Tarzan Spanish at best, but that doesn't allow me to throw in *a traves* ('across' in Spanish) or *unten* ('below' in German). Such practice is verboten. Though these exotic clues of Auster, aka Shirl O'Brien, are totally *bons*:

> *King Charles possibly upset Spain and the Spanish (7)*
> *Sprinter, the German, remains inside (6)*

The first combines anagram and charade. The second is a container. Because exotic is less a recipe than a chance to warn you about this crossword ploy. Without great fuss, Auster's clues expect you to know the definite article in a foreign language – Spanish and German respectively – and not much else. SPANIEL is the King Charles in question, where a jumbled SPAIN annexes EL. While DASHER does the job in Clue 2, seeing DER (German's masculine *the*) enclose ASH, or *remains* to create a *sprinter*.

Crossing the border, my next two clues presume a soupcon of French:

> *Seduced the French professor (3,2)*
> *Lament route, oddly or French-ly! (3)*

Another article lesson, this time leading to LED ON, or LE + DON. The second clue is RUE, an alternation formula.

When you're in the erudite hands of Araucaria, or wrestling a denser puzzle such as *Beelzebub* or *The Listener*, your bilingualism will be more greatly quizzed. And that leads us back to the Master answer, QUIZ, a word which owns a most curious backstory.

WHO'S WHO OF CLERIHEW – creating words and verses

Several querulous words call on Q, from question to query, inquire to inquest. Even the bickering trio of quarrel, squabble and quibble can often pivot around a question. The reason for this Q-connection traces back to Latin, where *quaestio* meant question, and *quaestors* were treasury officials asking how every last *centavo* had been spent.

(As for why the Romans plumped for Q as their inquisitive signature, don't ask. Numerous English words have similar clans, such as the GL-words of illumination – *glint, glow, glisten, glitter* – or the SL-words of ooziness, the –ACK words of impact, or the W-words that dominate questions themselves. This area of language is known as sound symbolism, or phonaesthemes, where cognate terms cluster under a similar banner, gaining strength through association.)

Most likely then that QUIZ is one more cousin in the nosy Q-clan, but when it comes to derivations, who can resist a piece of Irish folklore? James Daly was the man in question. The Dublin theatre owner bet a chum in 1790 that he could create a new word inside twenty-four hours. The bet was made, impelling Daly to hire a gang of ragamuffins with a peculiar brief. I can just imagine the conversation:

'I want you to scrawl QUIZ all over town,' said Daly. 'That's Q-U-I-Z.'

'What's it mean?' asked a waif.

'Exactly.'

Come first light, when Dubliners woke to the graffiti, theirs was the same question. What was it? A secret test? A pseudonym? The hubbub became a quiz of sorts, and so the stunt endowed a new word to the *Oxford*, and Daly made a tidy profit. Allegedly.

Codswallop, I'm thinking, but the story has stuck with me for years. Some kids long to fly to Mars or drive fire engines, but I've always yearned to coin a word. Hundreds have managed the feat, from inventors (Laszlo Biro) to scientists (Georg Ohm), from Milton (*pandemonium*) to Shakespeare (*unreal*). Journalists have left their fingerprints too, with such words as blitzkrieg, metrosexual and flying saucer first appearing in newspaper copy.

Then again, you may have uniqueness, a maverick perspective or burst of radical thinking on your side. If a grim existence is not Orwellian, it's likely to be Dickensian or Kafkaesque. If I said the Daliesque dreamscape was the breast I'd ever seen, then that would be a Freudian slip.

So what would be my original word? At twenty I lacked the flair to invent a notable salad. My crossword job was only just beginning – a little premature for injecting self-made neologisms into the mix. And that's when the verse idea hit home.

Edmund Clerihew Bentley was the trailblazer. The humorist had stylised a poetic genre that I introduced to the English class I was teaching. 'Look at this,' I told them, handing out a photocopied sheet.

At just four lines, the clerihew is a ragged biographical poem with a rhyming pattern of AABB. To give you an example, here's Clerihew himself, in clerihew form:

Edmund Clerihew Bentley
Wrote humorous novels and columns intently.
But his lasting claim to fame
Is inventing this style of ill-scanning ditty that bears his
    middle name.

When not teaching English, back in the mid 1980s, I was fixing up a manuscript, the book called *Marzipan Plan* that was written back in Rome. The story was set in a crummy carnival, where the tattooed woman speaks a tongue that nobody recognises, a gibberish to everyone around her. What makes her seem stranger still is that she devotes her spare hours to reading offbeat scripture written in her own language. Verses in fact, each of seven lines. Here's a taste of one:

Vanar thrame mitpa doma
Ep elg luldi onuc paun
Rarkue nac obar moda
Nus gwid vanar losp u pan
Omun omun logro choth
Shembla fhavo eubi hotch
Plell orh peeg lunthum spovern

I called theses strange little poems 'qerlams', a word I hoped would reach the dictionary one day, or at least do the rounds of Year 8 English classes. If you take a closer look at the mumbo jumbo, you'll notice how the line-ends rely on anagrams instead of rhymes, with a mixing pattern of ABABCCD. In other words, the third line ends with a blend of the first line's final word, and so on. Line D's final word in this case, the qerlam's finale, scrambles the seven lines' initials – an acrostic with a twist.

Twist, no doubt, is the right word. I still have ambitions of endowing a word to English, but nowadays I'm less hell-bent on a plan. Naming the poem at the time, I felt obliged to enlist a U-less Q, since I'd spent too long during Scrabble games despising Qs for needing their sidekicks.

Needless to say, Operation Qerlam was a fiasco. The book did OK but the verse never found its niche in the lexicon, unlike quiz or pandemonium. Probably best to summarise the fiasco as a clerihew:

David Robert Astle
Only has till
2040 or so, mixing letters at his desk,
To work out what it means to be Astlesque.

LAZY DOG – pangrams and alphabet jigsaws

Harking back to QUIZ, our answer for 13-Across, I'm prompted to move to the next related subject.

Stop. Have a second read of that last paragraph and what do you notice? Don't worry. It's not easy to see. Then again, if you share my obsession, you can't read a shopping list without this kind of thought simmering in your head. Milk cartons, cereal boxes, comic strips: anything that has letters will instigate an alphabet search. Studying English in my final year of school, I spent as much time memorising the lines of Donne and Eliot as seeing if 'The Love Song of J. Alfred Prufrock' contained a Q.

So the opening paragraph, you're thinking, holds every letter. Or does it? Take a closer look, and you'll see there's no Y, making the sentence one letter short of a bona-fide pangram, those quick-brown-fox creations that use all of the alphabet. The Master Puzzle follows suit, omitting a single letter. For all its KASBAHs and GEN-Xs, the pangram ambition fell one letter shy. The quirk is like a Nina, a wrinkle in the cloth only fellow obsessives would see. So which letter is it? Creeping closer to a completed grid, treat that question as your bonus quiz.

Pangrams, to return to brown foxes and the lazy dogs they hurdle, remain the Holy Grail for word-lovers. Years have been sacrificed to the cause of producing the shortest possible, a sentence holding every letter at least once, and still making sense. Among the more notable attempts, with letter count provided, are:

*AMAZINGLY FEW DISCOTHEQUES PROVIDE
    JUKEBOXES. (40)*
*SIX BOYS GUZZLING RAW PLUM VODKA QUITE
    JOYFULLY. (40)*
*JAIL ZESTY VIXEN WHO GRABBED PAY FROM
    QUACK. (36)*

QUICK WAXY BUGS JUMP THE FROZEN VELDT.
   (31)

Constructors pay similar heed when making grids. You won't be able to squeeze every letter into a puzzle, but SQUEEZE and PUZZLE sure help. That's why I jumped at VENEZUELA. The homophone idea was fun, and as a solver I value any grid that lobs a few high-scorers (using the Scrabble term) into critical junctions.

Nothing worse, wrestling with a puzzle, to run into SENSELESS and TSE-TSE at every turn, timid words built entirely of soft vowels and consonants. The music analogy is the songwriter who can't escape the cosiness of you/blue and me/see.

Amy Reynaldo, the Crossword Fiend blogger, labels the richest alphabetical specimens as Scrabbly, an adjective I'm happy to spread. In fact, with a bit of luck, Scrabbly may end up being the word Amy endows to English, a country mile ahead of qerlams.

RECIPE PRECIS: EXOTICS

The exotic clue presumes you have a modest grasp of other languages: just the very basics, really, with the various articles (LA, EL, LE, DAS, DER, DIE) as well as other staples, such as JA, OUI, SI and *un poco más*. While not a recipe, exotic clues will state their target language, sometimes more subtly by naming a city rather than a nationality. Beyond this etiquette, any other foreign word is *de trop*.

HALL OF FAME: EXOTICS

An idée (not fixe) about epic (6) [Cinephile, *FT*]
Inaugurate church with articles in Le Figaro (6) [*Times* 8595]
Rallying but get a drug for pain? (8) [Alberich, *FT*]
Genius taken for a mug in his native land (8) [Sesame
   crossword, May 2005]
Here in Paris models posed around homes (9) [Cincinnus]
Picture the White House for Latinos (10) [Paul, *Guardian*]

SOLUTIONS: Aeneid, launch, baguette, Einstein, domiciles,
Casablanca

QUIZLING 21.1

Israelis know the game as *Mapolet* – or avalanche. On the
other hand, Danes prefer *Klodsmajot*, alias klutz. In Rio de
Janeiro the same game's nickname translates as earthquake-
tower, while you and I know it as the Swahili word for build.
What game?

QUIZLING 21.2

Hip to a new era, the Vatican has converted modern words to
old Latin. Can you link apathy, casino, dancing, flirt, gateau
and shampoo to their translations below?

*aleatorium, amor levis, capitilavium, ludus saltatorius, placenta
farta, voluntatis defectio*

QUIZLING 21.3

Can you place an Asian currency beside an Asian hardwood to
sound out an Indonesian word adopted into English?

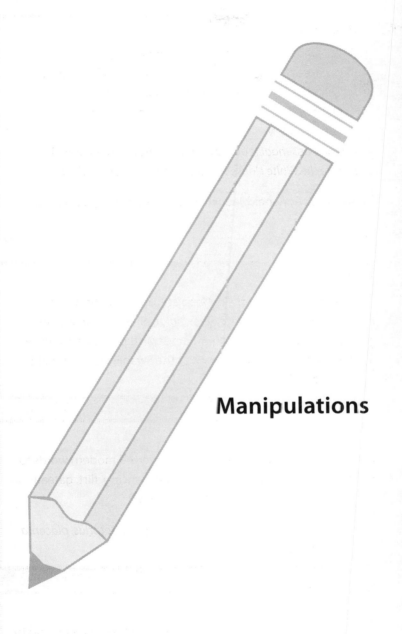

Manipulations

CHAPTER 22

Dope doubled his $500 in seven days (4)

Crossword-making is as lucrative as dog-walking. Next time you drive through South Kensington, admiring the homes of the rich and famous, know that puns and homophones didn't secure the collateral.

I live in a Californian bungalow, a world away from California, with three bedrooms, two kids, a Labrador cross and a wife whose annual salary, most years, puts my revenue in the shade. Are we happy? Last time I checked. Are we rich? Put it this way: does your house need painting?

It's only natural then, that money-making opportunities tend to catch my eye. In finance terms, I'm the dope in our Master clue, a chump aspiring to double his dough in a week, and usually seeing his efforts backfire. Over the years my list has extended to include: teacher, copywriter, deckhand, columnist, mango picker, book reviewer, journalist, proofreader, Tarzanagram.

It'd be nice if we could tiptoe past that last one, pretend I never mentioned it, but this chapter's themes of idiocy, money and manipulation insist we go there.

Say what you like about a puzzle income, but the job has catered to my gypsy disposition. Nowadays the Web has erased the need to be fixed in one spot, though crosswording has enjoyed that bonus for years. If I gathered no moss for most of my twenties, at least I could glean a wage.

The *Herald* was good enough to tolerate my itchy feet. In those early Wordwit days, when Ted Validas held the chair, I recruited Mum as go-between. For a year or more, Heather Astle was Lee Starheath, typing my air-mailed clues and sending them to the puzzle department. Bear in mind that these were different times, when an electric Olivetti was the height of technology, and parents were selfless by definition. Of course Mum took a modest cut of salary, plus the perks of personal updates from her eldest boy, slapdash travelogues sandwiched between pangrams and spoonerisms.

One such letter confessed to playing Tarzan. This was 1983. I was 21, a lunk with more muscles than sense, a fugitive from the European rugby tour. The rest of the team had flown back to Oz, leaving me to travel south to Torquay, the home of *Fawlty Towers*, to play a season with the town's local side.

The set-up was cosy: a new circle of friends, a bedsit with sea glimpses, the puzzle income, but after a while the heater began to swallow 50p coins like movie popcorn. Weekends of lager started to tear holes in the budget, and suddenly my knack for making riddles was not enough to keep the wolf from the door.

Enter Tarzan. The telegram racket was run by a girl called Helen. Her dog was Lester, and the park where he ran doubled as Helen's office. When I first responded to the ad in the paper I said I had a preference for gorillagrams, figuring it stood to be warmer. But when Helen insisted that my rugby frame was more in the Johnny Weissmuller mould, we settled on a 60 per cent cut, which was reasonable given that I had to drag my arse through the elements wearing nothing but two chamois as a costume.

The job was casual in every sense. Periodic phone calls, maybe twice a month, told me where and when I needed to appear. Thankfully, I could keep my Speedos on underneath the loincloth, but in zero degrees, an icy wind blowing off the Channel, that was small comfort. Hence the manipulation. To every gig I took my lucky pair of woollen gloves. To get from A to B on a second-hand moped, I first wore the gloves to save my fingers from falling off. On reaching B, I rolled the gloves into a ball and stashed them down my jungle briefs to save face, so to speak. Zero degrees can take its toll on a man, even Tarzan. I felt obliged to maintain appearances on behalf of the hero's franchise.

My debut gig was for a woman called Pamela. All I knew was that she was turning forty, she was having dinner at the Teignmouth Hotel in Teignmouth and the whole thing was a surprise.

Riding the moped, my plastic overalls keeping out the sleet, I started reviewing all the other idiotic schemes I'd attempted. Neck and neck with Tarzan would have to be an early TV appearance, a quiz show back in Australia. (That's the other reason QUIZ is in the grid, but I was too embarrassed to tell you.) *Sale of the Century* in 1981, no question, was my lowest public moment.

Getting selected was less about IQ than having an interesting job. Who cares if you don't know the capital of Chad, you make crosswords, yeah? That's quirky. Good fodder. So the audition staff found me a slot and I went home to memorise the wives of Henry VIII, only for disaster to strike.

In ten years of playing contact sport I'd hardly suffered a scratch. But on the eve of my quiz appearance I copped a flying boot to the eye, requiring thirty stitches. I rang the producers first thing on Monday and told them I'd had a mishap but thought I was all right to appear. In hindsight that was optimistic.

I gave the make-up girl a heart attack. She did her best to camouflage the surgical wire, slapping pancake on the

Mercurochrome, using wax pencils to replace my missing eyebrow, but nothing in her bag of tricks could remove my concussion. Again, I was the dope trying to double his loot – and lost. My reflexes were shot. Those few times I managed to beat the buzzer I thought Jonas Salk created Peanuts and Jane Austen invented the pneumatic tyre. It was a nadir.

Novelty telegrams, by comparison, ran a close second in the Stupidity Stakes. Huddled on the moped, the sleet getting thick, it dawned on me that I had no telegram to deliver. Apart from saying happy birthday to a stranger, maybe leading the table in song, I was a messenger without a message. After the Tarzan yodel, what did I have? The panic set my crossword knack into overdrive. *Think, apeman, think!*

On arrival, the publican led me to a backroom where I peeled off my slicks and clipped on the chamois. I rolled up the gloves and improved my contour. I coughed and warbled to lessen the panic, my mind racing through the pun reserves, trying to compose a piece of wordplay to see me escape this torment unscathed. Pamela, I was told, was in the bistro next door.

> Sound FX: Tarzan howl
> [Crossword-maker in loincloth enters crowded bar. He has no idea what Pamela looks like. He asks the barman, who points to a table by the window. The crossword-maker beats chest, wails to ceiling.]
> Crossword-maker (in Cro-Magnon voice): Me Tarzan, you Pamela. Me swing on vines all day, you divine. Tarzan live in jungle, Pamela tree-mendous. Me created by Edgar Rice Burroughs, Tarzan digs Pamela …

It was a train wreck, with three cheers to finish. I gathered my cash, my rags, and didn't think hanging around for a Guinness was the smartest idea. Besides, the rain was getting heavier, my sniffle was worsening, and I had a crossword to make.

IS THIS YOUR CARD? – manipulation clues

Manipulation is a subtle recipe, sneaky, evasive. In showbiz terms, the formula is close magic, the sleight-of-hand stuff you need to see in slo-mo before you can figure out how it works.

We've talked about deletions, where BASIL may lose heart to become BAIL, or a RABBIT can run short to be RABBI. By the same token, containers embrace the idea of insertion, such as GUESS gaining INN to reveal GUINNESS. And soon we'll enter the reversal realm where words change direction. Yet falling between all these is manipulation. Neither pure anagram nor straight deletion, manipulation is more a tweak, a shuffle of the shells to make you lose the pea.

The clearest way to explain how this recipe works is to divide the subtle operation into two types – the switch and the swap. At first glance, they may sound like synonyms, but these next two subsections will help you set the styles apart.

The switch

Neo in the *Financial Times* made the first manipulation switch, and the second clue was crafted by a retired Tarzanagram:

> *Prison caused change of heart – that's the aim (4)*
> *Row ending early for depleted foursome? (4)*

These two are twins, not just in answer lengths, but also in how they operate. For British solvers at least, *prison* is GAOL. After a *change of heart* – not with new letters, but a flip-flop of the vowels – you'll create GOAL, meaning *aim*.

The next switch deals with a heteronym. Remember them? Does DOES, say, equal female deer or hairstyles? Here the booby trap is *row*. I want you to think of the aquatic kind, boosting the deceit by involving a *foursome*, a common boat quota, but the truth is more about uproar – a RIOT in fact.

So what does the wordplay tell you? The key phrase is *ending early*. The ending of RIOT is T. Make that T appear earlier and hey presto: RIOT turns into TRIO.

Big deal – that's just an anagram. True, but manipulations are suaver in their moves. Instead of getting you to scramble, they advise you to slide a letter. Or a few letters, like this dark gem from Alberich, also of the *Financial Times*:

Cautious and vigilant when leaders advance (9)

Most readers won't crack this clue, not cold anyway. It's hard but beautiful, and worth a look to see the guile of manipulations.

Leaders advance, the phrase, whispers the idea of nudging two or more letters deeper within a word. The MA in MANOR, say, could advance in line to make NORMA. But what's the word here that undergoes this change? Well, it's nine letters long and probably means *vigilant*.

That word is ATTENTIVE, though not your final answer. Don't neglect *cautious* at the start of the clue, the likely definition. Advance the leaders of ATTENTIVE several slots and TENTATIVE emerges. Tough but beautiful. In fact, we really are paddling in the deep end here, so don't panic if you can't get to the bottom of these clue styles.

Let's recap. We've looked at a letter switch, then a switch of letters plural, leading us on to a third switch option – moving the order of whole words. These two samples will help you to see this wholesale approach, the first courtesy of Paul, the other of yours truly:

Stand by for armed robbery? On the contrary (6)
Where silks may embellish space romance? Vice versa (9)

Treating words like freight cars, these manipulations are asking you to re-shunt the sequence. In both clues, the last two phrases – *on the contrary* and *vice versa* – are the signals for this switch. *Armed robbery* is a HOLD UP. Display the crime *on the contrary* and you make UPHOLD, or *stand by*.

The treachery in the second example is *silks*. The material, right? Sorta. Here the material is slang for Queen's Counsels, the highest order of barrister. And where do silks embellish? Try a COURTROOM, which vice versa becomes ROOM/COURT, or *space romance*, just as the White House can turn into the house white, or an offshoot can shoot off. Which brings us to the second manipulation style.

The swap

Maybe the best analogy to help you grasp the difference between the two manipulation modes is to imagine that switches are internal, like two classmates exchanging seats for the school photo. Swaps, on the other hand, are external, where a classmate gives up her chair so that an outside student can join the lesson. Let's take it back to Tarzan:

Apeman dumping Liz, finally, for model material (6)

In equation terms, the clue is saying TARZAN – Z (*Liz finally*) + T (as in Model T) = TARTAN. Keeping with the ape world:

Ape altered face and ass (6)

The equation: MONKEY – M + D = DONKEY.

Never will you be expected to scramble a word that's not presented in the clue. Such a sin is known as the indirect anagram. Elusive as manipulations can be, they give you clear pointers to the words you need, and a specific command on how to alter those words.

That said, this swap style can test your mettle, asking you to intuit the missing word (TARZAN or MONKEY) and then make an external trade. Your latest Master clue does just that:

Dope doubled his $500 in seven days (4)

With no cross-letters to build on, this clue is not one you'd readily consider. However, that familiar phrase of *seven days* can only mean WEEK. Is that the answer? As it happens, yes. But why?

Cryptic clues are sprinkled with words suggesting letters. T, we've just discovered, can be denoted by model, as well as *time* or *bone* (T-bone), *temperature* or *tonne*. Don't forget *shirt* too, as in T-shirt, or *junction* (T-junction) and *true*. In our Master clue the shorthand relates to numbers.

Roman numerals are a clue-maker's bonanza. Thanks to Caesar and co., a girl like LIV is permanently 54, while MAGNETISM is 'seating' rearranged within 2000 (or MM). So what is our fool doing in the Master clue? He has $500, or D. Double that and you get M, the Roman thousand. So how does WEEK play out? Or has the maths lesson fooled you?

Dope is more than just a ninny. The word is also slang for marijuana. Can you think of another synonym ending in D? (The WEEK theory should help here.) That's right, WEED. But WEEM is not the solution, let alone a word, so how does that K bob up? The answer lies in business slang, as seen in this sentence: *Puzzle making pulls in some 26k per annum, explaining why some compilers need to teach, or write books, or dress up in chamois occasionally.*

RECIPE PRECIS: MANIPULATIONS

Manipulation clues rely on one of two tricks – the switch or swap. The switch sees one letter changing places, so to speak. If IRAN's leader is demoted, then RAIN may be the result. No external letter is enlisted; unlike in the other trick, known as the swap, where a letter in a keyword is traded for an outside letter in order to spell the answer. Again, if IRAN has a leadership change, then anything from BRAN to GRAN is a possible outcome. Look for signs to suggest either action – rearranging within, or borrowing from without.

HALL OF FAME: MANIPULATIONS

Child the result had this couple married much earlier (4) [*Times* 8587]

External path, first to last (5) [*Times* 8611]

Horse and cart back to front? It's monstrous (5) [Puck, *Guardian*]

Canadian province with idiot president, degree going to head (8) [Paul, *Guardian*]

Singer from Switzerland replacing German in Bond movie (9) [Cincinnus, *FT*]

Acquire site and relocate a pub (3,6) [Gemini, *Guardian*]

SOLUTIONS: item, outer, hydra, Manitoba, goldfinch, gin palace

QUIZLING 22.1

What simple English word becomes its own past tense once its initial is transferred to the tail?

QUIZLING 22.2

Exchanging a letter per step, and mixing the new combination, can you progress from EMBRYO to FOETUS? But wait, there is a mild complication – you need to go via MOTHER. (Remarkably, our own five-step operation includes a slang for man, and 'to rear a child', with the other step inferring rest.)

QUIZLING 22.3

What four-letter word for layer
Becomes another player
In the laying art
Once L's the new heart?

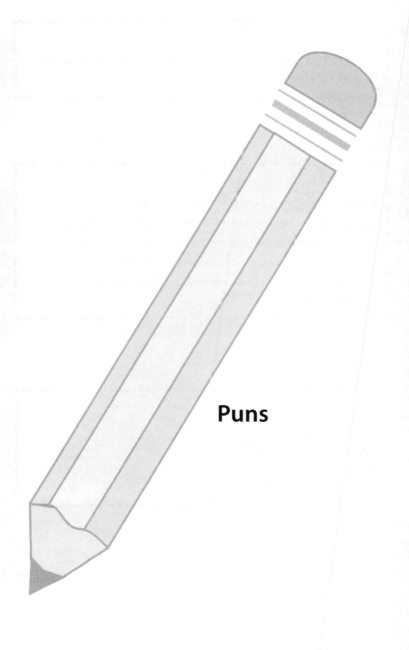

Puns

CHAPTER 23

Swinger's bar for partner pickups?
(7)

Knock-knock.
Who's there?
Sarah.
Sarah who?
Sarah reason you're not laughing?

Maybe because puns are the lowest form of wit. But if that's true, doesn't that make puns the foundation of all humour?

Knock-knock jokes are *toc-tocs* in the Transvaal, *klop-klops* in Amsterdam and *kon-kons* in Kyoto. The stuff of cute graffiti, headlines, slogans and kids' jokes: puns separate us from the beasts.

Virgil cracked them. Homer and Dante lapped them up. *Don Quixote* is built on wordplay and swordplay. In Act II of *Macbeth* a boozy porter does a knock-knock routine: the gag reflex is certainly an enduring one.

To a child, puns present the elements of risk and creativity, testing both semantic and social boundaries. (Though remember, no matter how far you push the envelope, it will always remain stationery.) Compared to the bigotry of so much adult humour, puns imply a wonder of how language operates. Instead of racism or sexism, the punster would rather describe two silkworms racing down a leaf, only to end up in a tie.

Puns fall into three main baskets. The first includes our silkworms or the talkative yak – a wisecrack based on double meaning. Like the coffee shops that trade as Ground Zero or Daily Grind.

The second sort mucks about with homophones, like pirate earrings costing a buccaneer. Or subeditors forging such headlines as:

EMERGING OLYMPIANS COME FOURTH
CIRCUS FIRE: HEAT IN TENTS
HAVANA BALL

Lastly, there's the manipulation kind where words or names have been reshaped. A sick pig, say, needs *oinkment*, and the sick bird, *tweetment*. Or take a gander at these take-away joints:

Just Falafs
Kebabylon
Marquis de Salade

Vaudeville veteran Les Dawson reckoned that puns were the quickest way to lose an audience, while John Cleese, another star in the English galaxy, is attributed as saying that comedy has three rules:

no puns;
no puns;
and no puns.

Clinicians at the Levity Institute recognise this syndrome as 'punnus envy', an affliction common among groan-ups, yet not crossword lovers. We can't resist a wry game of gotcha. In fact the pun warrants its own recipe. Two chapters in fact. Brace yourself.

GROAN-UP HUMOUR – cute clues and misdirection

Americans call them cute clues, where a standard definition is dumped in favour of a comical slant, a more oblique
tangent to the answer. Ben Tausig, a Gen-Xer who syndicates
his puzzles widely in the States, has a flair for this clueing
mode. Take these four, for example:

Proverbial battlers = SEXES
Apple for the teacher? = IMAC
Country album = ATLAS
Go home = JAPAN

Each has the potential to be styled into a riddle, so elegant
is the wordplay. (If the last clue bamboozles you, think about
Go, the Japanese board game.) Better still, this cute mode of
clueing can rejuvenate a weary solution, like ATLAS, which
tends to recur at short intervals. You'll also notice, in Tausig's
quartet, that only one entails question marks. This rightly
suggests that seasoned US solvers don't insist on punctuation to declare the mental twist.

Though when the twist is kinkier than usual, like these
next four from a bevy of American setters, the question mark
is mandatory:

Something gays and straights have in common? = LONG
   A
Drive in the backseat of a car? = LIBIDO
Holiday cut short? = XMAS
Star of Westerns? = BADGE

By definition, not all of these can be described as pure-bred
puns, yet they certainly throw fresh light on their answers
in the same way that riddles do. As we know, riddles pivot
on a skewed way of thinking, often a misdirection – another
reason why most US bloggers plump for the tag of cute clue,
or daffy definition, rather than the stricture of pun.

In cryptics, the label can be called the oblique definition, or a tee-hee, even a riddle clue, with a pun often residing at the centre. Unlike makers of US quicks, the cryptic setter will almost always enlist the question mark, as these three from Rufus in the *Guardian* illustrate:

> *A young crab?* = NIPPER
> *Well off?* = SOUND ASLEEP
> *Hold hands?* = STEVEDORES

Pun clues are indeed nippers. Their surface sense encourages you to look one way while the answer stalks you from behind and – *ouch*.

Of all puzzle setters, Rufus (Roger Squires) is born to this clue style, as he once graced the stage and TV screen as a magician. He therefore knows the art of misdirection, getting the crowd to glance left while he dabbles with mechanics on the right. As a member of the elite Magic Circle, Rufus is also accomplished in patter, that other silken quality of good puns, lulling you with words you take to be innocuous, only to learn they pack a punch.

Notice too how the Rufus trio boasts brevity. As a whole, puns tend to be shorter clues since the formula doesn't demand the two customary strands, as wordplay and definition are woven into one allusion. *First-class student* (a Rufus clue for INFANT) is entrusting the quip to bear both elements.

That said, length is not always the giveaway. Some prolong the gag, or take their full measure, as this *Times* bundle goes to prove:

> *Digitally produced image* = FINGER PAINTING
> *Materially unaffected by psychotherapy?* = SHRINK
>   RESISTANT
> *Hail fellow? Well, Met* = WEATHER BUREAU

Maybe it's what you feared – one pun clue without a question mark, while another holds one in its centre. But the etiquette is usually reliable, even if the clue length can fluctuate.

Take our Master clue, for instance. Hardly skimpy, compared to the cunning of Rufus, the five-word specimen at least sports a question mark. Let's take a look:

Swinger's bar for partner pickups? (7)

Where are your thoughts? Shadowy liaisons? Kiss-and-no-tell? That's the plan, of course: the wrong direction. You won't be shocked to hear the clue has nothing to do with sexual antics, despite the surface sense. Indeed the answer is more aligned to an earlier headline, the one about the circus fire.

Change the kinky backdrop for the Big Top, and all the key words – *swinger, bar, partner* – take on a new glow. If partners are being picked up, it's not over sleazy one-liners, but different lines suspended from the upper reaches of the ring. TRAPEZE of course is the answer you're chasing, and one step closer to sealing the grid's second quadrant. Handily, the Master Puzzle's other pun clue is 30-Across, along the frame, but before we go there let's take a break from the circus and throw the spotlight on a lesser known aspect of the puzzle story – the romance of partner pickups.

DOWN WITH LOVE – hidden proposals

Emily Cox and Henry Rathvon are lifelong partners and makers of some of the best cryptics in the world. This Pennsylvania pair have been creating deviant grids for the *Atlantic Monthly* until recently, as well as a weekly cryptic in Canada's *National Post*. At the time of writing, their work runs monthly in the *Wall Street Journal*. For some strange reason, US (or Canadian) cryptics are reluctant to succumb to pun clues, opting for every other recipe, including some of these exquisite anagram clues from the Cox and Rathvon stable:

Les, Tom, Dicky and Harry = MOLEST
For Callas, a fabulous place to sing = LA SCALA

When not crafting clues, the couple collect fossils from the Devonian period, listen to calypso music and play cupid for their solvers. Once anyway, back in September 2007.

The story began with an email from a young communications officer named Aric Egmont from Cambridge, Massachusetts, who wished to propose to his girlfriend Jennie Bass, a medical student. Every Sunday Aric and Jennie loved to collaborate over the quick in the *Boston Globe*, a feature created by Cox and Rathvon. Any chance, asked Aric, of lacing a proposal into the crossword? Romantics at heart, Cox and Rathvon warmed to the idea.

Popping the Question, the eventual puzzle, wove half a dozen nuptial phrases into the grid, from LET'S TIE THE KNOT to MAY I HAVE YOUR HAND. These longer entries crossed covert references to Jennie's family, friends and other passions. The last themed answer was clued as *Generic proposal* (a pun of Jen + Aric), being Aric's cue to kneel with ring poised and ask WILL YOU MARRY ME.

'She screamed and hugged me,' Aric recalled in a follow-up article on the coup. 'It took her a minute to say yes.'

I once hatched a similar plot, creating a secretive toast for the wedding of Naomi Taylor, one of the many Taylors to oversee Fairfax puzzles. On Naomi's big day, my puzzle revolved around something old, something new, something borrowed, something blue, and the reception at the reception was apparently rapturous.

Lee Glickstein of California, a sporadic setter for the *New York Times*, also turned to puzzles to do his bidding. His plan was to tie the knot with his partner, but just in case she had other plans, Lee turned his byline into Ken Stegicelli, masking his true identity on the page. The puzzle hinged on the all-important question, to which thankfully his beloved said yes, causing Ken to revert to a jubilant Lee and go book a chapel.

Our last star-crossed story has a bittersweet ending and involves the giant of Australian crosswords, Lindsey Browne. In his salad days, just after the war, LB fell in love with Nancy Moore, aptly a mixture of YON ROMANCE. In cryptic fashion, LB confessed his feelings with an inbuilt acrostic, the first letters of every Across answer spelling I LOVE NANCY MOORE. A few weeks later, once his paramour had twigged to the secret message, Lindsey crafted a sequel: WILL SHE MARRY ME? Not long after that, brimming with the news, LB let his sharper-eyed solvers know the outcome: THE ANSWER IS YES.

The *Herald* was less than thrilled, quashing any future updates in Lindsey's work. These were puzzles after all, not journal entries. Hitched and happy, the couple had four kids, only for cancer to strike Nancy down in 1959. The diagnosis was a brain tumour, compelling LB to sink his meagre puzzle income into a flight to Sweden, hoping the world's best surgeon at the time could work a miracle. Alas, Nancy lost her battle, leaving Lindsey with four small children, and next to broke.

The cure? More journalism. More cryptics. And a TV quiz called *Pick-A-Box*, where the cruciverbalist did a lot better than my damp squib and scooped the prize pool. Invited back by public demand, LB later appeared on a family edition with his second eldest, Adam, and won a further jackpot. Owing to countless hours of researching clues, Lindsey had the perfect mind for trivia. In a tumultuous span of years, crosswords had given him a soulmate, and later the where-withal to manage in her absence.

Little by little LB recovered from the grief and climbed out of poverty. Then one day he went to a tennis event in Sydney's eastern suburbs. There, a young social worker named Elspeth Knox, a lover of crosswords and almost starstruck, asked this handsome man on the baseline, 'Are you LB?'

'*C'est moi*,' he said.

Despite such pompous beginnings, Elspeth saw past Lin's airs and found a real sweetness, as well as a devoted father. 'A male chauvinist he may have been,' laughs Elspeth now, 'but he never swore. He told me that swearing demonstrated a lack of imagination or an ignorance of the great richness that is the English language.'

Elspeth agreed, and the two became fast friends. For only the second time in his life, LB was smitten, and a crossword, of course, seemed the traditional way to ask for the young woman's hand – this time keeping the powers that be in the dark. The response? ELSPETH SAID YES.

RECIPE PRECIS: PUNS

A pun is like a comical query, testing a word's nuances, and hence often flagged by a question mark. The other signature is brevity, since wordplay and definition are entwined. One more tip: look for words that carry several meanings (shutter, for example, can be a louvre, or part of a camera, or maybe a door) and see where each tangent leads.

QUIZLING 23.1

Mix the ten letters missing from the riddle below to make its punny two-word answer:

WH## BO#K DO YO# BUY # #AU#Y GRA##A#IAN?

QUIZLING 23.2

A famous English actor. Turn the last letter of his first name into a Roman numeral, and you spell a type of pain that bad puns can produce. Now turn the first letter of his surname into another Roman numeral, and you get a word for glee. Who is our man?

QUIZLING 23.3

What eight-letter word means potentially difficult, as well as provoking amusement? And what other word – a three-letter synonym of problem – also means to remedy a problem?

CHAPTER 24

... Twister for openers? (8)

Scrabble was my first true love. You could almost say I was singular about it. The passion began in my early teens, lasting the length of high school. Mates would be roaming the real world meeting girls or forming garage bands while I'd be setting up the Scrabble board, seeing if my right hand could outscore my left. For general studies in Year 12 each student gave a talk about a personal interest. I chose Scrabble, or Scrabble chose me, and I stood there like a loon on day release, reciting the fifty-nine words you can make with RETINA plus a blank.

CANTIER
CERTAIN
CRINATE
NACRITE

The class feared I was speaking in tongues, and who could blame them? ANESTRI, RESIANT: half the words were hokum, even to me. But if STARNIE or STEARIN promised 70 points, plus the bingo bonus of 50, then that's all that mattered. Language in my teens amounted to racking up points.

I entered tournaments, meeting other verbal misfits in community rooms around Sydney, carrying tiles like holy sacraments. Between games I swotted three-letter words ending in AE and devised ways to dump surplus vowels. I became close friends with DZO (a Tibetan yak) and XU (a former coin of Vietnam). I played cab drivers and professors, retirees and prodigies, creating dense knots of words that looked like pretzels written in Klingon.

At twenty I made the state's top echelon, though I had a nemesis, a bloke called John Holgate. With square glasses, wispy beard and a riotous vocab, John was everybody's nemesis. The Australian champ ran the medical library in Paddington Women's Hospital, though I'm sure his primary occupation was digesting words ending in J.

We met a couple of times in his hospital lair to fashion a new board game. Words of course were central to our plan. The board's shape resembled an eye, with each player needing to complete a circuit before entering the retina for the last challenge. Knower's Arc was a working title, and it never went anywhere. Though I did. Overseas. With a football team. And for most of my twenties, I hardly drew a blank in anger.

The reason was GAE, the Scottish verb for go. Or WAE, their word for woe, or with, or a Spenserian wave. Either/or, I was sick of knowing words purely in order to get a score. AGE and AWE were words I could abide, but GAE and WAE belonged with DODO and MOA.

When I did eventually return to the game, it was strictly a pastime between friends. Scoring was done on the backs of envelopes, and wine was essential. A long lyrical word like COYOTES was preferred to OOCYTES, which seemed too desperate anyhow. Aesthetics, in a way, counted more than mathematics.

John Holgate kept in touch, usually disguised as John Le Gotha, sending letters to the *Herald* to comment on Wordwit puzzles, and Ted Validas replied warmly. Puzzles of course couldn't afford to have answers like NACRITE or CRINATE, which saw the slow erosion of my obscure jargon. My Scrabble links fizzled as well, and soon Mr Le Gotha stopped corresponding altogether. In fact we didn't see each other for two decades, when an extraordinary coincidence threw us together in 2008.

The occasion involved eight bodies stuffed into barrels. The barrels occupied an obsolete bank vault in a small corner of South Australia called Snowtown, the end point of a notorious serial killing back in 1999. I'd written a short play about the case – *After the Avalanche* – and flew to Sydney for an open reading of the script.

Other plays, other crimes, were involved on the day. The reading was run by a theatre company who had invited submissions for scripts about an Australian crime. I'd chosen Snowtown, while other writers tried their luck with Ned Kelly, the missing Beaumont kids, a stolen bike outside Safeways or the disappearance of publisher Juanita Nielsen.

For readers unfamiliar with the last case, the nutshell version is that Nielsen, a fierce opponent of corrupt land deals in urban Sydney, had vanished in 1975, presumed murdered. By sheer chance the script readings were being held in the Cross, the same postcode where Nielsen was last seen, though the eeriness didn't end there.

The moment I entered the building I heard the siren song – the coin-like clatter of Scrabble tiles as they spilt from board to bag. Climbing the stairs, I walked into the past. The prim rows of tables with racks and boards: a Scrabble tournament was in full swing, the Trans-Tasman Challenge no less. A sturdy bloke of 50, dressed in black tracksuit with a kiwi embroidered over his heart, said, 'Yer right, are ya?'

'I used to play this game,' I said.

'Yeah, well – ' His way of saying bugger off. Then I recognised the grizzled features of Holgate in the throng.

'That's John,' I said. 'We know each other.'

'He's playing,' said the bouncer, softly.

Time to go, I thought. 'I'll drop back later.'

The script readings were down the hall in a room of beige carpet and plastic chairs. Late November, the day was hot, and by the time the fourth play was going, the room was stuffy.

Night and Day at the Carousel Cabaret focused on the murder of Juanita Nielsen. Actors Anonymous, the group in charge, had cast a doppelganger of the missing editor. She stood in the make-believe nightclub, script in hand, rebuking the mobsters in the cocktail booth when her body started swaying. She staggered, clutching her chest as if she were shot, then slumped to the floor. People leapt to her aid. 'Does anyone know CPR?' bellowed a director.

Better than that, I knew a network of smart people in the next room. I bolted down the hall and burst into the tournament, blurting, 'Is there a doctor here?'

No, but there was Glenda, a Kiwi nurse. The only hitch, she was halfway through a game. In her eyes I could sense the addict's dilemma: do I save a life or make a killing with my blank? Her Aussie rival deemed a life to be more important and froze the clock, encouraging Glenda to go.

John Holgate came too – he knew a bit about medicine, mainly of the gynaecological kind, as well as a lot of arcane anatomical terms like AXILLA and NUCHAL, though less where these parts were located. As Glenda helped bring Juanita Nielsen back to life, John and I chatted.

'So this is what you do now?' he said, glancing round the room.

'This and crosswords. I'm into scripts at the moment.'

'Plays, you mean?'

'Dramas. Black comedies. Not a Gaelic verb in sight.'

John's eyes lit up. 'You still remember them?'

'Gae, hae, kae – scary, eh?'

'You'd be welcome back any time. Melbourne has a very active Scrabble scene.'

'Nae,' I smiled, 'but thanks. It's great to see you.'

Juanita survived, by the way, and Snowtown was pipped by Ronald Ryan, the last man hanged in Australia. Once the ambulance arrived, Glenda won her *contestus interruptus* by a comfortable margin, though Holgate and his compatriots seized the trophy, 179 wins to 108. Zingers played across the weekend included MEGAVOLT and HAZINESS, not to mention the usual suspects of WAE, VUG, CWM and DZO.

TOURNEYS WITH A TWIST – crossword slamdowns and Lollapuzzoola

Scrabble is not the only word-game to inspire its own tournament. When Holgate and I first locked horns in the Hakoah Soccer Club, back in 1978, playing JO and QI till the KINE came home, a man named Will Shortz saw a gap in crossword culture.

Shortz of course would go on to edit crosswords for the *New York Times* in 1993, but his passion for puzzles is lifelong. He's the only known person to hold a degree in enigmatology, a course he helped construct at Indiana University in the early 1970s, studying the ageless appeal of conundrums. After graduating, Shortz wore several puzzle hats, chiefly on magazines, and then came the dream of the American Crossword Puzzle Tournament, or ACPT.

When the word went out, Shortz had no inkling how many might attend. But on that first chilly morning in February, 1978, the mercury nudging zero, some 149 diehards appeared with pencils and registration forms. Thirty years later the ACPT draws 700 competitors, the event so big it's recently been forced to shift from Stamford to Brooklyn.

Now in his fifties, dapper as ever, Shortz still hosts the gig, explaining the ordeal to competitors: they do six crosswords in the first day, then there's a championship play-off on Sunday – across three divisions – to see who wears the chequered tiaras. Tyler Hinman is the boy most likely, bagging his first of five Open titles when just 20. To see this guy attack a grid is to watch a house being built in time lapse, every last piece thrown into place. (In 2006, the movie *Wordplay* captured this feat, as well as shadowing three other super-solvers.) Tyler has an IT degree and now works as a Google programmer. To quote Will Shortz, 'Not all smart people solve crosswords, but all crossword solvers are smart.'

Yet ACPT is not the only tournament on the radar. We've already read about the *Telegraph* showdown, while *The Times* of London has sporadically run a tournament since 1970. Roy Dean, the first winner, not only won a silver cup but an ongoing job as compiler.

Yet the joker in the pack has to be Lollapuzzoola, a US event first staged in 2008. The newborn contest doesn't just boast a remarkable link to Scrabble, but also to Twister, the game suggested by our current Master clue.

Ryan Hecht and Brian Cimmet are 'two nerds with microphones'. They produce an indie podcast called Fill Me In, a weekly look at the *New York Times* crossword. Ryan is an actor and Brian a pianist. Each has two cats plus an understanding wife. And a few years back, they hatched a thing called Lollapuzzoola, a crossword tournament with a dash of lunacy. The event is held in a retrofit church in Queens, New York, a sacred site to anyone with a love of words.

The Community Methodist Church on 35th Avenue is where Alfred Mosher Butts invented Lexiko in the 1930s. If that means nothing to you, consider that the game was later renamed Criss-Crosswords, before being christened Scrabble in 1948. Remarkably, Alfred's old Scrabble club still congregates in a room off the nave. The street itself is nicknamed

Scrabble Avenue, while the actual sign reads like a homage: 35 $t_1h_4 A_1v_4e_1n_1u_1e_1$.

The maiden Lollapuzzoola featured a crossword by Barry C. Silk that dwelt on the Scrabble theme, with MAGAZINE RACK and ROOFING TILES referencing the church's history. Another challenge required an organist to play snatches of tunes, with LA BAMBA and SEND IN THE CLOWNS serving as central answers. Yet Mike Nothnagel had the craziest idea, making a puzzle called *Compromising Positions*.

Solvers initially struggled to connect the entries – KNOT THEORY and HIT THE SPOT. But then they noticed the smaller words sprinkled in the flanks, words like BLUE, LEFT, HAND and GREEN. Sound familiar? As Ryan Hecht explains, 'We used those terms as starting positions for the Twister game. The top three finishers of the puzzle got to play for a chance to win one hundred bonus points.'

According to one eyewitness, Michael Smith, alias Philly-Solver in cyberspace, 'Some nimble minds were not as nimble of body.' Crosswords may merit their reputation for keeping our brains in shape, but there's nothing like gardening, swimming, yoga or Twister to maintain all our other parts.

To stretch the segue, and turn back to puns, be aware that this recipe may yet make the greatest demands on your agility. Where most clues bend letters, the pun contorts whole concepts. If I say BOXER, do you think pug or pugilist? Maybe the answer is otherwise. A boxer could mean a packer (one who boxes), an undertaker, a trifecta punter, a comic-strip artist, even a crossword-maker, such is the formula's elasticity.

Then to push you further, as you can see from our current clue, is the mystery of the ellipsis, that line of dots connecting our Twister conundrum to the previous 29-Across. How do the dots work? I'll explain …

TWISTED THINKING – puns and the ellipsis …

There's a fail-safe way to separate the tyro solver from the pro, and it boils down to what question comes up when crosswords are discussed. Here are the five tells:

What bloody language are they written in? (non-solver)
Is every clue an anagram? (non-solver with potential)
How can you pick the definition and the other bit?
   (promising beginner)
My favourite clue was XYZ. What's yours? (steady
   achiever)
How do those three dots work at the end of a clue?
   (experienced achiever with aspirations)

Of course, other questions will get asked. Among the FAQs are these perennials, my standard answer attached:
Which comes first – the words in the grid or the clues? ('Either /
or, usually words then clues.')
How long does it take to make a crossword? ('An hour to interlock, then a few more hours to fine-tune the clues. Themed
grids usually take longer.')
How the hell did you get into the whole business? ('Gae, hae,
kae … sorry, what did you say?')

To return to that curious string of dots, what editors call an ellipsis, I have a simple message. Relax – the dots are overrated. They loom too large in the mind of many anxious solvers. Tim Moorey, author of *How to Master the Times Cross-word*, puts it in plain English. The ellipsis, he writes, 'is merely a way of connecting two clues (sometimes more) to present a longer than normal clue sentence.'

Hence the pair of dotted clues in our Master Puzzle, 29-Across and 30-Across, can be dovetailed to read: *A weir worker set Twister for openers?* But since we've already solved that same charade for ADAMANT, it's safe to say that each linked fragment can be tackled on its lonesome.

Usually. That's the unstated qualification to Moorey's simple message, since two clues can be joined for other reasons. In the Master example the link is purely grammatical. For ADAMANT, we have a clue that seems to invite more info: *A weir worker set*. Set what, you ask. The clue is ripe to be extended, and 30-Across can oblige, as the pun is lean and can finish what 29-Across began, completing the sentence that ADAMANT started.

Elsewhere, the link may be an overlap, where a definition element might be shared. Here's a pair from my own swag:

Issue shocking female … (5)
… setter, objective on the outside (4)

The first clue is a basic anagram made scarier by the dots. SUSIE is the answer, with the word *female* the definition. Importantly, this same word flows into the succeeding clue. So here we need to read this clue as *Female setter, objective on the outside*. ENID is the *female* we seek, since *setter* is I (the crossword-setter) enclosed in END, or *objective*. This way, the word *female* serves two clues as definition.

Tim Moorey, then, is right. The ellipsis marries two part-clues into a whole, but this union can be based on grammar, or mutual definition. Or, as our next examples show, a mutual slice of wordplay:

Sterile noble discussed … (6)
… business party with right man in bull market? (7)

Here homophones get a call-up, with BARREN your first solution, an echo of BARON, or *noble*. The audio signpost, *discussed*, then serves the second clue where we need to utter a synonym of *business* (MATTER). The rest comes from *party* (a frequent indicator of DO), plus R (*right*), which gives us MATADOR, or *man in bull market*.

And that, judging by your groan, is a pun. Keeping to the mantra of simple connection, let's treat our current ellipsis as the bridge in a halved sentence, rather than as a signal of any word overlapping. Ditching the dots from our mind then, we're faced with the clue:

Twister for openers? (8)

The question mark, we know, points to mischief, as much as the Twister arrow will get your body stretching. So what twists? What opens? Pun clues should provoke those questions. Don't get trapped by tunnel vision. Think outside the box. If BOXER can be CRATER, or SHUTTER a gate, so can TWISTER be a DOORKNOB, and soon you'll find whole new hatches opening within. Knock-knock.

HALL OF FAME: PUNS

Candy eaten after chin-ups? (3) [Ben Tausig, US]
Punishment that's capital to a point (8) [Paul, *Guardian*]
Cultivated swimmers are spotted here (5,4) [*Times* 8530]
The entertainment here is taking off (5,4) [Alberich, *FT*]
Sluggish transport? On the contrary! (6,5) [*Times* 7940]
Ashes held in this? (4–7) [*Times* 8133]

SOLUTIONS: Pez, sentence, trout farm, strip club, bullet train, tree-hugging

---

QUIZLING 24.1

Each line combines two definitions of the same word. One points to the straight version, the other the pun version that needs to be said aloud. No room for pigs to suppress = STIFLE (STY-FUL). Be careful – the straight clue can come first or last.

Prohibit blue cradle? (7)
Greek god minus 'omburg (5)
Genuine goose spin (10)
Newsreader's guide to traffic jam (7)
Pub ghost examiner (9)
Spotted seabird wine (8)
Trivial broth umpire (11)

QUIZLING 24.2

If the surfie is wiped out, and the baker pie-eyed, how drunk did these other four get at the gala? Some have more than one answer (as indicated in parentheses). You may well create your own fitting descriptions.

Meteorologist (1)   Panel beater (3)   Taxidermist (2) Soldier (3)

QUIZLING 24.3

Can you reconnect these 14 fragments to spell a pun-ful cosmological question? No mixing is needed.

AN CH DZ EC EL EN HM
IA IC NS TO TR UL WO

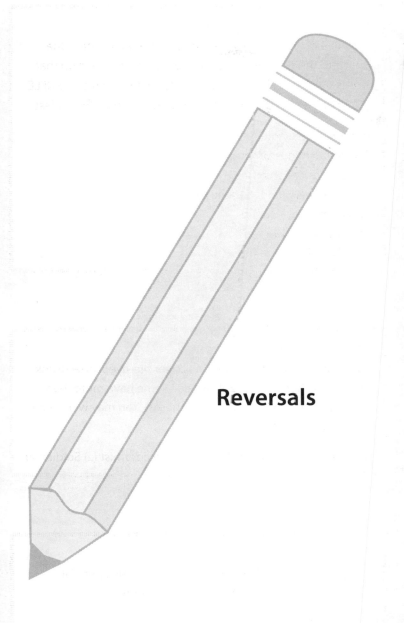

Reversals

CHAPTER 25

Snub regressive outcast (5)

Till now we've been dealing in English and the secret language of words – anagrams, codes and the rest. But in these next two chapters we'll be talking in a tongue called Hsilgne, flipping everything we know and seeing what words reveal in reverse.

Spun around, words can declare wonders. WOMBATS, say, must need their claws to STAB and MOW. Two more animals, ELK and CAT, can U-turn to spell TACKLE, while LAPTOPS are popular with dogs, since SPOT, a common mutt, lies tail-to-nose with PAL, a popular pooch food.

That connection was captured by an Australian racehorse called SIR LAPFONAC, which managed to run a few events at country tracks before stewards woke to the reverse logic and demanded a name change. And some years back, in the same vein, a greyhound did the rounds of Florida with the faux-Aztec name of CILOHOCLA.

Without a stick of proof, I firmly believe that C. S. Lewis coined his mystic kingdom NARNIA owing to the realm nestling in a reversed MOUNTAIN RANGE.

In the Greek alphabet, OMEGA is a paradox, pairing as it does AGE with MO, an eternity sleeping beside a nanosecond. Meanwhile IOTA, a word that also means a tiny piece, can swap initials to be become the equally small ATOM in the rear-view mirror.

Felons, be warned. If running from the law, don't run backwards. BAN, a word for outlaw, only offers NAB, a word for arrest. Later, feeling loveless in GAOL, you'll find cold comfort in forfeiting love (or O) and reflecting on LAG, a vernacular word for prisoner. Appeal against your sentence and you may be NULLIFIED OR REVOKED (which cradles OVERRODE, a third synonym, in reverse).

What was your crime, by the way? Did you try to sneak past the GATEMAN with a bogus NAMETAG, or SCAM MACS at a swap meet? Are you a YOB BOY with a DAB of BAD, or do you LIVE EVIL? Perhaps you secreted ACID, the illegal drug, inside the legal version, MEDICATION? Maybe you chanced on the drug-lab formula, where POT can be switched to make a harder drug:

POT reversed = TOP
TOP = first-class
First class = CRACK

No less bizarre, PAT can change its central vowel to morph into PET, a synonym. Or take a spin, becoming TAP, a second synonym.

If we shift our focus to food and drink we'll find that the onion guards an amazing truth. A member of the BULB family, this tear-jerker reveals BLUB on the rebound. A Chinese waiter, meanwhile, asking if you'd like the WONTON to be served, may well invite the soup in reverse – NOT NOW. And should you be drinking at table, as laudable an Australia winery as DRAYTONS may be, I'd be wary of its flipside, since a red or white may be rendered green.

For Bob Smithies, a young lad growing up in wartime Lancaster, a similar retro-moment took place in his local fish-and-chip shop. There, Bob was waiting for his haddock when he spotted GARTONS, the vinegar on the counter, and giggled. Dangerously, you'd have to say, since the impulse to manipulate words soon developed into Bob's fixation, the boy growing up to become one of the trickier *Guardian* setters, a man known as Bunthorne.

As Orpheus can tell you, there's a genuine risk in looking backwards. You may stumble on wonders and go seeking more. As a kid doing chemistry I loved the fact that TIN sits forwards in PLATINUM and backwards in NITROGEN. In geography, you can look at LEBANON and intuit Cain, since he was the NON-ABEL of the Eden story; or realise that a landscape as dry as the GOBI spells 'one wetland' when lying east to west. You can come to see that BALSA, which is light, can be flipped to be A SLAB, which isn't.

Years later, living in Melbourne, I was riding on tram with a mate, both of us dressed in tuxedos, bound for a fund-raiser in the city. Maybe the novelty of the outfit sparked the question, my friend asking, 'Seriously, what made you get into puzzles?'

By way of answer I pointed to the window. A decal was pasted across the glass, saying YARRA TRAMS. 'Read that backwards and that's what we're wearing.'

DEN RUT – reversal clues

Dylan Thomas knew the charms of Hsilgne, creating the town of LLAREGGUB for his radio play *Under Milk Wood*. In the same year, 1954, jazz composer Sonny Rollins released a tune of fast samba patterns called *Airegin*. The retro-virus was in the air. Even Dracula, in a movie of similar vintage, opts for the alias of Count Alucard to put the villagers' fears to rest.

If it's good enough for poets and the undead, then it's good enough for puzzle-makers. Already, by default, you've met half a dozen reversal signposts in the first section, all those words suggesting a direction switch. These include *turn, spin, flip,* and several combinations using *back*, like the opener in the batch below. The first two clues stem from my own puzzles, while the next two come from the desk of Bob Smithies (alias Bunthorne) and a setter named Cincinnus:

> *Corporal punishment goes back (5)*
> *Monstrous female gets abstemious rule rejected? (6)*
> *Dr Seuss is involved with raising children (6)*
> *A bit of advice about depression (3)*

To crack the first clue, you need to reverse PARTS (or *goes*) to make STRAP, the *corporal punishment*.

Once again, looking at the second clue, the reversal signpost (*rejected*) is planted last, casting suspicion on *monstrous*, or *monstrous female*, as the definition, while the middle section must be the fodder to switch.

Could OGRESS work? What about MEDUSA? Flipping the letters, ASUDEM feels warm, but still doesn't reflect the wordplay – *gets abstemious rule rejected* …

GORGON any good? Spin it and there's your breakthrough: NO GROG. The question mark is the customary warning of the extended leap, a whole phrase on the turn rather than a solo word.

So what is Bunthorne asking us to turn in the third example? Let's take a closer look: *Dr Seuss is involved with raising children (5).*

Scan the clue and guess what word is signalling reversal? *Raising* seems the prime suspect, but how does *raising* denote backtracking? The answer lies in the vertical, as this was crafted to supply a Down solution, and the rules of reversal vary depending on whether a word is lying or standing in the gird.

Physically, it makes sense. If you consider a wordplay block as a caterpillar, lying right-to-left in the grid, then the bug needs to retreat, walk backwards or turn around, to become a fully-grown answer. Likewise, if the caterpillar is traipsing down the grid, then the bug has to head up, go north, scale or mount to metamorphose into your answer.

The second crucial point about Bunthorne's clue is formula. Unlike the first two samples, this is a hybrid clue, blending the categories of reversal and hidden. *Raising*, you now know, alerts us to the idea of an upward reversal. Couple this with the clue's central phrase – *involved with* – and the hidden mode enters the frame.

Difficult clue, but this is Bunthorne. When Bob passed away in 2006, his obituary listed the man's many passions, all of which his puzzles reflected. You name it – jazz, wine, Dickens – and you'd often need it, entering his grids. Here the topic is paediatrics, or is *Dr Seuss* a ruse? Raise the cluster of words and ISSUES will emerge, another word for *children*.

As we'll discover in the next chapter, the reversal formula is a popular mixer with other recipes, and the reason for delaying its appearance in the book. When encountering hybrids, you should always keep the idea of reversal alive, and sweep the wordplay for any talk of moving up or back.

Leaving us with the final example: *A bit of advice about depression (3)*. Breezy on paper, this clue from Cincinnus is handpicked for a reason, namely the dilemma of a central signpost.

Remember the muddle this problem sparked with anagrams? If your cue to scramble sits amidships, then which side is the mixing fodder? Reversals can suffer a kindred curse. In this clue *about* is a subtle signal to U-turn, which is also treacherous, since *about* has also been a steadfast signpost among containers.

Can you sense the oxygen thinning? In the last few chapters we've learnt that recipes can blend, and now we're seeing how certain signposts – like *about* or *off* or *without* – can flag alternative approaches. This is how it should be, scaling the giddy peak of Mount Cleverest. The higher we climb the smarter we have to be, the more caution we need to exercise.

But at least our earlier answers have given us the footholds to help with the final assault. And where hybrids are involved – like Bunthorne's example – or dilemmas emerge – like this latest clue – then we have the experience to get over the challenge. As every PHRASE unravels, we inch closer to becoming a SHERPA.

Here's my TIP then, my *bit of advice about depression*: step light, keep flexible and don't fall down any great PIT, your answer. In a sense, the clue tells you which word needs reversing, the signpost of *about* welded tighter to the first definition. Though in the end we needed to make a leap of faith, and look – we survived. And the summit is beckoning.

Before we advance, though, let's grapple with our Master clue:

Snub regressive outcast (5)

In the grid our toeholds offer R_P_ _ .(Any suggestions?) Remember, we need a word that's flippable, just like PARTS gave way to STRAP. Two words in fact, where one means *snub* and the other *outcast*, with *regressive* your signpost.

Yes, a central signpost again, but now the toeholds come into play. Without them, LEPER (an *outcast*) could be as legit a solution as REPEL (to *snub*). Fill it in. Adjust your crampons. The peak is peeking through the clouds.

RECIPE PRECIS: REVERSALS

Depending on how your answer lies – Across or Down – the reversal clue will tell you to turn your letters back – or up. On the horizontal, watch for such signposts as *around, back, go west, mirror, receding, reflected, retiring, retreat, return, reverse, revolutionary, wheel* and *withdraw*. For the vertical, look for *climbed, flipped, hang-up, head over heels, invert, lifted, mounted, over, overturn, raised, rose, up* and *upset*. Gnivlos doog.

QUIZLING 25.1

What word for careless can be made endless
And reversed to make mates cheerless?

QUIZLING 25.2

If every word in the English language is spelt backwards, which 'word' would appear last in this bizarre new dictionary?

QUIZLING 25.3

Explain why 50 in 09 reversed
Is a weather pattern by which our world is cursed.

CHAPTER 26

Pacific islander immune to revolution (7)

As a bub you're loved by Mum – or Mom maybe – plus your dad, your nan and pop, even a big sis if she's around. More than loved, you are deified. In the eye of kin, your every peep is a wow, every deed you do a minor aha. Developing into a tot, going from boob to pap, you learn to poop in the toot. No longer on the tit, you have enough pep till noon when you hit the cot for more zzzz.

Living proof we are born to palindromes. That last paragraph had 23 of the suckers, words spelt the same in either direction. Twenty-three and you're barely two years old. Stats don't lie.

KAYAK is a palindrome, as is RACE CAR. Both modes of transport are identical in reverse, just like A TOYOTA.

Compare this to words in our previous chapter, where STRAP and BULB render new results when spun. Dimitri Borgmann, a brilliant logologist (or word buff), called this versatile bunch of words *semordnilaps*, where DOG is GOD when chasing his tail.

Try breaking the ice at your next cocktail party by saying, 'Did you know that semordnilaps are also known as volvograms, backwords, semi-palindromes or anadromes?' And see how far that gets you.

Each term is just a fancy label for a city like POTSDAM,

a mad stop on your next Eurail adventure. When TURNED is turned, the wordsmith can imagine a randy lion racked by DEN RUT. Maybe the poor beast is pining for the giant harlots found backwards in STRATAGEM.

Palindromes, on the other hand, are spin-proof. The word derives from Greek, meaning 'running back again'. Twirl RADAR all you like – palindromes are incorruptible.

Believe it or not, a figure named Sotades the Obscene, a poet dating back to 300 BC, is the reputed father of the palindrome, but that's like saying Homer invented the comma, or Aristotle the dangling participle. The palindrome has long been a strand in the human tapestry.

Related in style, a popular writing method in ancient times was called boustrophedon, which literally means ox-turning. If you imagine a bullock pulling a plough, working his way along one furrow, then turning to haul the plough in the opposite direction, then you have the essence of the boustrophedon, where a writer like Sotades might start his first line in standard fashion, left to right, only for the next line to pivot at the end, and travel right to left.

As for why this style was hip among Hellenic scribes, the debate continues. Maybe the reverse line reduced smudges on the papyrus, or abrasions on the tablet, or maybe the vogue rested in our ancient fetish for language looping. Across Greece and Italy, within the grounds of ancient temples, many fountains carry the palindrome of *Nipson anomemata me monan opsin*, which translates as 'Wash the sins, not only the face'.

On conquering Britannia, the Romans built new temples and cities, with one site near Gloucester presenting an opaque palindrome to archaeologists. Known as the Sator Stone, the puzzle was unearthed in 1868 in modern-day Cirencester, a market town north-west of London. Was it a spell? A code? Here's how the original enigma appeared:

SATOR
AREPO
TENET
OPERA
ROTAS

Viewing the square as one line of text, reading left to right, the stone reveals a palindrome, but why? And what did it mean? Theories bloomed in academia. Translation depended on where you divided the words. Either it meant 'The sower Arepo holds the wheels at work' or 'Arepo the sower holds the wheels with force'. Question being: who was Arepo? Was this a word game or did the inscription carry a deeper significance?

As you can see, the five rows match the five columns. Several scholars suspected the text to be an incantation. The idea was bolstered by the ABRACADABRA precedent, this classical word of magic having that near-palindrome knack of being arranged into a pyramid of letters, spelling itself by degrees like so:

A
A B
A B R
A B R A
A B R A C
A B R A C A
A B R A C A D
A B R A C A D A
A B R A C A D A B
A B R A C A D A B R
A B R A C A D A B R A

This two-way patterning is a hallmark of many sacred words – think hocus-pocus or even TENET, our own expression of faith and a word that lies in the heart of the Sator Stone.

Without doubt, one of the more radical guesses about the stone's meaning was made by a German professor who reckoned the text to be a code adopted by the first wave of Christians. With so many Colosseum lions to feed, the followers of Christ needed to keep hush-hush, which explains their use of the secret fish symbol of Yahweh and the clandestine catacomb services beneath the Eternal City. The Sator Stone, said the professor, was one more link in this secret chain. The central piece of evidence for this cultish idea was an anagram. Rearrange the stone's 30 letters and you can create a symmetrical cross, with the phrase PATERNOSTER crossing itself at the central N. With a slight catch. Do the maths, and you'll realise that two As and two Os are missing from the new combo. The professor argued that these were the Alpha and Omega of the Lord's message, a divine punctuation that went to open and close the message. This last liberty alone tended to unglue the theory.

So who was Arepo, the wheel holder? Historians scoured the annals for any mention of the name, but found nil. Maybe the verse was a metaphor? Yet whichever creed was implicated, it wasn't Christianity, as news of Pompeii came to light.

Amazingly, seventy years after the Sator Stone was found in England, a twin was uncovered in Pompeii. The discovery went to cool the Christian theory, given how early in the millennium Vesuvius had erupted and how strong were the pagan vestiges of Pompeii itself. In fact, the fluke of finding a replica stone now urged scholars to favour the wordplay notion. Rather than a piece of scripture, the square was deemed a nifty alignment, a palindrome broken into a tidy box, a feat so neat it warranted chiselling. Arepo and his wheel, in fact, could well comprise the world's first crossword, or at least evidence of mankind's enduring passion for the secret life of words.

NEVER ODD OR EVEN – palindromes from home and away

There she was, a beautiful woman in the grove, tempting the man to approach her with an extended hand and to say, 'Madam, I'm Adam.'

Our first scrap of human dialogue, and it's palindromic. As was the woman's reply: Eve, a name immune to revolution, joining the elite of Anna, Hannah, Elle, Viv and Bob. Meanwhile Anita is forever destined to wash the bucket in Spanish-speaking countries, trapped in the palindrome of *Anita lava la tina*.

Finns hold the record in the single-word category, with their majestic *Saippuakauppias*, or soap merchant, owning pride of place in the Babel dictionary. And should a Swede ever say, *'Ni talar bra Latin'* (or 'You speak good Latin'), then you can probably recite the Sator Stone better than most.

Perhaps the world's best palindrome is French, the jury swayed by the rarity of a Q, as well as the sentence owning the whiff of scandal: *Engage le jeu que je le gagne* (or 'Begin the game so that I may win').

Best known is the 1948 line by Leigh Mercer, an Englishman who saluted a certain engineering feat with some engineering of his own: *A man, a plan, a canal – Panama!* This gem has been spoofed a dozen times, with the pick coming from US sportswriter Roger Angell: *A dog, a plan, a canal – pagoda!*

Maths professor Peter Hilton, once employed as a codebreaker at Bletchley Park, reputedly had a hand in forging one of our sleeker palindromes, despite its length: *Doc, note. I dissent. A fast never prevents a fatness. I diet on cod.*

Dmitri Borgmann, the late word-buff of Illinois via the Ukraine, stylised several longer examples, with his most fluent effort invoking Rome: *A new order began, a more Roman age bred Rowena.*

Longer palindromes exist, of course, with most getting silly after crossing an invisible line. Or they read beautifully, only for a leftover spanner to wreck the works. Here's one by Anon, by far the most prolific palindromist in the Western canon, which opens with an easy grace only to founder by the finale: *We repaid a no-name Pacific apeman on a diaper, ew!*

Which leads us into Polynesia, the focus of our latest clue. After double meanings on the Amazon, charades in Omaha and codes in the Kasbah, we need to swing the binoculars towards a tropical island. Let's view the clue:

Pacific islander immune to revolution (7)

To get REPEL, our last answer, we obeyed the signpost, *regressive*. Here the wordplay invokes the spin-proof quality of the palindrome. HANNAH and ANNA can stand on their heads with impunity. DR AWKWARD can come and go as he pleases. Two clues from my own collection affirm the same truth:

Chopper blade can spin either way = ROTOR
Stand-up act unchanged = DEED

The first is pretty clear, while the second belongs to a Down entry, allowing the signpost of *stand-up* to work, telling you to 'erect' the solution for zero effect. Our current clue travels the same road. Also reading down, the answer won't change for being thrown upward.

After so many palindromes, you also know that if the answer ends in N, it must have N at the start. Ditto for the U in Position 5 of our answer – the same vowel can safely occupy Position 3 as well. Which gives you the promising array of N _ U _ U _ N.

The Pacific solution is NAURUAN, a native of Nauru. According to the World Factbook, your typical islander is likely to speak English, plus his own Micronesian tongue, though probably not the lingo of southern India: Malayalam.

EVE ON REFLECTION – reversal clusters and ambigrams

Backwards or forwards, the words SENILE FELINES give the one message. We call this a palindrome. Whereas a name like EDISON is dubbed an emordnilap, as it spells NO SIDE in reverse, a departure from the source word.

But really, aren't we splitting hairs? Who cares if HANNAH spells herself from right to left, compared to her little brother, LIAM, who goes postal on reflection? Both names defy the natural order of things. Volvogram, schmolvogram – I'm happy to treat both kids as palindromes. Both make sense in two languages: English and Hsilgne.

PAM and EVE, for instance, are both remarkable girls. Both names can change direction – PAM spelling MAP and EVE staying EVE. The first girl has changed wholesale, while the second is notable for resisting change. Or maybe she has changed. EVE, I mean. Let me explain.

Most words are nonsense in reverse, or hold sensible shreds within the bunkum. By way of experiment, let's flip four more Pacific islands. Suddenly Tonga, Tuvalu, Fiji and Tahiti turn into AGNOT, ULAVUT, IJIF, ITIHAT. Mumbo-jumbo mainly, though a few words emerge in the back-wash: NOT, LAV, HAT plus the domestic cleaner JIF. These little flukes fuel the stuff of reverse hybrids, where the setter breaks the answer into smaller pieces, with one piece viewed in reverse. TAHITI, say, might be sliced into HAT + IT + I, with the solver asked to switch the opening fragment.

Those same four islands also confirm the treasure of PAM and EVE. For a word to make sense in reverse is unusual, whether that means retaining your own identity (EVE), or drafting MAP. This rarity alone throws the two categories (palindrome and emordnilap) into the one remarkable box. But straying deeper into the topic, we come across a nagging question of geometry: how 'same' is normal EVE from EVE-in-reverse?

For starters, the letter E faces east, compared to a J, which looks to the west, or right-to-left. Hence, to achieve the EVE illusion as a physical stunt, the E's of EVE would need to perform an about-face. (Picture EVE as a complex shape, rather than a girl's name, and you may see what I'm driving at. Think geometry – not semantics.) The E's need realigning for the palindrome to work purely. To get Zen for a moment, can the same girl return from the girl who made the outward journey? All this may sound inane – or insane – but orientation lies at the gist of some deep-geek wordplay we're about to explore.

TOOT might be closer to being a truer palindrome, as none of the letters needs realigning. Sorcery of this kind enters the genre of mirror-writing, where puzzle-makers and graphic designers treat words as physical constructions, each with their own contours and axes of symmetry. Fog up your bathroom mirror (a 'mirror rim') and vertically write TOMATO. Note how the fruit appears the twin of its own reflection.

SWIMS is another minor miracle. Capsize this page and now read the word. What do you see? That's right: SWIMS. This is known as an inverted palindrome.

Step by step we are nearing the mind-spinning science of ambigrams, the visual equal of palindromes that arose in the *Strand Magazine* of London, in the early 1900s. The feature was entitled Topsy-Turvies, with words like *honey* and *chump* written in strategic script. Overturn the magazine and the words appeared intact.

Madison Avenue pushed it further during the 1960s, coining the term ambigrams along the way. With a few deft touches, DMC (DeLorean Motor Company) could read the same when the logo is revolved. A talented artist could even massage asymmetrical words like *wavelength* or *blacksmith* into ambigrams when the script is capsized. (Check out *Angels & Demons*, the Dan Brown thriller, and you'll see that the first-edition cover can be read spine-left or spine-right.)

To finish on matters reversible, we turn to a pilot named Douglas Corrigan. While the Texan never invented a palindrome, or crafted an ambigram, his deed of 1938 went on to inspire one of the century's great pieces of retro-journalism.

Corrigan was entrusted with the task of flying a single-engine plane from Brooklyn, NY, to Long Beach, CA, a four-hour flight that took our pilot some twenty-seven hours to complete. Corrigan blamed thick cloud and a wonky compass when asked to explain why the plane touched down in Ireland rather than California. Instead of mainland USA, the aviator had crossed the Atlantic by mistake. Though closer scrutiny of the 'bungle' reveals a measure of intent on Corrigan's part, the pilot being found to have carried surplus fuel and food supplies.

Genuine gaffe or not, the bloke came home a different man, much like BOB-in-reverse versus BOB flying eastwards. A ticker-tape parade marked his return, and he went on to write a best-selling autobiography as well as sponsoring a wristwatch that spun anticlockwise. But the headline to enshrine his name appeared in the *New York Post* on 5 August of that year, reading LIAH YAW-GNORW NAGIRROC.

HALL OF FAME: REVERSALS

Overseas race (5) [Taupi, *Guardian*]
Direct from both directions (5) [Mudd, *FT*]
Communist party rising is more unusual (5) [Gemini, *Guardian*]
Also a revolutionary pick-me-up (7) [Crux, *FT*]
Pretentious Brazilian returning greeting in Paris (7) [Viking, *FT*]
Irregular design – zigzag on reverse (7) [Bonxie, *Guardian*]

SOLUTIONS: speed, refer, odder, reviver, bonsoir, wayward

QUIZLING 26.1

Hannah is one of few six-letter names that read the same either way. What's the only common six-letter word with this property? (As a clue, think of one sunbather versus another.)

QUIZLING 26.2

Complete this palindromic sentence:
Anne, I vote more cars race [where to where]?

QUIZLING 26.3

Written vertically in capitals, TOMATO appears unchanged as a reflection. What famous American Indian of eight letters can perform the same trick?

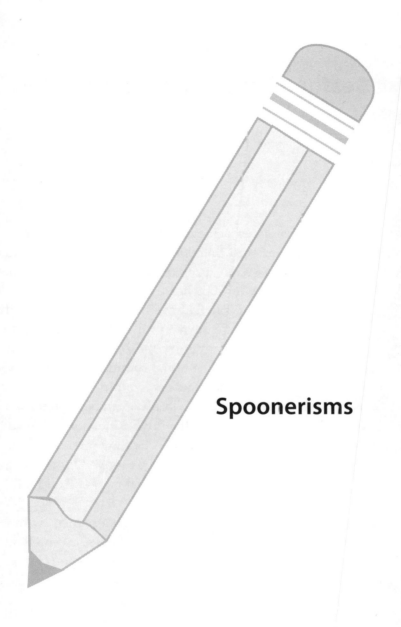

Spoonerisms

CHAPTER 27

Seafood nibble causing pains for Spooner (4,5)

'Not many men have achieved immortality by a happy slip of the tongue,' read one obituary of Reverend William Archibald Spooner – writer, preacher, lecturer, but most of all: bird-watcher. Sorry, word-botcher.

Remarkably, Spoonerism (later to drop its capital) reached the *Oxford Dictionary* while the man still lectured at the same university. With debatable accuracy, the definition reads: 'the accidental transposition of the initial sounds, or other parts, of two or more words'. The debate is twofold.

For starters a *single* word like lockjaw can be spoonerised into jock law, and then there's the iffy business of *accidental*. Spooner fluffed his words, no doubt. Orating for sixty years, from pulpit and lectern, a fellow can be forgiven for tripping over his tongue. But where does a verbal goof end and folk-lore begin?

Numerous sources suggest an undergrad named Arthur Sharp to be a generous font of these verbal gags, invented on campus for the sheer fun of wordplay. Queer dean for dear queen, and so on. Many gems appeared in a collection edited by Sharp, who also went on to become a preacher.

According to the same obit, published in the *Herald* in 1930, Spooner was only ever recorded as making the one eponymous booboo, and that was in 1879 when naming the upcoming hymn as 'Kinquering Kongs, Their Titles Take' instead of Conquering Kings.

Mind you, Spooner was fond of his own legend. Through press stories and humour columns, not to mention the dictionary honour, the man became an accidental celebrity. Or maybe a deliberate one? The debate goes full circle.

Factual or fudged, the famous slung-tipper (tongue-slipper) has been attributed with these examples:

> To a lazy student, the reverend says, 'You have hissed all my mystery lectures and tasted nearly three worms. I must ask you to leave Oxford at once by the town drain.'

> At a wedding, he advises, 'It is now kisstomary to cuss the bride.' And during another service, he tells a parishioner, 'I believe you are occupewing my pie. May I sew you to another sheet?'

> Spooner spends a day looking for a pub called The Dull Man in Greenwich, when the tavern he wanted was The Green Man in Dulwich.

Notice how some of these entail the exchange of internal syllables rather than the swapping of initial consonants, as typifies the modern spoonerism. Today, if a crossword-solver spoonerises *tailpipe*, they'd end up with PALE TYPE rather than the nonsense of TILE PAPE, despite either tweak being a Spooner trademark.

Speaking of pale types, the reverend was a man with paper-white skin. Not quite albino, Spooner was an unusual character to behold. Colleague and biologist Julian Huxley described his friend as 'one with very pale blue eyes and white hair just tinged with straw colour'. Chronically short-sighted, Spooner had to hold books centimetres from his nose. Such eye strain, the spectacles, the striking pallor would inspire another Oxford don to create a famous character. Can you guess who?

Here's a further clue: Spooner had seven children by his wife, Frances, and was often seen hastening from hall to chapel or back again. Observing this was a maths professor called Charles Dodgson, alias Lewis Carroll, creator of the *Alice* books and himself a wordplay genius. Staggering to think that the notable fluffer of words can brag of his own fluffy avatar in world literature, namely the White Rabbit.

Then there's the other issue of Spooner's brain. Without getting bogged down in clinic-speak, so much of Spooner's life embodied what we call the Absent-minded Professor Syndrome. Each of these reputed episodes stands as evidence:

> Asked whether he likes bananas, Spooner replied, 'I'm afraid I always wear the old-fashioned night-shirt.'

> According to cohort Huxley, Spooner remarked of a missing college fellow, 'I'm afraid that when he hears what we did at the college meeting yesterday, he'll gnash his tail.'

> 'Her late husband,' said Spooner of a church widow, 'was eaten by missionaries.'

It's bizarre to reflect that the one clue category to salute an individual commemorates an Englishman who ostensibly suffered a cerebral disjunction. Even if these scraps are hearsay, so much of the Spooner story suggests the man's miswiring.

Conjecture is rife, of course. Did Spooner suffer from a medical condition or was he a natural at rubberising words? The diagnosis is moot and the clinic is shut – but the irony remains. It reads like a cryptic joke, in fact, having history's greatest word-botcher central to a hobby praised for keeping words and memory intact. Or so runs the anecdotal evidence. What are the white mice of Brisbane telling us?

CRACKERS AND CHEESE – mental stimulus and ageing

The Queensland Brain Institute is a neuroscience centre on the banks of the Brisbane River. Much like an office block of the mind, the Institute is dedicated to investigating how we think and how best to thwart the onset of dementia.

One area of research has been messing around with mice, seeing how their neurons fare as a result of exercise. 'Put an old animal on a running wheel,' said Professor Perry Bartlett, the centre's CEO, 'and production of new nerve cells goes up more than twofold.'

Subsequently, the mice are better equipped to tackle a maze, the vermin equal of a puzzle. In the same article, Bartlett echoes the idea. 'Keeping the brain in good shape through a combination of physical exercise and cognitive activity as basic as doing a cryptic crossword could be part of the key.'

The crunch of course is 'could'. CAT scans and mouse wheels can only reveal so much about the neural pathways. In 2003, American neurologist Dr Joe Verghese and his colleagues at the Albert Einstein College of Medicine in New York published the results of a marathon study. The team kept tabs on 469 elderly citizens, none with dementia, and followed their fate for the next two decades, measuring their mental capacity at regular intervals. All the subjects gave details of how they stretched their brain and/or their body during that period.

On the brain side, the activities rating highest were puzzles, reading, board games and playing musical instruments, with dementia less likely to occur among the subjects involved in these pursuits.

'According to our models,' Verghese wrote, 'elderly persons who did crossword puzzles four days a week (four activity-days) had a risk of dementia that was 47 per cent lower than that among subjects who did puzzles once a week (one activity-day).'

On the body side, the best deterrent against mental fog was ballroom dancing, beating general exercise, housework and babysitting. (Bear in mind, these were people over 80, so hang-gliding was out.) Though all categories rated favourably, a foxtrotting cruciverbalist with good social networks (and perhaps plenty of Omega-3) may have a better chance than most of making sense in their twilight.

Playwright Michael Frayn puts it well in the *Chambers Book of Azed Crosswords*. To introduce these devilish puzzles, Frayn writes, 'Here are a hundred of the precious pills all at once. And if one a week keeps the geriatrician away, a hundred together (perhaps taken in conjunction with a few bananas and bars of dark chocolate) must surely be the elixir of youth.'

Though perhaps a *Times* clue from 2008 says it best. You may need to readjust your nerve cells to the anagram mode:

Of outstanding ability till brain decays = BRILLIANT

B-CHORD ON THE KEYBOARD – spoonerism clues and phrase answers

'Hey Dad,' said my son, Finn, sniggering among his Year 8 cronies, 'say this quickly.' He slides a sheet of paper towards me and I read the familiar verse:

I'm not a pheasant plucker,
I'm a pheasant plucker's son.
I'm only plucking pheasants
Till the pheasant plucking's done.

More than likely I peddled the same gag when I was fourteen, given that the spoonerism's a staple of smutty jokes, lame riddles and cryptic crosswords alike.

From a setter's point of view, the spoonerism is a renegade alternative when more obvious approaches misfire. HIGHBORN, another word for privileged, or blue-blooded, is one such entry. The awkward clump of consonants rules out an anagram. Double meaning? HIGH has all sorts of tangents – school, intoxicated – but BORN far fewer. Maybe homophone: HI BORNE (*welcome carried*)? This is the clue-making process – the steady elimination of wordplay options until the right one emerges:

Aristocratic Spooner to purchase trumpet

Thankfully, from a solving point of view, every spoonerism clue will cite the word-botcher by name. While you may encounter a break from this rule, Spooner (the name) is your true watermark.

Kinder than that, many spoonerism clues provide the actual words you need to manipulate. In my HIGH-BORN clue, for example, if the crossword was geared to a simpler level, I might consider:

Aristocratic Spooner to buy horn

These next two show similar mercy:

On-line guide might sap Spooner (4,3)
Was Belle Spooner a biographer? (7)

The first clue hails from 2000, when terms like *online* and *sitemap* (your answer) had yet to shed their hyphens. BOSWELL of course satisfies the second clue, an overhaul of *Was Belle*.

Perhaps the time is right to talk about spelling in regard to our latest category. So far, in the three samples we've seen – HIGH-BORN, SITE MAP and BOSWELL – the transition from one phrase to the answer has entailed a shift in letter patterns. *Might sap* yields SITE MAP, and not SIGHT MAP as a purer swap might involve. Same as HIGH-BORN, which gives *buy horn* (and not the bogus phrase of *bigh horn*). In other words, the sound pattern survives the transit, though often the letter clusters capturing those sounds will vary. And just as importantly, no homophone signpost has to warn you of this spelling drift.

With that in mind, let's move away from the spoon-fed spoonerism, where the actual words in need of mangling are presented, and look at clues where the words are given indirectly. Like these:

> *Handy brew handy, according to Spooner* = NEARBY
>   (spoonerism of BEER NIGH)
> *Spooner's crone snoozes in mining dumps* = SLAG
>   HEAPS (HAG SLEEPS)

Indirect spoonerisms call for heavier lifting. It's even tougher when the fodder you need to manipulate is rolled into a single definition. Here's one such clue from my own backlist:

> *Free squat for Spooner? (3,2)*

If the question mark doesn't warn you of a looser-limbed approach, then brevity is a further alarm. What word for *squat* has two syllables for starters, enough to tweak at least? Thinking from the other direction, what phrase meaning 'free' owns the letter pattern of (3,2)?

LET GO could work. Test your hunch and spoonerise it. There's your reason for the question mark. GET LOW has been translated into *squat*, the solver needing to take that extra leap of imagination.

Some compilers abstain from spoonerisms, while the *Guardian* trio of Paul, Araucaria and Orlando are recidivists. I'm a sucker for the reverend's charms as well. Come Shane or Rhine, the Master puzzle had to have one:

> *Seafood nibble causing pains for Spooner (4,5)*

Warning: this is a hard nut to crack. A key reason is the paucity of information, taking a leaf from the *squat* clue. Does PAUSING CANES mean anything? No. Do we need a new phrase meaning CAUSING PAINS? Not quite.

Coincidentally, another spoonerism from my archive uses seafood as well, its answer a piece of encouragement:

Draw confidence from Spooner's fishcake = TAKE HEART
(hake tart)

Regardless of difficulty, at least you know the recipe involved. On top of that we have some helpful letters, making the endgame a fairer battle. The layout is this:

C _ A _ / _ _ _ C K

Different solvers make different marks to signify a phrase, either in the grid or in the puzzle's margins. Since this is our first phrase, I thought it timely to show you one technique, using slashes to measure out the spaces. Flukily, the very first phrase to appear in a crossword, as condoned by pioneer editor Margaret Farrar, was thought to be SOFT-SHELL CRAB.

Does this bit of trivia help you? Any tasty phrases spring to mind?

Standing in a fish-and-chippery some eighty years ago, a boy called Bunthorne saw the fluke of GARTONS Vinegar. Six months ago, waiting for my own cod to fry, I started dreaming up the Master Puzzle in my head. That's when I saw the richness of CRAB STICK. Like few other phrases, the snack can be switched into a pair of synonyms: STAB and CRICK, two kinds of hurt. And if that's you groaning in the background, relax. The pleasure of solving the spoonerism recipe will long outlive the pain.

RECIPE PRECIS: SPOONERISMS

Spooner is your trigger. Should the reverend's name bob up, start switching whatever initial clusters are on offer. The direct version gives you the keywords cold – like SANE CHORE to yield CHAINSAW – while the indirect kind alludes to the fodder in need of flip-flopping – in this case *rational task* may indicate SANE CHORE, and then you apply the spoon. (Notice in both examples how the CH transfers as a single piece, not just the C.)

QUIZLING 27.1

What simple warm-up exercise,
Seeing athletes leave the ground,
Can be spoonerised to make
A 'shock' beside confound?

QUIZLING 27.2

When spoonerised, this eating area found in most modern malls creates a word meaning 'spoke lovingly' beside a word meaning 'acted aggressively'. Name the venue.

QUIZLING 27.3

In the reverend's deck of playing cards, where the king of clubs is the cling of cubs and so on, what cards can pair with the four clues below?

Bath hint   Helper's nook
U-boat noises   Floozies' fowl

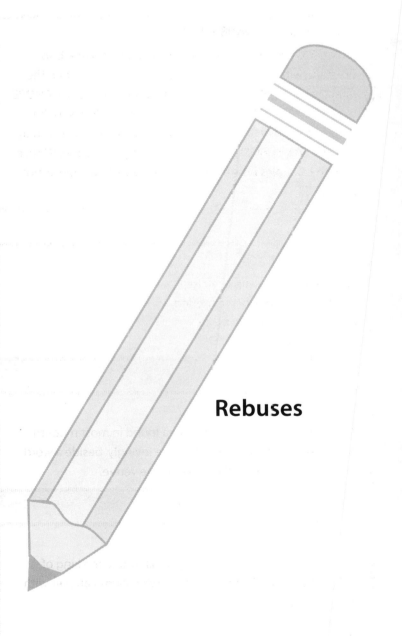

Rebuses

CHAPTER 28

M_ _E (4,2,4)

My physical fix for the first few years after school was rugby. After six years of the three Rs sport was a welcome antidote and I swigged it deep like an ice-cold beer.

Coming and going over six seasons I racked up 100 games with the Gordon Rugby Club, a place that saw me evolve from smart-mouthed teenager to smart-mouthed twenty-something with a drinking problem.

Well, not really. Just Saturday nights, when the novelty of booze combined with the blokey camaraderie. They were wonderful times, those parts I remember.

Being on the field was even more addictive. Skill-wise I wasn't on the Wallaby radar but I made up for my deficits with exuberance. Yet for all the sweat and grunt my principal legacies to the club were not sport-related, but verbal. With an ear for parody, I took to bastardising songs, overhauling lyrics to suit a tribe of North Shore numbskulls in the post-match celebrations. Some of those numbers may still resound under the grandstand today, who knows?

The *Tartan Times*, a scandal sheet I scribed with a second-rower named Scoop, was another landmark. As the name suggests, Scoop was in charge of the dance-floor gossip while my beat was the Wisecrack Department. If I wasn't spoonerising SMART FELLA, I was turning All Black legends into lewd anagrams.

My proudest legacy, however, was doubtless the introduction of SCHULTZ BAKING POWDER. Before I go there, however, I should outline the basic principles of rugby, the line-out included.

The sport is known as brutal poetry, with Team A trying to plant the ball down Team B's end, and vice versa. Part of the tussle entails what's known as a line-out, where the eight bulky types from Team A stand cheek-to-jowl with their rivals from B, leaping for a ball that is tossed in from the sideline. To best disguise where the ball is going, a code is required, and our code for several seasons was SCHULTZ BAKING POWDER.

The phrase is not original, but a coinage of Dmitri Borgmann, our palindromist extraordinaire. In case you haven't noticed, SCHULTZ BAKING POWDER has 19 letters without a single repeat. Even better, the three words allowed the line-out code to pinpoint three locations. Imagine the call was 'Limerick-65'. Ignore the numbers, a total red herring, and focus on the word's initial. Since the L of LIMERICK is in SCHULTZ, the thrower knows to hit the first position. If the call is '1–2–9', then ONE, starting with O, means the final position, as O is found in POWDER. Opponents had no chance. So sound was the code that most grades in the club adopted the subterfuge, though not all.

The farce occurred on a drizzly day at Chatswood, our home ground. We were playing Randwick, our mortal enemies, with ten minutes left on the clock. Rain was thickening, and a finals berth was up for grabs. Mud made the game a test of wills. Every yard was vital, every maul, every line-out. A clumsy tackle saw Drano, our best jumper, wrench his ankle. Medics fetched a stretcher to cart him off.

Enter a plumber called Lurch, not the sharpest knife in the drawer, but his height was the key. If he could win the line-out jump we might steal the edge.

'Call is Charisma-99,' I yelled.

'What?' said Lurch.

I took out my mouthguard, made the message clearer.

'Ninety-nine what?' Lurch yelled back.

'Change call,' I belted out, thinking spelling was the hitch. 'Call is Horse-81.'

Lurch waved his hands. 'Hang on,' he said to the referee. He turned back to me and said, 'Where's the fucking ball going?'

'King Kong-34,' said our jumper at Position Two, and the ball flew in.

At the next break Lurch asked about the code. 'Schultz baking powder,' I whispered, and Lurch blurted, 'Huh?!'

The Randwick players relished the confusion. I sensed my own talent was at risk. Every week, in close selection disputes, the coaches chose the best side for the paddock. And one reason I gained a regular place in decent sides was my Rain Man ability to decode enemy systems. In many ways I was a Station-X geek a few generations out of sync. Randwick was my Third Reich, so to speak. Even in this current mud battle I'd already cracked their code, reducing their throws to tatters, yet here was a plumber blowing our advantage as precious time was ebbing away.

'Who the hell is Schultz?' Lurch wanted to know.

'He's a code,' said the hooker.

'Time on,' said the referee.

I turned to the ref to explain the problem – a bit of gamesmanship, and the ref knew it. Probably in his early fifties, the bloke was a wry character, with a cowlick falling on spectacles the size of Art Deco ashtrays. At first I tried the soft-shoe, told the ref that Lurch was new to the system. He needed briefing, I said.

'Brainwashing more like it,' said Cowlick. 'Get on with it.'

We had no option. The line-out was set. I filled my lungs

and called 'Titanic-26' only for Lurch to swivel around and yell, 'Does Schultz have a T?'

The game was falling apart. Our code was compromised, our vision of finals melting in the rain. Lurch had a solution. 'Just throw it to me and see if I can get it.'

Like I say, rugby is a test of wills. In the end, we may have won that battle. That part I can't recall. Though I do know that Mr Schultz kept a low profile for the campaign's remainder.

GSGE – rebus clues and the elusive definition

Give me a dollar for every time I've heard the Scrambled Eggs Clue and I'd be living in the Bahamas. Seems that every mug's idea of cryptic brilliance is GSGE. Answer: SCRAMBLED EGGS.

If not that clue, then maybe HIJKLMNO, which equals WATER. Get it? H-to-O. And number three on the punter's podium is NOEL, or more precisely: ABCDEFGHIJKMN–OPQRSTUVWXYZ.

In recipe terms, such clues are called rebuses, where a word or phrase is depicted by an array of letters and symbols. Literally, rebus is Latin for 'by things'; this draws on the notion of signs and alignments doing the customary job of words. Other books call them pictograms. Before I was a published puzzler I couldn't resist loading my apprentice grids with rebuses, such as:

MOMANON = man in the moon
1D 2R 3A 4C 5U 6L 7A = Count Dracula
PREIST = clerical error
but but but but BUT = last but not least

GAMES magazine, the puzzle-making bible during the 1980s, labelled these gimmicks Wacky Wordies. Part of the *Playboy* stable, the magazine began life in 1977. Crossword guru Will Shortz edited the title for a time, and the same mag nurtured many fine constructors including Mike Shenk, Henry Hook and Brendan Emmett Quigley. Avant-garde grids, space-age visuals: *GAMES* was my pornography, and just as awkward to buy. Distribution was patchy. Cover prices fluctuated. The magazine went from bimonthly to monthly to new owners to hiatus, but was always worth hunting down. Even today, my desk adjoins two milk crates full of back issues, and many of the ideas from *GAMES* seed the new crop of brainteasers we see across the Web and newsstands today. Picking through the pages I found these Wacky Wordies:

r/e/a/d/i/n/g = *reading between the lines*
GLIBNESS = *mixed blessing*
JU144STICE = *gross injustice*
O _ ER _ T _ O _ = *painless operation*

Rebuses, you can see, lack a definition. The whole thing is wordplay. SKπY doesn't talk about illusory rewards or distant dreams. Instead, it's a cute way of denoting PIE IN THE SKY. Worse than that, to get pedantic for a minute, you'll note that the same rebus ignores a homophone marker, obliging the solver to transfer PI into PIE. But that's the roguish charm of the rebus, a devil-may-care attitude that dodges convention.

Getting back to GSGE, I know that it's the punter's pet clue. First up, the joke is there to get. Anyone can see EGGS in the mixture, and the idea of scrambling (letters or eggs) occurs just as promptly. In chess terms, GSGE is a three-move checkmate memorised by amateurs with no deeper love of the game.

It's a bar trick. A gimmick. GSGE is something a drunk uncle scribbles on a coaster and asks the kiddies to solve at Christmas time. The fact that outsiders embrace it says more about their unfamiliarity with the cryptic rule book than anything else. As God is my witness I'd be prepared to give the dollar back if the same GSGE-lover was made aware of how cryptic clues require a balance of wordplay and definition, and thereby agree that HIJKLMNO is one element short, for all its cuteness.

Agreed, then, that the rebus is a heretic recipe. And rare too. More than wacky, the formula divides the public as much as gangsta rap can split an audience. Some solvers despise the tack, while those in the GSGE camp, as well as some veterans, adore them. I'm split as well. If a rebus is original, and the answer makes me smile, then call me a fan. But if a setter has lifted the idea from mothballs, or the answer is a stretch – no thanks.

Historically, the rebus has amused us for centuries. Antique puzzle books devoted whole pages to this picture play, where letters are gained or lost so rendering a final message. This style, with letters pinched or added, is more in the manipulation mode, but at that time the genre was dubbed a rebus and it still exerts a hieroglyphic cool.

Let's take a look at a few rebus samples. The first two stem from *Guardian* regular Paul, while the last two are mine:

Husky GAG? (6)
D-d-dog? (8)
_ ettle t_ _ bi_ _ (5,3)
estiMAte? (8,5)

Paul is showing more mercy than your average rebus-monger, providing a definition in his two clues. The answer to the first is HOARSE, which means *husky*, and entails HORSE (or *GG*) around A: a visual interpretation of a container clue. Meanwhile his second clue implies CERBERUS, the three-headed dog that guards the gates of Hades.

My own clues *allude* to a definition, going closer to the terse rebus tradition. The first answer is SHELL OUT, as the letters of SHELL have been dropped from *settle the bill*. And the last is EDUCATED GUESS, where *estimate* (GUESS) has its tertiary degree highlighted by capitals.

Ready to make a stab at 3-Down, our lone rebus in the Master Puzzle? More or less, you say. Let's have a look:

M _ _ E (4,2,4)

Wily, this one, mainly due to the lack of definition, or even the hint of one. More in the GSGE mould, the clue is all wordplay without any nod to meaning, though we do have some cross-letters for assistance.

The answer's last word obeys the pattern of L _ S _ . Is it LAST, LOST, LESS? These last two, LOST and LESS, murmur the idea of missing letters, just as the rebus dashes imply. Something-something-LOST, or something-something-LESS? Even if undefined, we know the answer must be a familiar phrase, more or less.

Bingo. The pictogram captures MORE minus OR, hence MORE OR LESS. Half of you will be booing, declaring the clue unfair, but rebuses shrug the customary niceties, and no Master Puzzle worth its name could omit this polarising recipe.

More or less, this chapter's done, though we can't leave without the punch _____ to the _____-out story.

TWO SHOCKS IN SHORTHAND – Pitman and the other man

Doing a journalism degree, I thought it wise to attend a short-hand course during the summer. Given the choice of Pitman Script, the scrawl adopted by most stenographers, versus Pitman 2000, a dummy version for lazy reporters, I went with the latter. Most of my colleagues at the school opted for the tougher stream, being a little more committed to their careers. I should also add that 99 per cent of these same colleagues were female . I felt like a sultan in his harem.

Over time I learnt how to doodle with guessable meaning

and tap out forty words per minute on an asthmatic Under-
wood. When summer school shut, the girls and I swapped
addresses, CAJUSTSE (just in case). A few months later, eager
to host a picnic for my twenty-first birthday, I dug up the
contacts and sent out invitations.

With one catch. In a fatal bid to be clever, I put down all the
details in shorthand, a rebus for the gang to unravel. Twenty
young women, I thought: a perfect foil for the twenty young
footballers also attending, plus the twenty bohemians from
uni. The ideal party mix, except none of the girls showed up.
Not one.

Only later did the penny drop. I'd used the wrong shorthand. My Pitman 2000 squiggle for PICNIC resembled a
sozzled worm to their eyes. Basically, I'd sent a love letter to
twenty sweethearts in fluent Neptunian. Or, harking back to
Mr Schultz, I'd hollered a line-out code to twenty gorgeous
Lurches and consequently the ball was missed.

But that's not the only rebus shock during that period. While
Lurch went on to make millions fixing people's pipes, I then
decided there was more profit in crossword-making, assuming
the *Herald* would employ me. Sprucing up those early grids
during 1982, my last year of college, I sent them to the paper in
the cocky belief that they wouldn't be able to resist.

I was wrong. They resisted for a year at least, with the
editor, Ron Nichols, and the vaunted LB both sending back
reasons why my stuff fell short of the mark. A common beef
was my rebus fixation. RUMEONGIN may well translate as
LONG TIME BETWEEN DRINKS, wrote Ron, but can't you
find a better way to clue it?

Maybe plumbing was a better option after all, or breaking
codes for a spy office in Canberra. But slowly I weeded out
the rebus plague and tested the mainstream recipes, only to
draw more flak.

Trim your fat. Quell the puns. Disguise your wordplay.

Fairer definitions etc.

Back to the drawing board. New grids, new clues, followed by more criticism. Naturally, LB's counsel was easier to hear – the setter a demigod in my eyes – but who was this Ron geezer anyway? Did *he* make crosswords? We'd never met but that didn't stop the man's rebukes. After the third round of heat I decided to take positive action. The *Herald* building, by coincidence, was a block from campus, where my journalism course was winding up. One afternoon, after a tutorial, I skipped across to the Fairfax bunker on Broadway, in Ultimo, asking to see a man called Mr Nichols.

'Is he expecting you?' asked the woman at the counter.

'No.'

Given my lowly status, I wasn't expecting him to even step out of the lift to talk to me. It was almost a rebus moment, seeing a familiar character in an unfamiliar setting, out of context, out of harmony with the norm. Certainly, my brain felt out of whack as a diminutive chap with a cowlick crossed the floor, his hand extended, the glint in his eye magnified by those ashtray glasses of his.

'G'day, ref,' I said instinctively.

'Call me Ron,' he said with a smirk. 'Ron Nichols.'

I tried to speak. My tongue was stone. I was b-o-u-n-d (spellbound).

RECIPE PRECIS: REBUSES

The layout says it all. The rebus clue is unique in its weirdness, an assembly of dashes or typefaces, perhaps a cluster of letters and numbers. With no definition, as a rule, the game is in your hands, as you try to find the word or phrase that lends meaning to the miscellany before you.

SIX OF THE BEST FROM MY REBUS ARCHIVE

SIX OF THE BEST FROM MY REBUS ARCHIVE

wHaTEveR (2,3,4)

PEEP (4,4,4)

pASPalum (5,2,3,5)

FI_TH   WH_ _L (5,2,7)

C O S M O S

C O S M O S (8,9)

A$$ ASS (1,4,3,3,5,3,4,6)

SOLUTIONS: in any case, look both ways, snake in the grass, spare no expense, parallel universes, a fool and his money are soon parted.

QUIZLING 28.1

Can you intuit what familiar seven-word phrase is represented by the text symbol below?

:-$

QUIZLING 28.2

What five Graham Greene novels have been roughly encoded below?

SHUS (3,5,8)   R (3,3,2,3,6)

B

ORE (8,4)

TT (3,5,2,3,6)

nuestro hombre (3,3,2,6)

QUIZLING 28.3

Look closely. That's not an O in each cluster below, but a zero. With that in mind, can you reveal the river, the flavour, the country, the plant and two monsters on display?

0E C0R CA0 PHOE0 SA0CH MAR0AN

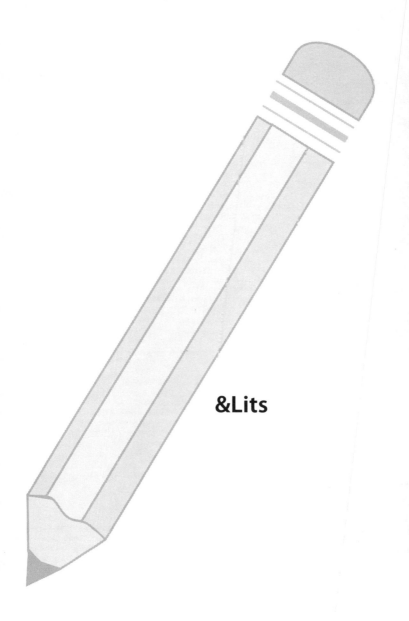

&Lits

CHAPTER 29

Central period in time-spread one spent!(7)

Thankfully, after making me jump a few more hurdles, the *Herald* found a place for me, with just ten crosswords a year. I came to learn that Ron Nichols was a delightful man, while the rebus was a runt compared to the splendour of the &lit.

Don't be daunted by the strange label. You've already met the &lit category, back when we solved ETC, and you survived. In one regard, the &lit formula is the simplest on offer, due to the fusion of wordplay and definition into one unit. At least that's my rough-and-ready explanation. Ximenes does a better job, as he's the man who christened the genre in 1966.

The term &lit is short for 'This clue both indicates the letters or part of the required word … and can also be read, *in toto*, literally, as an indication of the meaning of the whole word, whether as a straight or a veiled definition.'

To remind you, here's that clue for ETC again: *Partial set closer?! (3.)*.

The clue can be read as a definition for ETC. Second to that, the same definition embodies the wordplay; all three words serve dual roles.

But don't go thinking &lits only use the hidden tactic. Till now every category we've tackled has adhered to its own formula. Containers have contained and homophones have sounded, every clue keeping to its separate box. From this moment, however, those boundaries will evaporate as we enter the realm of &lits and hybrids.

Hybrids wait around the corner, the labradoodles of the cryptic pound, but let's first grasp the versatility of the &lit. Depending on a setter's approach, the &lit clue can play with puns or deletions, codes or even rebuses, whichever ploy that accomplishes the feat.

Spoonerism is a category. Reversal is a category. Whereas &lit is an ideal, the pursuit of oneness. Almost every clue we've met has faithfully carried the two necessary burdens – definition and wordplay. Both are separate, despite meeting harmoniously at a clue's midriff. The &lit clue takes intimacy to a new level, like the commingled souls of John Donne's lovers, where the two partners merge into one organism, either lover fulfilling the role of the other. The border is lost.

Here's a glimpse of the anagram &lit – both these samples were made by US duo Henry Cox and Emily Rathvon:

Is a bit less wobbly! = STABILISES
Hunan caterer's site, perhaps! = CHINESE
    RESTAURANT

See how each signpost (*wobbly* and *perhaps*) unifies with the fodder to conspire as part of the definition? In the same vein, MESSAGE IN A BOTTLE could be defined by the wordplay *Drifting item belongs at sea!* Make those 16 letters ITEM-BELONGSATSEA at sea (or confused), and you'll end up with the phrase the wordplay describes.

Not to be outdone, charades can also become charade &lits, as with this gem deriving from *The Times*:

Stop heading for takeaways! (4)

One approach to cracking &lits is to treat each serving as an oblique definition. If you *Stop heading for takeaways*, what are you doing? If that doesn't work, break the clue into pieces. When clocks or engines *stop*, they DIE. *Heading for takeaway* is a deft means of signalling the letter T, the head-letter of *takeaway*. Join these two pieces in charade style and you make DIET, or *Stop heading for takeaways*.

Adhering to a strict &lit diet, these next two morsels are the container kind, again from *The Times*:

Sweet best to keep cold! (4–3)
Something carried about in box! (7)

Your first answer is CHOC-ICE (C for Cold inside CHOICE, or *best*), while FREIGHT (RE in FIGHT) solves the second. Succinct and elegant, &lit clues are like hen's teeth, as the ideal of fusion is elusive. Speaking from experience, they usually entail some minor epiphany at the drawing board. You suddenly see how a word like THEOLOGY, say, contains EGO, which seems the answer's counterforce. The leftover letters are THLOY, which gives rise to the anagram &lit:

Ego hotly disputed by this study!

That's the epiphany, realising for the first time how the answer's definition shares a compatibility with the wordplay. Priest-like, you marry two souls into one.

No doubt, after meeting a few &lits, you've realised how the exclamation mark is a staple. This is despite the lament of F. Scott Fitzgerald, author of *The Great Gatsby*, who warned all aspiring writers that 'The exclamation mark is like laughing at your own joke.' I can only imagine the great man was chiding novelists, since clue-writers have little choice but to tag &lits with the offending item. In Cryptopia, punctuation is etiquette. Though not quite a golden rule, the exclamation mark is certainly a dominant trait of the &lit formula.

Not that every exclamation mark is automatically a sign

that the &lit is in operation. Ximenes was once censured by a solver for stabbing his clues with far too many of the emphatic little critters. The solver, conceded Ximenes, had a point. The setter assessed his own work to see the plague of screamers (as printers dub exclamation marks) and consequently vowed, 'Now I try to use much more restraint in this matter and to use them only when I am exclaiming, or for a technical purpose ....'

Because that's the gist. Occasionally a clue will shout by virtue of its message, with no &lit implicated. Here are two examples from my own bottom drawer:

> *'Tax!' yelled lunatic with triumph* = EXALTEDLY
> *Retro French artist almost curses!* = EGAD [DEGAS
>   minus S, reversed]

Now and then the exclamation mark admits a clue's own cheek, like Paul's racy double meanings in the *Guardian*:

> *Molest a little higher!* = TOUCH UP
> *Mad? They must be cracked!* = NUTS

Of course, when the stars align and the setter is moved, cheekiness plus the rigours of &lit can coalesce. For me that moment came with WONDERBRA:

> *Naughty piece in fashion wardrobe!*

To decode the wordplay: naughty piece is N, joining WARDROBE, which, once fashioned, tailors the underwear.

If it calms your nerves, we can use the word 'literals' as a label for &lits, since that's the way to tackle them – *literally*. You register the exclamation mark, and you read the clue as its own definition. Think about what the clue might suggest and see if any wordplay supports your early stabs.

So far, among the Master clues, we've bumped into three

screamers and each of these clues – KASBAH, GEN-X and ETC – own strong &lit tendencies. Connoisseurs can argue about their purity, but all three cases see the answer's definition carried largely by the wordplay. Our current clue, 10-Across, is our final encounter with the exclamation mark, and again the &lit balance seems on offer. In the next section, let's do some literal un-mingling.

MEANWHILE … – double- and triple-barrelled &lits

Glance at the grid and you'll probably pounce on the answer of our Master clue. With every cross-letter in place, no other word fits the pattern. It has to be INTERIM. But that's less solving than sealing the gaps. For any fan the joy of cryptic crosswords rests in the clues. If this were a quick puzzle, I'd understand your haste. Why bother reading a prosaic definition if you've already hunched the answer?

But a cryptic is much more than a single puzzle. Each clue is in fact a tiny puzzle in a larger challenge. If nothing else, the pleasure of sampling these smaller conundrums should prompt you to see how INTERIM is reached:

Central period in time-spread one spent! (7)

Okay, let's work backwards. We have the answer, so how does the clue get us there? In the &lit tradition, the overall clue reads as an approximation of INTERIM, the time stretching between two points. Too approximate, perhaps, to please a sober dictionary, but sound enough on the puzzle page. So there's the definition – *in toto* as Ximenes decreed. What about the wordplay?

Focusing on the pieces, you see that *central period* gives us RI, the middle pair of *period*. The next part, *in time-spread*, could be read as anagram fodder plus signpost. Is that the recipe in action? Reviewing what we've collected, RI + INTIME, the outcome of INTERIM is teasingly close, but we have too many letters. Checking the fodder we have INTERIM + I. So how do we lose this surplus I?

Here's where the clue's tail comes to the rescue: *one spent.* Spending is another word for depleting. Once 'I' is disbursed from the eight, we have the raw material for INTERIM. The clue, we've discovered, uses two categories – anagram and deletion. Some may call this clue style a complex anagram, others would plump for hybrid, while this chapter prefers the triple-barrelled label of anagram/deletion &lit, just to underline how far we've come.

Not that our trip is over. Putting to bed the last &lit, we now face the labradoodles in the pack – alias the hybrids. The species might seem friendly enough but that would be to overlook the creature's natural curliness.

RECIPE PRECIS: &LITS

The pinnacle of clues, &lits mean 'and literally', as the wordplay literally acts as the definition. *Many set free!* (for example) doesn't just define AMNESTY, but the wordplay yields the same answer. Unlike other categories, the &lit clue obeys any recipe, so long as the wordplay and definition are fused. Brevity and the telltale exclamation mark serve as your best guides.

Hall of Fame: &Lits

Leading pairs to animal home involved him (4) [Aardvark, *FT*]

Original back to nature author! (7) [Puck, *Guardian*]

Difficult case (section), ending in operation! (9) [Paul, *Guardian*]

Alternative, say, to the op? (10) [*Times* 8641]

Besides the previous filling, might this prevent another? (10) [Paul again]

Result of a piercing tool! (10) [Henry Hook, US]

SOLUTIONS: Noah, Thoreau, caesarean, osteopathy, toothpaste, impalement

---

QUIZLING 29.1

When a Kenneth Grahame character
Gains the tail, ST,
The SYNONYM for a second character
Among the willows you'll see.
Name both animals.

QUIZLING 29.2

What six-letter ailment sees the last five letters describe the physical attributes of the affliction's initial?

QUIZLING 29.3

Autologues are words that literally describe themselves. Ampers& spells ampersand, and inh_man is another way of saying heartless. Can you work out the reasoning behind the way these six words are depicted?

| LONDON | e_punge | paci_ _ _ _ |
| hero | bl_nd | d r u g g e d |

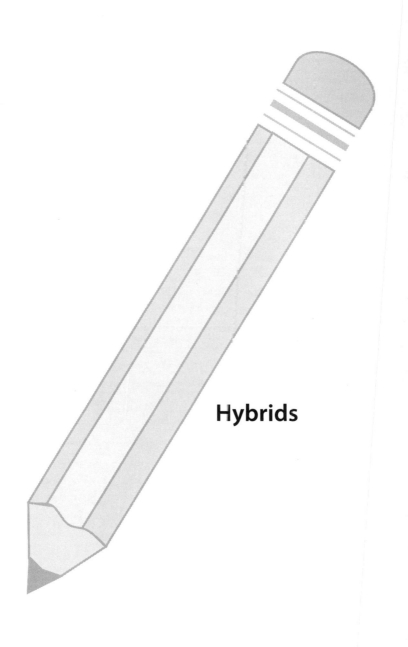

Hybrids

CHAPTER 30

Almost completed month hosting upstart libertine (3,4)

'Know any good crossword songs?'

The gauntlet had been thrown by a school in Melbourne. They wished to run a trivia night with a crossword dimension. About 100 people took part, dressed in black and white, determined to crack a crossword, clue by PowerPointed clue. To make Crossnight a proper success, all we needed was the right kind of music.

Plenty of artists, from Bee Gees to Pink, have cut a number called 'Words', but could we go one better with a direct crossword mention? Come the night, students burnt a disc of twenty songs with a cruciverbal hint, including:

'Looking for Clues' – Robert Palmer
'Hip to be Square' – Huey Lewis and the News
'Across the Universe' – The Beatles
'Down on the Corner' – Creedence Clearwater Revival

Hip hop of course has lent a new chic to wordplay. There's even an artist called DJ Clue, and a guy called Method Man whose remix called 'The Riddler' is all about my favourite lime-green psycho. But finding songs with rock-solid mentions of crossword puzzles was a taller order.

The night went well, by the way. We raised a few grand for a remote health clinic, solved a few clues, but the music challenge lingered. Over the weekend, I combed lyric data-bases to uncover this bizarre medley:

- 'Crosswords' by Tim Finn, formerly of Crowded House. The track describes a couple out of sync with each other – he's down, she's across. In bed, he'll turn, she'll toss.
- 'Crossword' by Jethro Tull – 'your brain on the train to test'.
- In 'My Old Man', Ian Dury and the Blockheads sing about solving a crossword at the airport. Or failing to solve one.
- The Partridge Family released an album entitled *Crossword Puzzle* in 1973, complete with themed grid on its canary-yellow cover. (Just as Neil Diamond, three years earlier, had converted his face into a dot-to-dot portrait on his *Shilo* LP.)
- Confucius, reckons Tori Amos in her 'Happy Phantom' song, does his crosswords in pen, while in 'Drug Me', the Dead Kennedys claim that crosswords are a government conspiracy to sedate the masses.
- INXS mentions crosswords in 'Simple Simon', not to be confused with XTC, whose 'Mayor of Simpleton' shuns them.
- The all-German metal-heads called Cryptic Carnage have some crossword references in their backlist, such as 'The Wizard', 'The Guardians Awake' and 'High Hopes'.

By all means, hope away. There's nothing wrong with optimism in the face of our next challenge: the hybrid clue. Just bear in mind the words of lyricist Stephen Sondheim, writer of such shows as *West Side Story* and *Sweeney Todd*, as well as his own cryptics during the 1970s. His belief: 'The nice thing about doing a crossword is you know there is a solution.' Sounds obvious, though compare that certainty to all life's other problems. Crosswords are built for breakthrough, that piñata euphoria.

And keeping with music, our current clue has a faint underscore of Mozart. Time to segue to the second movement to see how the clue's composed.

UP FOR THE RUMBLE – slash method and hybrid clues

The reason that rookies fear hybrids is because of the lengthening of the mental question list. As a rule, facing a cryptic clue, the solver asks two questions:

Where do I draw the line between definition and
    wordplay?
What recipe is involved?

Along come hybrids, with recipes plural, and the list gains a third question:

Where does one piece of wordplay end, and the next
    recipe begin?

Clue division, in other words, needs an extra slash or two. Before we grapple with the *upstart libertine* in our latest clue, let's slash a beastly schoolmate, as created by Crucible, a *Guardian* setter:

Beastly schoolmate misbehaved, caught out (9)

Divided into its correct pieces, Crucible's clue would look like so:

Beastly/schoolmate misbehaved/caught out

Section One is the definition. Two, you can tell, is the anagram, with fodder adjoining a signpost. The tail is a deletion, telling you to remove the *caught* (or C in cricket shorthand) from a scrambled SCHOOLMATE. In earlier chapters we encountered this style under the banner of compound anagrams, where SUDOKU minus U can be jumbled to make KUDOS. So there's nothing to fear. We've done the miles. We've met one type of hybrid and beaten it already.

To expose the mechanics further, let's break the school-mate clue into an equation form:

Synonym of beastly = scrambled SCHOOLMATE – C

Distilling the elements further, we can fuse the recipes into a single challenge:

Synonym of beastly = scrambled SHOOLMATE

LOATHSOME is the solution. You ready for another? Just recite that mental list – instead of two tasks, the hybrid demands three. Here's one from my own collection:

Hawaiian bloke held out long iMac? (3,3,9)

It's a stiffer challenge this time, with no anagram involved. So, Question 1: Where's the definition? Question 2: Which recipe can you see? Question 3: What other recipe(s) remain? To give you a boost, I can tell you that the segments fall this way: *Hawaiian/bloke/held out/long/iMac*

Cross-letters would be a big help, of course. Let's imagine that our mystery phrase is among the last to join the grid, much like our current hybrid. Hence we know that the middle word is AND. Meaning we're seeking a *Hawaiian*, or an *iMac*, that's (3, AND, 9).

But which formulas are on display? Here again is the equation approach, with one of three ways of reading what we see:

Phrase meaning *iMac* = synonym of *Hawaiian* + MAN
(or man's name?) on the outside + word meaning
long

> Phrase meaning *Hawaiian* = synonym of *bloke* around
> out (or word meaning out) + synonym of *long* +
> *iMac*

> Phrase meaning *Hawaiian* = synonym of *bloke* inside
> synonym of *held* + word for *long* + *iMac*

Feeling peckish? The answer is HAM AND PINEAPPLE, also known as a Hawaiian pizza. The breakdown goes like so – HA(MAN)D+PINE+APPLE. Hybrid clues resemble pizzas in a way, the Four-Seasons kind. If standard clues follow a single recipe, then hybrids combine at least two styles. The kitchen may deliver a Mexicana/Vegetarian – two flavours in one – but ultimately the contrasting slices combine to make the whole.

The moment feels right to wheel out the Master clue:

Almost completed month hosting upstart libertine (3,4)

With a lack of shuffle markers, you can scratch out anagram. Then again, a container clue looks probable, owing to *hosting*. Second, we can suspect *upstart* as a pointer for U, which already appears as a cross-letter.

The grid suggests that the first word is either DAN, DEN, DIN, DON or DUN – each a viable word or name. Which candidate is favoured by the wordplay? If we seek a *libertine*, then the phrase to yield the opening word must be *almost completed*. How does DONE minus E seem? Can you name a Lothario called DON? Mozart composed an opera about the rogue, one Señor Giovanni, based on the Spanish legend and also the subject of the Byron poem. DON JUAN is your hombre, but how does the rest of the hybrid pan out?

> *Almost completed* (DONE – E) *month* (JAN) *hosting*
> *upstart* (around U) = *libertine*

There you have it, a deletion/charade/container all nestled into one, plus a splash of libretto and libido. And like Mr Juan, you proved equal to the hanky-panky.

READ MY LIPS – nobbled novels and lipograms

John Gadsby hails from Branton Hills, an imaginary township short of vigour. Not that Gadsby is all passion and pop, but gradually this chap brings back that missing X-factor by inspiring young folk to add a bit of razzmatazz.

Sound odd? That's because the paragraph above lacks an 'E', the most common letter in English. And that was a mere forty words. Imagine 50,000 words, the Gadsby story from go to whoa, and you'll understand the feat that Ernest Wright accomplished in 1939. His novel – *Gadsby: Champion of Youth* – is a full-blooded lipogram, or text excluding certain letters. Arising in Greece, this strange practice was born of literary discipline and/or masochism. Wright himself is a puzzle to unravel, dying, aged 66, days after his opus hit the streets. He would have published *Gadsby* sooner, but none of the major players thought the gimmick worth the risk, obliging the author to self-publish. (What must have burnt Ernest even more was that the name of the vanity press – Wetzel – boasted two of his taboo vowels, just as his own name did.)

The story of course is written in the present, as the -ed ending of the past participle was too restrictive. A stickler to the last, Wright also dodged such abbreviations as St. (for street) and Mr (Mister). In essence, working from a Tampa nursing home, Wright only had half the dictionary on which to draw. Since his passing, the novel has grown in stature, with French writer Georges Perec paying literary tribute with his own 50,000-word lipogram called *La Disparition*, published in 1969. The work shadows a band of klutzes seeking the missing Anton Vowl, the whole mystery devoid of E.

And if that's not mind-blowing enough, consider the feat of Gilbert Adair, who translated Perec's work into English, sans E, under the title *A Void*.

All this talk of omission and avoidance is apropos of the J in DON JUAN. As you'll recall, the Master solution carries the alphabet, bar one letter. An accidental lipogram, if you like. Or a thwarted pangram, with J the twenty-fifth and final unique letter to be recruited. As hard as I tried, plying the final three answers to come, I couldn't find room for the exiled F. Ironic really, given the arrival of an infamous libertine. Of all sagas, even Perec or the brilliant Ernest Wright would struggle to translate *Don Juan* without recourse to the F key.

RECIPE PRECIS: HYBRIDS

A catch-all formula, the hybrid clue sweeps up two or more recipes. Spooky as that sounds, every rule we've met so far is still in effect. If reversal teams up with anagram, then the two signposts (of recession and renewal) need displaying. Same with homophone and deletion – expect cues for sound and removal. Be alive to each word and try to distinguish which is signpost, which is link, which fodder, and which definition. That way, you can break up the clue correctly, using the equation method if handy, and stalk the solution step by step.

QUIZLING 30.1
The title of which major hit written and performed by Bob Dylan only uses letters (as often as necessary) from the singer's own surname? (And what song title by a British songwriter, released a year later, also follows the Dylan restriction?)

QUIZLING 30.2

Can you dredge up a well-known European river that not only sounds like a horse, but also can be mixed to spell a creature frequenting rivers?

QUIZLING 30.3

We have an American state in mind. Delete its opening M, and the remainder can be mixed to spell a particular European. Which state?

CHAPTER 31

Disorientated, guided east of tall grass zone one slashed (10)

We have B _ M _ O _ Z _ E _ to fill, so let's stop beating round the bush. Enter BAMBOOZLES – the obvious answer – and on we go.

Or wait. Maybe BAMBOOZLED is what we need. Champs can come unstuck making tournament slips like that, bungling one square in their haste to complete the whole. Both words fit – but which is right?

We have two ways to check: the definition's case and the wordplay. A past-tense definition must have a past-tense answer. New solvers – and setters too – can overlook this golden rule. Without considering wordplay yet, check the definition's tense, and you should confirm that last iffy square:

Disorientated, guided east of tall grass zone

Disorientated has the necessary –ED ending. We're BAMBOOZLED no longer.

Remember this when parsing clues. *She* in isolation cannot signal HER or HERS. The case must agree. With verbs the trick is valency, a fancy word for how any word combines with others around it. As you know, verbs are divided into two camps – the transitive and intransitive kind, with quite a few swingers who sneak across the border.

In lay-speak a transitive verb requires an object to receive the action. If you chase, then you must be chasing something. Different from when you run, which doesn't require a fugitive as such. People can run for the sake of it, no object needed. Of course run is one of those bed-hoppers that can answer to intransitive (*The athletes run*) or transitive (*The school runs the carnival*). These nuances matter when deciphering the definition element.

Imagine *eat* is the straight part of the clue. This could mean NIBBLE or DEVOUR, even ERODE or CORRODE, but misfires as a synonym of CATER or SATISFY or STRESS (as in *to be eaten* by worry). A verb can't perform a function outside its job description, or turn back on itself from clue to grid. If the setter offers *itch*, then the solver shouldn't think SCRATCH.

Don't worry. I won't be reciting the subjunctive any time soon. Too many souls more learned than I (or is it me?) have wandered into the Grammar Jungle never to return. Language is treacherous, as a cryptic puzzle demonstrates. Even fake ones, such as the outlandish case involving English writer Sir Max Beerbohm.

The hoax occurred in 1940, ensnaring thousands. For all his literary prowess, Beerbohm battled to solve the *Times* crossword, finding its clues 'disastrous and devastating'. So he plotted revenge, making a cryptic that looked like the real thing yet made little sense on closer scrutiny. Next he persuaded the *Times* editor to collude, the bogus puzzle running in June as a replacement for the real McCoy.

The typeface was right. The pattern had symmetry. Everything seemed hunky-dory, even the tone and mood of Beerbohm's clues. *A Manx beverage*, for one, had to be a deletion clue (since Manx cats have no tail), but where was the definition?

I'm in the old Roman bath was another booby trap, possessing all the container hallmarks, yet solvers across London found no joy in NIMERO, or CAESIMAR, or any other combo that might lead to a sensible solution.

Pitying the solvers in advance, the editor ran Beerbohm's own confession on the same page as the phoney puzzle. As to whether every solver noticed the admission, that could be measured by the level of screams and teeth-gnashing across the capital. This was disorientation on a grand and sadistic scale.

Versus our current clue of course, a legitimate hybrid with BAMBOOZLED the lock-in answer by virtue of the letter pattern, plus the clue's tense. Though before we delve into the intricate whys, let me continue to explore the idea of bafflement, as there are those times in Puzzleville, composing clues, when a dictionary can pull a Beerbohm on you, creating more questions than answers. As it happens, the prime example relates to the tall-grass world of horticulture.

WOOD FOR THE TREES – opaque definitions and Hookworm Syndrome

The word was *imparipinnate*. I turned to the *Macquarie Dictionary, Third Edition* (the *Herald*'s adjudicator), but the entry was less than lucid:

(adjective) pinnate with a terminal leaflet

Naturally I looked up *pinnate*, which wasn't much better. The first definition made sense (*shaped like a feather*), but the second bamboozled:

(of a leaf) having leaflets or primary divisions arranged on either side of a common petiole or rachis

So I looked up *petiole*, which seemed pretty clear:

the stalk by which a leaf is attached to the stem; leafstalk

Inspiring me to check out rachis, only to enter more brambles:

> the axis of an inflorescence somewhat elongated, as in a
> raceme

Adding further to my woes was the subsidiary definition:

> b. (in a pinnately compound leaf or frond) the prolongation
> of the petiole along which the leaflets are disposed

To a mug gardener, that last bit sounds like the stem that veers off the stalk, holding the smaller leaves, but I could be wrong. You can't approximate at the coalface. The solver needs to know if they're chasing a stick or a leaf, and *botanical term* – the phrase – is so general as to be odious. In the end I scrapped IMPARIPINNATE, the only word to fit my tortured pattern, and trudged back to square one.

As a rule, composing definitions is the simpler side of the job, though brevity can be a challenge. Facing STEM CELL one day, I turned to the *Collins Third Edition* which gave me a mouthful in return: *undifferentiated cell that gives rise to specialised cells, such as blood cells*. Well and good if the cell-word wasn't mentioned three times.

Because the other no-no, after long-winded definitions, is to define the solution using words that are actually within that very answer. Borrowing *pinnate* to explain *imparipinnate* is equivalent to a clue-maker defining CAR BOMB as *explosive device wired to car*, or INCONSOLABLE as *incapable of being consoled*. I don't mean to be churlish. Both *Collins* and the *Mac* are fine dictionaries, but even the best can err on the side of recycling.

Tiny words can sneak through the cracks, too. You can't clue TIP OF THE ICEBERG as *the small noticeable part of a more complex problem*. Why? Because the definition carries two words (*the, of*) that also appear in the target phrase.

The other peril to avoid as a clue-maker is the Hookworm

Syndrome. Back at uni I secured my first puzzle job crafting a crossword for the student newspaper. A big part of the credit must go to Mr Hammer. This was 1980. The media faculty was full of part-time Trotskyites and belligerent lesbians, those born with placards in one hand and megaphones in the other.

Fresh out of school, besotted by the anarchy, I was swept along by the constant protest. *Less fees! More rights!* One day we occupied Mr Hammer's office, refusing to move until certain undertakings were met. I can't recall the bugbear, nor the dean's first name, but we sat in his suite and chanted angry slogans, most entailing radical wordplay.

Hammer and Sickle. Claw Hammer. Sledge Hammer. We worked all the angles. I warmed to the puns, and next week composed a 15x15 grid for *NEWSWIT*, the campus rag, loaded with all the combos we missed: *hammer and tongs. If I Had a Hammer, Hammer Horror* and more. The lesbians loved it. Rabble-rousers stopped me in the hall to commend me on the HAMMERSTEIN clue, the hybrid that managed to blend our dean of studies, Boris Karloff and *South Pacific.*

The gig turned regular. I had free rein, and added all sorts of undergrad rubbish, slowly getting the feel for a puzzler's responsibility. The art of losing gracefully. The Piñata Principle.

I dabbled with alcohol – the theme – and shaped Crosswit to resemble a beer bottle. I went wild with rebuses and learnt how to be subtle without being unfair. Partway through the series I ran a clue for HOOKWORM: *Catch bait for parasite?*

'Nu-uh,' said Baz, my mate-cum-critic. 'Not a good clue.'

'Bad taste?'

'Bad clue.'

Hookworms, Barry reckoned, are called hookworms owing to their hook-like shape. So having *catch* as a clue for HOOK was weak enough, but plumping for *bait* to signal WORM was out-and-out shabby.

'Might sound picky, but you're really just defining each part without doing any wordplay. It's like, it's like ... I dunno. It's like HOOKWORM. Do something different next time.'

He was right – it did sound picky. But the comment stuck, and Baz's wisdom has lingered, much like hookworm. (Five years later, for a brief while, I asked Barry to babysit my puzzle correspondence while I was travelling, until I discovered his standard reply to all enquiries was *Dear Solver, Get a life. Yours, Wordwit*.) But my friend knew his onions when it came to clue science, his snub on campus now a commandment: *Thou shalt not use definition as wordplay*.

Easy, you'd think, but the trap is subtle. You can halve PIGEON into PIG and EON, and experiment with ideas of glutton or porker (PIG), plus time and ages (EON), but don't expect the same impunity when clueing GUINEA PIG. The fat little critter is named after the pig – so glutton and porker both seem a rehash.

On a subtler level, for a setter to toy with the LABOR chunk lying in ELABORATE is also dubious. Both notions draw from the one well. LABOR as toil (in its US guise) and LABOR (the Australian political party) share their root; while ELABORATE is also part of the work-related family, given its Latin meaning 'worked out'. A delicate piece of filigree is elaborate for the very reason that it has been worked into shape. Ditto for an elaborate plot, a fancy wedding dress, or a hybrid clue for that matter.

HYBRID TANGO – wordplay sequencing

Disorientated, guided east of tall grass zone one slashed
(10)

We know where the definition sits, as we know the answer. But how does the wordplay play out? Write BAMBOOZLED on paper and apply the logic in reverse, seeing how the answer renders the clue, rather than vice versa.

Fittingly, this clue is elaborate. Leaner hybrids will step a solver through each wordplay, much like the DON JUAN example: DON + JA(U)N. But this clue prefers to take two steps forward, then one step back. Let's slash the definition and focus on the wordplay:

guided east of tall grass zone one slashed

Jumping out is *tall grass*. If you're thinking BAMBOO, then you're on the money. Now to reckon with the tail: ZLED. A practical way is to swap what we've already confirmed within the clue:

guided east of BAMBOO zone one slashed

Compass points are frequent on the cryptic page. Whenever a word like point or direction appears in a clue, summon the map. Just as talk of notes and keys can signify the tonic scale (do, re, mi etc.), or A through to G.

Yet here, cruelly, ironically, *east* is tied to orientation. Anything east of BAMBOO will lie to its right. (A similar stunt was pulled in the QUIZ clue, where the word *behind* directed you to park the Z after the QUI.) But back to BAMBOOZLED, can you see how ZLED stems from the leftover wordplay?

Guided is another word for LED. This lies *east of tall grass* (or BAMBOO). But what about that pesky Z? How's this explained in *zone one slashed*? The verb should nudge you in a deletion direction.

Can you see it? When ONE is slashed from ZONE, you're left with a Z, the final step in a complicated dance. On paper it goes like so:

Disorientated (BAMBOOZLED), LED east of BAMBOO
   Z

Disorientated? That's why I'm here to guide you. Don't expect to undo these harder hybrids at first blush, or second blush. But glean what you can. And rely on the purer clues to give you the cross-over letters you need to tame the hybrids. After thirty years of grappling with tricky puzzles, I can promise you that tall grass is not the only place to get bamboozled, yet that's half the fun.

QUIZLING 31.1

Grass skirt possesses a triple-S, as do these other solutions.

Cinderella souvenir (5,7)   Holy burner (4,5)
Proles' battle (5,8)   Harvard for one (8,6)
Where queens lie (5,3)   Sewer's X? (5–6)
It's dishwasher-proof (9,5)   Fastener (5,4)
Tasmanian moat? (4,6)   Horny bunch? (5,7)
Sheriff often (7–6)   Where you swear (7,5)

QUIZLING 31.2

Call yourself clever if you can sever
An Italian city's head,
And switch the remaining thread
To reveal the vernacular for spectacular.

QUIZLING 31.3

Can you switch one letter of Queensland's AIRLIE BEACH to its immediate predecessor in the alphabet, then 'develop' the new combo to spell two African republics?

CHAPTER 32

Press disrupt opening about Russian writer (8)

dizzy as a butterfly
with praise before
the catcher's expectant mouth
love …
i love to love …

the holy attender understood
only music
as a rope down the throat
tied to …

a net

Peter Valentine broke his poem into three clusters for a reason. Every word in the first group, from *dizzy* to *love*, comes from the Across clues of the *New York Times* crossword published on 30 January 2006. The second verse ransacks the Downs, while the answer grid has provided the coda – *a net*.

The title of this curious work – *love, once noticed* – stems from either clue or answer. Crossword poems were invented by Valentine back in 2002. One day, tackling a tricky Thursday puzzle, Peter stared blankly at the page. He saw the rich wash of language and tried to create something beyond the day's clues. 'My poems pay attention to the incidental details,' he told Nikki Katz, author of *Zen and the Art of Crossword Puzzles*.

You can read more of Peter's magpie creations at www. hungrybutscared.com. Or maybe you'd like to craft your own crossword poem based on the Master puzzle. Here's my own effort, entitled 'Creepy Binoculars':

Why laugh for ignorance?
Press on, absorbed in remedy,
one twister completed, bar final pains.

Weather chaos. Expose new means to focus.
Be partial and avidly get closer
To superb revolution.

Climb trapeze, more or less.

Emily-Jo Cureton, another New Yorker, has adapted crosswords in a different way, selecting answers to prompt an illustration. On 26 August 2008, for instance, two Down entries (BROCCOLI and HYSTERIA) prompted Cureton to draw the vegetable bound in a straitjacket, the image framed by the crossword-in-progress.

Cureton maintained her crossword fetish for most of 2008, finding inspiration in the least likely answers. The phrase 'EAT UP', in combo with ORBS, saw the puzzle morph into a video screen where Pac Man munches dots through the maze. On other days, conjoined twins infer SOME PEOPLE/MISS THE CUT. (To see more, visit the virtual garret at www.emi-lyjocureton.com.) But be prepared for chills. The artist's gift is in finding darkness inside the black and white, for example in her image of the lamb standing frozen in a wolf's gaze to represent OVINE and ALONE.

Talk of sheep leads us back to another poem, this time a ballad written by Bluey the Shearer. His real name is Col Wilson, a bush laureate who couches his opinions in rhyme. A few years ago, on country radio, Bluey recited a poem named 'Friday Cryptic Crossword'. Here's a grab:

This 'DA', the setter, he's not in it for gain,
He's a dedicated sadist who loves inflicting pain.
When he isn't setting puzzles, how does he fill his day?
Dreaming up new tortures to be used by the CIA?

Seems one man's aqua therapy is another solver's water-board. Crosswords can do strange things to people, some of whom are tormented artists. Or Russian writers, maybe, like the shadowy figure cited in 4-Across. Time to migrate from New York lofts and outback sheds to Moscow, seeking the scribe embedded in our second last hybrid.

ALPHABET SOUP – unique sequences and database skewing

With a V to end the answer, the Russian mention should come as no shock. Here's the clue we need to consider:

Press disrupt opening about Russian writer (8)

When Mikhail Gorbachev stood down from power in 1991, I sighed. Not just the engineer of perestroika, the leader had such beautiful letters. So many Western statesmen own a glut of namby-pamby Os and Rs, but Gorby could hit a puzzle with both barrels. He still can, of course, emeritus-style, but I lament the exit of any V-ending bigwig. English can't make enough.

Brezhnev, Kasparov, Nureyev, Pavlov – Mother Russia has been generous. My heart sinks when a red star rises on the horizon, someone like Putin or Sharapova, only for their sur-names to end with a whimper. In the crossword caper, the tail is critical, as the wilder a word's finale the more leeway you gain in the interlock. Putin (*input switch*) and Sharapova (*A-Sharp medley + over, we hear*) aren't too shabby, but small potatoes compared to that exhilarating V.

It can get pathetic, trust me. I live so much for crisscrossing that I cheer on any horse in the Melbourne Cup, Australia's biggest race, that owns unusual letters. One November, back in 1986, the publican presumed I'd won the trifecta when the winner was announced. How could he imagine I was prancing the bar for purely verbal reasons, a horse like AT TALAQ giving future grids new hope?

Movie titles with odd patterns (*Antz*, *X-Men*, *EdTV*) get me going too, as do TV shows with peculiar sequences: CSIMIAMI, NYPDBLUE, NIP/TUCK. If they last a few seasons, that's all the better, cementing their future as grid fill. Like At Talaq, the prime weirdos are proven stayers.

In America, where interlocking is even more intense, the hunger for quirky combinations is acute. Best way to show you is by placing our last two ten-letter answers on top of each other like so:

MOREORLESS
BAMBOOZLED

Pretend that this block is the bottom-left corner of a grid, no spaces between them. To make a crust, the US constructor needs to create words that flow downward into each column, ending in the letter-pairs of the ten vertical slots the pairing offers. Savage business. That's why you need a welter of eccentric phrases. Let's step through this exercise to get a feel for the interlocker's art.

Reading left to right, looking at the vertical couples we have as end-pairs, we have the softer combinations (MB, RM, EL and SE), and then the gnarlier (OA, EB, OO), and finally the real hair-pullers (LZ and SD). Keep in mind that American puzzles require a setter to use each square twice, both horizontally and vertically.

LSD will do for the last couple, while the LZ obstacle could be leapt by SCHULZ, the creator of the *Peanuts* comic. Or maybe SKILLZ, the gamer slang for proficiency. Now you see the importance of gathering stuff with offbeat patterns, and why the Russians are in a class of their own.

Eric Albert, an enterprising compiler from the US, has a strong nose for rare combinations. Back in the early 1990s, when computers were anvil-sized, Albert fed his database with umpteen words and names, each one rated according to their individual make-up. In the case of SCHULZ or GORBACHEV, both entries scored zero, the optimal ranking known as Fabulous in Albert's system, a category set aside for words and well-known names abounding in strong consonants. NEW YORK, on the other hand, rated a single point, filed under Great: a common place name with less common letters, though not as bold as the first two examples. This radical approach, coupled with Albert's computer program, was a giant leap forward in crosswording.

Prior to the Albert model, most American setters relied on grey matter only, or on limited software tools that filled a grid with little sense of panache. Say you wished to create an interlock to occupy a 5×5 grid. Ask your brain, or ask ye olde computer, and the outcome may look like this:

S T U N G
T E N O R
U N T I E
N O I S E
G R E E T

Not too bad. But due to Albert's hard work, giving two points to JAWBONE (Very Good) or seven to ELLS (Boring), US setters have acquired alphabetic muscle. Thanks to this new system, where Fabulous fill scores zero and Very Yukky (Phil C, say, for Phil Collins) rates twelve, the software has a deeper challenge – not just to fill blanks, but to attain the minimal score. Updated, the 5×5 may pop out this way:

C L U M P
L U N A R
U N Z I P
M A I Z E
P R E E N

As a cryptic-setter, I use computers for a puzzle's stubborn junctions, where nothing in my lists or imagination seems to end in LZ, for instance. A quick key-tap, entering the letters in any crossword finishers (a growing niche of sites and software deals), will see the *Peanuts* creator save the day.

That's also why my word-watching never sleeps. Every waking hour I filter-feed magazines and conversations in hope of puzzle-ripe patterns. Take the world of music, for example. I may not like the tunes of DINOSAUR JR or OUTKAST, but I adore those letters. In the classic realm I cherish TCHAIKOVSKY and PROKOFIEV – those wonderful Russians again – by virtue of their wacky spelling. So let's unpick this fabulous man of letters:

Press disrupt opening about Russian writer (8)

Said another way, can you name a word meaning press, of any length, that ends in V? I'll speak for you – *nyet*. So *Russian writer* must be the definition.

We've met NABOKOV already, the Russian wordsmith, but he falls a letter short, in tandem with CHEKHOV. Name any others? If you know your literature, you're home and hosed, assuming your hunch obeys the recipes on show. Let's look for signposts to see what we're dealing with here.

Could *press* be an anagram signpost? Maybe yes, though some solvers and setters could object. If so, that would cast *disrupt* as your fodder, with no V in sight. Wrong theory.

How about *disrupt* then? Is that the anagram signal? More convincing, yes, but again the fodder looks scarce. Besides, our established letters (UGNV) aren't too evident in the clue, another blow to anagram conjecture.

Disrupt has better odds of being a container signpost, as ads disrupt a telecast just as surplus letters may disrupt a word. But what disrupts what? Consult the grid again. Don't neglect those strong letters, and think of a small word meaning *press*, I urge you. Ah, URGE. There's the gap. In she goes, but disrupting what? Our doodling looks like this:

_ U R G E N _ V

Either you know this novelist or you don't. If I told you that the nineteenth-century author of *Father and Sons*, Ivan Turgenev, shares my birthday along with King Edward VII and a Puerto Rican rapper named Big Pun, would that be of any use? Letter-wise, maybe, as TURGENEV can now be written as T(URGE)NEV.

It's a hard clue. Not just as it's a hybrid, and a less familiar surname, but also because the cues for reversal (your second recipe) are low-key. *Opening* is a synonym of VENT. *About* is a muted signal to reverse, one of those sly prepositions that kick you in the shins. When URGE *disrupts* VENT that's *turned about*, you solve the penultimate clue.

I'm only guessing here, but TURGENEV would probably score two points in Eric Albert's software, the mighty letters countered by the author's slip from the public mindset. Just think: there's only 20-Down between frustration and fulfilment, assuming you can summon the divine powers of inspiration. Though beware. As Turgenev once said, 'Whatever a man prays for, he prays for a miracle.'

QUIZLING 32.1

Logically, what classic Russian novel (4,8) and Pixar movie (3,5) are favourites among such actors as Uma Thurman and Pete Postlethwaite, plus director Hal Hartley, and writers Ray Bradbury and Mary McCarthy?

QUIZLING 32.2

Starting with M, what pharmaceutical word meaning drug is a mixture of NO TIME around a street word for drug spelt backwards? Take all the time you need.

QUIZLING 32.3

What aggressive ocean predator (4,5) is a mixture of fundamental ship parts within a type of ship?

CHAPTER 33

New 24-across-coated pickup yet to be delivered (2,5)

If I say Lear, do you think jet or king? For a few years, just to prove my inner nerd, I tried solving 100 consecutive crosswords in *The Times*. The rules were simple:

    must be solved on day of publication;
    no mistakes;
    no cheating, including dictionaries, googling or
        phone-a-friend.

I started briskly. Reached double figures without losing stride. Six days a week, the clues kept coming, and I kept cracking them. The day I clocked fifty – two months of steady solving – I celebrated with a tall Guinness. (The champagne could wait for the real milestone.) This wasn't my first time on the mountaintop. I'd scored a quick seventy across the summer, only to wreck my chances with a hybrid:

Violent thief about noon to steal from a person collecting in the Highlands (5–6)

I had every cross-letter too. Getting the solution was only a matter of time, surely. These were the letters already in the grid:

M _ N _ O / _ A _ G _ R

Violent thief had to be MUGGER. In this case, *about* was a container signpost, unlike the reversal role it just played in the TURGENEV clue. Place MUGGER about noon (common shorthand for N) and then … and then … then what?

I went with MUNGO-BAGGER, lacking a dictionary to ease my doubts. The next day I learnt that MUNGO-BAG-GER meant nothing, while a MUNRO-BAGGER is a climber who tries to scale every peak included in Munro's tables, a list detailing every Scottish mountain over 914 metres. The wordplay is a charade built into a container: MU(N+ROB+A) GGER. In view of the summit, I'd fallen short.

But not this time around. My gaze was fixed. The key to solving continuous grids is resolve, of the stubborn kind. Don't guess. Isolate recipes and find where the definition is hiding. To quell any doubts, ensure the wordplay renders the answer. Luck doesn't play a hand. Mind you, to reach fifty puzzles in a row, you do need to make a few intuitive leaps, just like a Munro bagger crossing a crevasse, trusting you land on solid ground.

In my latest attempt, passing eighty by then, I'd almost slipped on BISH (a peculiar word for nonsense) and a strand of seaweed called CARRAGHEEN. I'd survived a chess obscurity called SMOTHERED MATE. But then I struck a royal pickle with a clue involving Lear:

Lines from Lear don't show fate, sadly, protecting a king
(3,5,2,4)

Once again, just like your last Master entry, I had every alternate letter! Just unches to go yet I couldn't nail the last phrase:

T _ E / _ K _ N _ / O _ / S _ A _

THE SKINS ON SLAB? THE SKUNK OR SHAG? THE

EKING OF SHAW? Let's agree the first word is THE. After that, who knew? I became so panicky I sort of cheated, combing every scene of King Lear in hope of that vital phrase. THE SKINK ON SCAB?

Relax, I told myself. Remember the mantra of LL Cool J – what is the trap? Where is the trap? Or take comfort in Azed's edict: a crossword has two elements – wordplay and definition – and nothing else. Put King Lear back on the shelf and focus on what the clue is giving you.

An anagram, maybe, with the signpost of *sadly*, making the fodder DONTSHOWFATE. (Remember the clump theory we applied to RUSSNED, our first clue together?) Twelve letters – we needed two more. Wait, what does the rest of the clue say? Protecting a king – likely a container was the second recipe …

Let's think. Scramble DONTSHOWFATE around AK (a king in chess), then we get the answer. Wrong again, as there's no English word spelt AK_N_. I went through Shakespeare again and once more found nothing. In the end I risked THE SKINS OF SEAL, since it sounded the least ridiculous, and opened the next day's paper terrified.

The truth hit hard. All this time I'd been romancing the wrong bloody Lear. The king bit was a red herring. The man I needed was Edward Lear, the maker of limericks, plus his other nonsense poems, including THE AKOND OF SWAT.

Who or why or which or what is the Akond of Swat, runs the opening verse, and the humiliation in my head.

Is he tall or short, dark or fair?
Does he sit on a stool, a sofa or chair …

I didn't care. I'd lost the fight. I fell in a heap and waited for the paramedics.

THE LAST LAPSE – endgames and cross-references

My AKOND OF SWAT was panic. I'd never crept so close to a century of puzzles, and that growing sense of anticipation eroded the poise I needed to rumble the clue. Likewise, if the Master Puzzle ranks among your first ascents, then the prospect of filling the final blanks can tend to fray your concentration.

Often, when solving four puzzles a day, I might scribble SCARPER into the gird, instead of SCAMPER, and ruin the finale. Anxiety and eagerness has a history of jinxing any trip. So let's guard against both and read the ultimate clue:

New 24-across-coated pickup ready to be delivered (2,5)

The last clue, and our first cross-reference, where another answer is needed to read the full message. While we did have the ellipsis pair of ADAMANT and TWISTER, joined by their mutual dots, that was more a marriage of convenience than a genuine cross-reference. Either clue could be cracked in isolation. But this baby is another matter.

24-Across is IRON. All that means, should you meet any more cross-references in your travels, is that you should plant the referenced answer into the clue. This practice is rampant in themed puzzles, and will crop up in normal stuff as well. So now we have a clearer clue reading:

New iron-coated pickup yet to be delivered (2,5)

New murmurs anagram. *Coated* suggests container. *Pickup* could be reversal. No wonder this clue is last. The categories are piling up.

The anagram idea, looking at those cross-letters, feels right. The letters of IRON can easily be moulded into a framework, with I and O as our two extremes. If that's right, what is the internal block being *coated*?

Could this be clued by *pickup*? We need three letters, as seven minus IRON equals three. Logically, too, looking at the pattern, those letters are U_E (as IRON can't account for these two vowels).

IN UTERO? Or said the cryptic way, IN(UTE)RO? Congratulations, you've just been delivered. You've bagged your Munro peak. You've solved the Master Puzzle.

OCTOPUS GARDEN – going slow and getting there

F, of course, is the letter we never used in the grid, though Fe for IRON is chemically close. F may well be your grading too, if the Master challenge is your first outing in the genre. (F for Fledgling, perhaps, or Fumble-fingered, Faint-hearted, Fresh-eyed.) At least that will be the case when you next strike out solo, hoping to climb a crag minus mentor. You've already seen how skittish I became, staring dumbly at THE SKUNK OF SCAB, and that's after years of addiction.

Solving cryptics is not brain surgery – it's even more delicate, but with far less at stake. Your own brain needs to be thoroughly wired to meet the challenge. You need sharp eyes and stubbornness. And for every clue you crack, you'll be a surer operator tomorrow.

Take this puzzle, for example. Thirty-three clues later, you know that $500 may mean D, or cheerleader C. A worker might point to ANT, and question marks can signal an inbuilt curliness. You know that words like *soundly* and *say* murmur homophone, and if the Reverend Spooner had been born near Albert Square then hairy clues may translate as *clarey ocze*.

You know swaps and switches are two brands of manipulation, even if you're bamboozled by which switch is what. That's OK. Go slow.

Lying inside almost every cryptic clue, you know, is the yin-yang model of wordplay and definition, and these can be tough to tell apart. Don't worry. That's the art.

You know that charades mean more than a parlour game, and that 'hybrids' can apply to more than cars with power points. On top of that, we know that nescience is a fancy way of describing the vast gaps in our knowledge, whether you've spent half your life solving and compiling these symmetrical universes or are daring to enter the genre for the first time. That's fine. We all start ignorant. Little by little, we get wiser.

The other image I carry with me when solving elusive clues is the octopus. By all reports this slippery creature is crafty in its camouflage and brainy too, using coconut husks as armour or waving its arms to imitate seaweed. At first sight the octopus is terrifying, yet it's harmless if treated with respect. Those tentacles look lethal but really they enable the animal to attach itself to objects from different angles, much like the eight-clue recipes – a multiple choice of approaches. As for that defence system, squirting a black cloud when lunged at, it's only ink. Just remember that. It might drift into different shapes, and seem like a new peril, but the brave can reach right through.

To test that new nerve, try the six mini-puzzles lying in the next section and see if the former mumbo-jumbo has suddenly gained a shade of familiarity.

Now that your brain is supple, bend it more, and find out what new regions it can reach – and I don't just mean Nauru or sixteenth-century Italy. The only place a crossword is black and white is on the page. That's what I discovered *in utero*, cocooned in the family Commodore, staring at ENSUE and wondering what other secrets might follow. I still wonder that, gazing at the next bed of clues. Every puzzle is a mystery tour, every clue a head-trip whispering any number of destinations. Now that you know these things, you have my permission to get lost.

HALL OF FAME: HYBRIDS

Fat not left by supplier of beef and chicken (6) [Cincinnus, *FT*]
Senior priest holding mass at two in old city (7) [Viking, *FT*]
Before turning haggard, throw up (10) [Henry Hook, *US*]
Insect is tucking into a dead bug (10) [*Times*, 8600]
Family doctor warns about seafood (4,6) [Orlando, *Guardian*]
Argument about bodyline pitch that's preposterous (6,6)
   [Moodim, *FT*]

SOLUTIONS: coward, Pompeii, heavenward, antagonise, king
prawns, beyond belief

TO SOLVE – OR DISSOLVE?

Congratulations. You've reached the end – or the beginning.
Even if you grasp a fraction of this book, you should have
enough to infiltrate the next cryptic puzzle, and the one after
that, making more headway as you go. Don't forget to work
backwards if unsure – check solutions with clues to see how
they marry up. And look back across this book as well, visiting
each recipe precis, and browsing the Halls of Fame. And look
forward too – as six mini-puzzles lie beyond this page, from
easy to slippery: the perfect chance to see how far you've
come.

QUIZLING 33.1

There's one girl in King Lear who has LEAR strewn through her own name, and another who arises from strewing two adjacent words in this sentence. Name both.

QUIZLING 33.2

What decor items might,
Elegantly encircle a light,
Where one half's a holy song swirled
And the other, the intact underworld?

QUIZLING 33.3

By breaking in half a word that is part
Of this puzzle's poetical start,
And filling the gap with a jumbled version
Of a second word in this diversion,
You'll spell a hyphenated word relating
To that which is awesome or exhilarating.
What's the word?

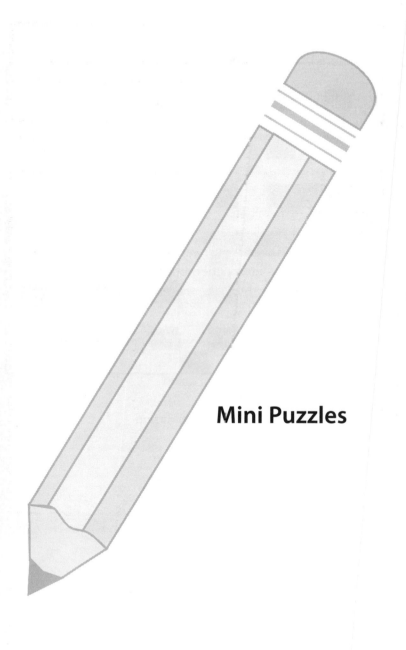

Mini Puzzles

Mini Puzzle 1

Level: friendly

Across

1   Ali Baba's opening ingredient? (6)
4   Sing inside mosque alcove (6)
9   Diet throwing out meat in gravies?! (13)
10 Mischief-maker altered Kremlin's façade (7)
11 Fruit: melon, bananas (5)
12 Test for booze in bar? Yeah, let's rock! (11)
17 Cross five Roman figures (5)
19 Spoken about bit of earth? (7)
21 Guitar legend arranged carols and chants, heartily embraced by St Nick (6,7)
22 Fuel runs out? Unlimited help required (6)
23 Complete in diplomacy (6)

Down

1   Fierce skinhead gave a wave (6)
2   House guest pens link (5)
3   Dahl novel covering one troubled lad (7)
5   Imitate chickens or another bird (5)
6   Puzzles offer cryptic meanings with no end of confusion! (7)
7   Regret a muffin top during Lent (6)
8   Prepared the corn fats for breakfast? (6,5)
13 Backward, though possibly poetic? (7)
14 Pressurise bigoted leader inside Arab nation (7)
15 Still bitter after record write-up (6)
16 Elastic factory storing iodine (6)
18 GP sits on a bee (5)
20 Pageant prize that's in a royal array, primarily (5)

Mini Puzzle 2

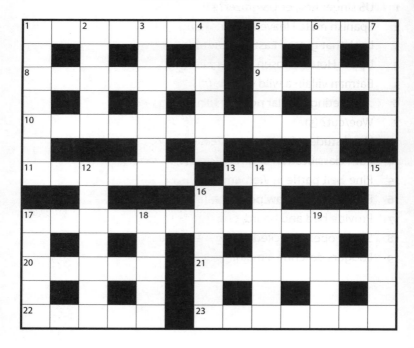

Level: friendly

Across

1   Opposition leader travels for fruit (7)
5   Half-judged as traitor (5)
8   He left blithe Buddhist reindeer (7)
9   Flatten in the vein of marsupial? (5)
10 Perforates leaves (6,7)
11 Relative one doesn't start – what a relief! (6)
13 Oil tax affected soup ingredient (6)
17 Caution copper suffering fixation (13)
20 Pay for cure (5)
21 Wild natives least modest (7)
22 Sucker caresses husky's tail (5)
23 Diet concerning private blokes (7)

Down

1   US singer Roy, or US grazer? (7)
2   Spanish mate I leave after morning (5)
3   Look that gutted Eastern newspaper (7)
4   Upper House chosen at every assembly (6)
5   Batman villain a wild card … (5)
6   … meeting regular nuclear villain with fangs (7)
7   Wee/cut? (5)
12 Head student becomes perfect with right adjustment (7)
14 Porn classification at times: topless, irksome (1–6)
15 Pine-belt battle in Vietnam War (4,3)
16 Feel the cold arrow pouch? (6)
17 Provide bed and board, one way or the other (3,2)
18 Scatty opener sacked, being malicious (5)
19 Lodgers describe a major girder (1–4)

Mini Puzzle 3

Level: tricky

Across

1 Sounded tender – acted dirty (6)
4 Cockney covering his bets on the side (6)
9 Some don't appreciate being readily available (2,3)
10 Allows curse about the French (7)
11 Limit small explosive (3)
13 John Hancock is repulsed by grand instinct (9)
14 Improbable airline cuts crackers (11)
18 Stirred, a poison must lose no volatile element (9)
20 Audience dumps jazz instrument (3)
21 Exaggerate general kerfuffle (7)
22 Reconciler half-turned to what's left (5)
24 That mess detailed London feature (6)

25 Dope rolled in dope (6)

Down

1 Nullify spirit (6)

2 Snitch rejected pitch (3)

3 One politician with 25-acrosses almost makes jam (7)

5 Yours truly penned hit play (5)

6 Regular discourse couches praise for one toga drama (1,8)

7 Blast each heavy breather (6)

8 Big, elegant, wild predator, in conclusion! (6,5)

12 A surgeon finally cuts into kneecap earning cigar (9)

15 Japanese warrior briefly disclosed about a retro spirit (7)

16 Happy to be twice spent (6)

17 Quietly left trade show, prepared to discuss missile (6)

19 Help to put ball in play (5)

23 Sound knowledge of court game? (3)

Mini Puzzle 4

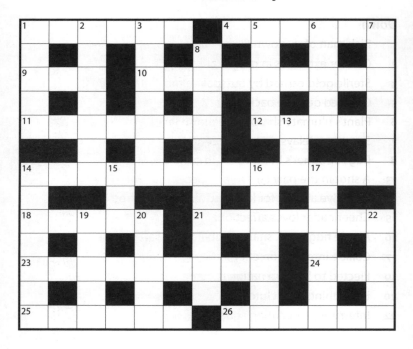

Level: tricky

Across

1 Recant mixed juice (6)

4 1-across ruined jog (6)

9 Snake's principal blood groups? (3)

10 Cattle base, we hear, in Sweden (9)

11 Crashing breakers wiped out a lunatic (7)

12 United claimed a European final, then fizzled (5)

14 Soldier, mid-fifties, can race poor hound (5–8)

18 A cricket team with over-meek openers revealing truth (5)

21 Porcelain saucer – a mica streak inlaid (7)

23 During brief month, shade colour (4,5)

24 Start off fascinated and fit (3)

25 Spell 4-across wrongly (6)

26   25-across struck Greek islander (6)

Down

1   Rich man of 19-down flipped an old coin (5)
2   Greater extremes in range cause vexation (7)
3   Sterile gold carried by outspoken pilot (7)
5   Crooked quiz we backed (5)
6   Plant's ultimate sharp projection?! (5)
7   Supremo delays part-renovation (7)
8   Bugs Spooner's band tutors, maybe (11)
13   A shot in the past (3)
14   Exclusive aircraft for king and I in Paris on time (4,3)
15   Cheerleader loves affectionate sound (3)
16   Above ridge-top, snare climbing companion (7)
17   Collide into section of embankment (7)
19   Elected to help up nation (5)
20   Bewitching host clutches silver pin in centre (5)
22   Interrupt prosecuting squad (3,2)

Mini Puzzle 5

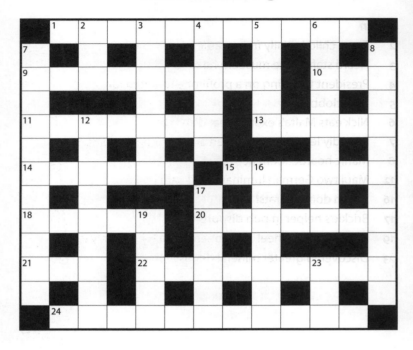

Level: gnarly

Across

1 Past accomplishments suggesting song on album? (5,6)
9 Engulfed in loathing, one Swiss city to crash for months (9)
10 Tree remains (3)
11 Traumas plagued Indonesian island (7)
13 Poet's concern mounted in cab? (5)
14 After success, go cold (6)
15 Journo sketch returned to boy (6)
18 Is a fact unlimited for Newton? (5)
20 Dealing with unknown quantities, say, left to regress in a couple of cups (7)
21 Objective tip (3)
22 Traveller to ruin Penny in fashionable circle (5,4)

24   Feel very low, suffering this?! (6,5)

Down

2   Tease child initially from cradle (3)
3   Heard staff judge museum head? (7)
4   President touching on a profit one forfeited (6)
5   Elite clobber (5)
6   Nick eats Malta's exotic meat dish (5,4)
7   Soundly leaves more clichéd author under cover (5,6)
8   Manic hoarder bent ace (3,3,5)
12   Maul two German luminaries, it's said (9)
16   Pooch doomed rats! (7)
17   Brickie's helper in pub dispute (6)
19   Humped one wheel component onto telly, evenly (5)
23   Discovered greater mineral deposit (3)

Mini Puzzle 6

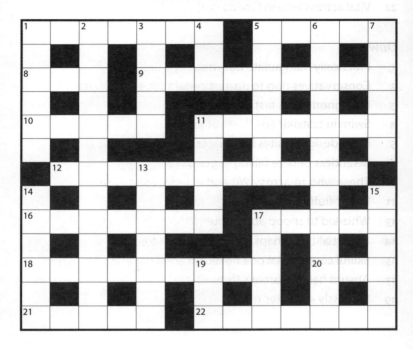

Level: gnarly

Across

1 Help to grab flightless bird for bozo (7)
5 Dispatches fellows in auditorium (5)
8 1-down spare field (3)
9 Truly deep vet, by all accounts (9)
10 State outright … (5)
11,12 … 'You're a sole ray of light' and 'You deserve top perch'?
    (4,3,11)
12 See 11-across
16 Give notion I scrapped to hooligan (4,3)
17 Called old after limp ending (5)
18 10-across SP_ _? (4,2,3)
20 Life story blazes in our heads (3)

21   Terrible line of monarchs, beyond the original couple (5)
22   Vital actress Mae in Florida (3,4)

Down
1   Practically manipulate bull in data centre (3,3)
2   Conservatives ring to disrupt certain reform sign (13)
3   Brat ignoring his first sin (5)
4   Swim in tzatziki? (3)
5   Mum designed sites for painter (7)
6   Relentless debate failing vagrant (13)
7   Those who 10-across 'Wit and writer, Dorothy?' (6)
11   Rock f-fluff? (5)
13   Whiz-kid to snoop about intermittent coddling (7)
14   Impartiality, perhaps, upheld inventor (6)
15   Skilful commercial one observed amid drivel (6)
17   Absurd heir apparent's throne? (5)
19   Endlessly saturates tree (3)

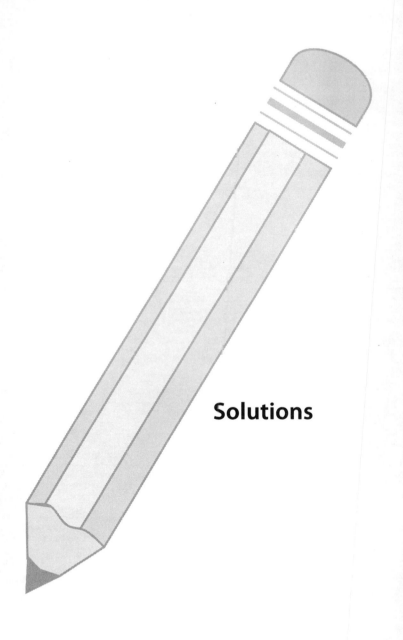

Solutions

Quizling Solutions

Quizling lists run horizontally, not vertically, like this:
A B
C D
E F

Q1.1
ASTOUNDING + T = OUTSTANDING

Q1.2
Niger, Nepal, China: reign, plane, chain

Q1.3
Mad/nuts, trim/neat, stir/tease

Q2.1
Alphabeticise them: BELOW, GHOST, FIRST, ADEPT

Q2.2
Far/close, deny/admit, loose/tight, holy/satanic

Q2.3
Harley-Davidson motorcycles

Q3.1
Restful, enormity, violence, funeral, adultery

Q3.2
Upsilon + eta = epsilon + tau

Q3.3
PANIC-STRICKEN

Q4.1
Sophie Dahl, Gisele Bündchen, Kate Moss, Linda Evangelista, Heidi Klum, Christy Turlington

Q4.2
Bemoans, canyons, funeral, needily, citizen, coyotes, inaptly, wraiths

Q4.3
Hate heat, cures curse, begin binge, green genre, plum lump, adobe abode, late tale, below elbow

Q5.1
Race/dash

Q5.2
Cap+one, Scarf+ace

Q5.3
St/ring, st/ash, st/ripe, st/ratify, st/itching, St/Eve, St/Ella, st/ride, st/roll

Q6.1
Highlighter, accordion file, foolscap, felt tip, hole punch, staple gun

Q6.2
Tarot

Q6.3
NOTHING

Q7.1
Neck +tie

Q7.2
SON + ART + AD + SUM = NOSTRADAMUS

Q7.3
COUSCOUS and COS (lettuce)

Q8.1
Hurl earl, Ulster holster, axe hacks, armour harmer, harder ardour, anchoring hankering

Q8.2
Just+in+timber+lake

Q8.3
W/asp, f/ox, f/owl, b/ass, t/ern

Q9.1
VA(CAN)T

Q9.2
CamemBERT, gorGONZOla

Q9.3
Gone Baby Gone, Minority Report, Tomb Raider, One Flew Over the Cuckoo's Nest, Clockwork Orange, Billy Elliot, Some Like it Hot, Eagle Eye, The Last Emperor, Educating Rita

Q10.1
Scarlet, carmine, carnation, caramel

Q10.2
Kenya (token/yam), Nepal (tone/palm), Peru (tope/rum)

Q10.3
National, scarab, retirees, available, excavate, embarrass, punster, clambake, mislays, bandannas.
(Other words are possible.)

Q11.1
Singin' in the Rain

Q11.2
Monica Seles, Chris Evert

Q11.3
Musical lass; metal compound; sacred order; base, vile; tempest or monsoon; swimmer's ingress.
(Other definitions are possible.)

Q12.1
SELECTED, REJECTED

Q12.2
Häagen-Dazs has a hidden agenda.

Q12.3
Look for a smaller word hiding inside the paired numbers when spelt: WOO (seduce), EVENT(contest), NET (clear) and REEF (gold, knot OR coral).

Q13.1
Drive, chip, hacker

Q13.2
Mushroom, boom, snowball, flourish, blossom and bloom

Q13.3
'Button up' is the same as 'pipe down'.

Q14.1
Rolling pin

Q14.2
Clip

Q14.3
Peer, affected, rider, entertain, steer, convention: SCRAPE

Q15.1
Kevin Spacey, Jacques Villeneuve, George Eliot, River Phoenix, Sandra Bullock, Corazon Aquino

Q15.2
Ale/ail

Q15.3
Assent/dissent (ascent/descent)

Q16.1
Spa spar, bury berry, laud Lord, your yore, whirled world, principal principle, needing kneading, peak pique, sauce source

Q16.2
Therefore (three/four)

Q16.3
Leek/pea

Q17.1
UK-'raine'

Q17.2
The list includes awe/or, eye/I, you/ewe, a/eh, auk/orc – and arguably quay/ki (life energy of Chinese philosophy) and eau/oh.

Q17.3
Lax, lacks, slack

Q18.1
A/bridge

Q18.2
Scarab, hornet, cicada, EARWIG

Q18.3
C/raven

Q19.1
Floridly and scabbarded

Q19.2
SQUEAKY (You can also create the rarer IMAGOES, CAESIUM, SEQUOIA, CAIQUES and SOMEWAY.)

Q19.3
Claire Danes (car/sedan)

Q20.1
GRANT (Harding, Carter, Obama, Clinton, Roosevelt); and
HAYES (Bush, Obama, Kennedy, Coolidge, Adams).
(Other combinations may be possible.)

Q20.2
What's Eating Gilbert Grape?

Q20.3
A capsized calculator holds the key. The animals are DOE,
BEE, EEL, DOG, IBIS, GOOSE, HEDGEHOG. Three can fly.

Q21.1
Jenga

Q21.2
Apathy/*voluntatis defectio*, casino/*aleatorium*, dancing/*ludus
saltatorius*, flirt/*amor levis*, gateau/*placenta farta*, shampoo/
capitilavium

Q21.3
Baht + teak = batik

Q22.1
Eat (ate)

Q22.2
EMBRYO-HOMBRE-MOTHER-OTHERS-FOSTER-FOETUS.
(Other gestations are possible.)

Q22.3
TIER (TILER)

Q23.1
What book do you buy a saucy grammarian? COMMA
SUTRA

Q23.2
Colin Firth (colic/mirth)

Q23.3
Ticklish, fix

Q24.1
Boycott, Atlas, propaganda, autocue, inspector, sauterne, superficial

Q24.2
Under the weather; smashed, wrecked, hammered; stuffed, had a skinful; tanked, bombed, shot.
(Other states of intoxication could apply.)

Q24.3
Would Zen electricians chant ohm?

Q25.1
Slapdash (sad pals)

Q25.2
Fuzz (or ZZUF) is the most common tail-ender.

Q25.3
Fifty (L) in 09 reversed (ENINO) spells El Niño.

Q26.1
Redder

Q26.2
The full palindrome is ANNE, I VOTE MORE CARS RACE ROME TO VIENNA.

Q26.3
HIAWATHA

Q27.1
Star jump (jar/stump)

Q27.2
Food court (cooed/fought)

Q27.3
Two of Clubs (clue of tubs), Ace of Spades (space of aides),
Six of Clubs (clicks of subs), Ten of Hearts (hen of tarts)

Q28.1
Put your money where your mouth is

Q28.2
*The Quiet American, The End of the Affair, Brighton Rock, The
Heart of the Matter, Our Man in Havana*

Q28.3
NILE, CLOVER, CANADA, PHOENIX, SASQUATCH,
MARZIPAN

Q29.1
Mole + ST = MOLEST (Badger)

Q29.2
Scurvy

Q29.3
capital letters; cross out; pacifist (no fist); bold type; no 'eye'
in blind; spaced out

Q30.1
Lay Lady Lay; Layla (by Eric Clapton)

Q30.2
Rhone (roan/heron)

Q30.3
Minnesota (Estonian)

Q31.1
Glass slipper, joss stick, class struggle, business school, chess
set, cross-stitch, stainless steel, press stud, Bass Strait, brass
section, process-server, witness stand

Q31.2
Genoa (A-one)

Q31.3
Change E to D, and you'll find Liberia/Chad.

Q32.1
Since all the surnames contain their first name from left to right, the gang's two favourites are *Anna Karenina* and *Toy Story*.

Q32.2
Medication (NO TIME around ACID)

Q32.3
Bull shark (HULLS mixed in BARK)

Q33.1
Cordelia, Goneril (one girl)

Q33.2
LAMPSHADES: Lamps (PSALM) + Hades

Q33.3
BREATHTAKING (THAT jumbled inside BREAKING)

Mini Puzzle Solutions

Mini Puzzle 1: Solution

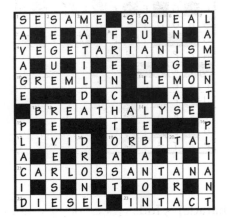

Across

1 Sesame (pun) 4 Squeal (hidden) 9 Vegetarianism
(anagram &lit) 10 Gremlin (manipulation) 11 Lemon
(anagram) 12 Breathalyse (anagram) 17 Livid (charade
of Roman numerals) 19 Orbital (container) 21 Carlos
Santana (anagram/container) 22 Diesel (charade/
deletion) 23 Intact(charade)

Down

1 Savage (charade/anagram) 2 Segue (hidden) 3 Matilda (charade/anagram) 5 Quail (double meaning) 6 Enigmas (subtractive anagram) 7 Lament (container) 8 French toast (anagram) 13 Reverse (lateral thinking) 14 Lebanon (container) 15 Placid (charade/reversal) 16 Pliant (container) 18 Drone (charade) 20 Tiara (code)

Mini Puzzle 2: Solution

Across

1 Oranges (charade) 5 Judas (deletion/charade) 8 Blitzen (deletion/charade) 9 Koala (charade) 10 Shoots through (double meaning) 11 Nephew (deletion/charade) 13 Oxtail (anagram) 17 Preoccupation (anagram) 20 Treat (double meaning) 21 Vainest (anagram) 22 Patsy (charade) 23 Regimen (charade)

Down

1 Orbison (charade) 2 Amigo (charade) 3 Gazette (charade/deletion) 4 Senate (hidden) 5 Joker (double meaning) 6 Dracula (anagram/alternation) 7 Slash (triple

meaning) 12 Prefect (manipulation) 14 X-rating (charade/
deletion) 15 Long Tan (double meaning) 16 Quiver
(double meaning) 17 Put up (palindrome) 18 Catty
(deletion) 19 I-beam (hidden)

Mini Puzzle 3: Solution

Across

1 Sordid (homophone/charade) 4 Edging
(Cockneyism) 9 On tap (hidden) 10 Enables
(reversal/exotic) 11 Cap (double meaning) 13 Signature
(reversal/charade) 14 Unrealistic (anagram) 18 Potassium
(subtractive anagram) 20 Sax (homophone) 21 Enlarge
(anagram) 22 Relic (reverse/hidden) 24 Thames
(deletion) 25 Nitwit (reverse/charade)

Down

1 Scotch (double meaning) 2 Rat (reversal) 3 Impasse
(charade/deletion) 5 Drama (container) 6 I Claudius
(alternation/container/anagram) 7 Gasper (charade) 8 Bengal
tiger (anagram &lit) 12 Panatella (container) 15 Samurai
(deletion/ container/reversal) 16 Upbeat (double

meaning) 17 Exocet (deletion/homophone) 19 Serve
(double meaning) 23 Law (homophone)

Mini Puzzle 4: Solution

N	E	C	T	A	R		C	A	N	T	E	R
A		H		U		C		S		H		E
B	O	A		S	T	O	C	K	H	O	L	M
O		G		T		C		E		R		O
B	E	R	S	E	R	K		W	A	N	E	D
		I		R		R		G				E
L	A	N	C	E	C	O	R	P	O	R	A	L
E		O			A		A		A			
A	X	I	O	M		C	E	R	A	M	I	C
R		N		A		H		T		P		U
J	A	D	E	G	R	E	E	N		A	P	T
E		I		I		S		E		R		I
T	R	A	N	C	E		C	R	E	T	A	N

Across

1 Nectar (anagram) 4 Canter (anagram) 9 Boa
(charade of blood groups) 10 Stockholm (charade/
homophone) 11 Berserk (subtractive anagram) 12 Waned
(container) 14 Lance corporal (container/
anagram) 18 Axiom (charade) 21 Ceramic (hidden) 23 Jade
green (container) 24 Apt (deletion) 25 Trance
(anagram) 26 Cretan (anagram)

Down

1 Nabob (reversal/charade) 2 Chagrin
(container) 3 Austere (charade/homophone) 5 Askew
(charade/reversal) 6 Thorn (charade &lit) 7 Remodel
(hidden) 8 Cockroaches (spoonerism) 13 Ago
(charade) 14 Lear jet (exotic/charade) 15 Coo
(charade) 16 Partner (reversal) 17 Rampart
(charade) 19 India (charade/reversal) 20 Magic
(container) 22 Cut in (hidden)

Mini Puzzle 5: Solution

Across

1 Track record (double meaning) 9 Hibernate (container) 10 Ash (double meaning) 11 Sumatra (anagram) 13 Meter (double meaning) 14 Wintry (charade) 15 Edward (charade/reversal) 18 Isaac (deletion) 20 Algebra (charade/reversal/container) 21 End (double meaning) 22 Marco Polo (charade/container) 24 Yellow fever (anagram &lit)

Down

2 Rib (deletion) 3 Curator (homophone) 4 Reagan (charade/deletion) 5 Cream (double meaning) 6 Roast lamb (container/anagram) 7 Ghostwriter (homophone) 8 The Red Baron (anagram) 12 Manhandle (homophone) 16 Doggone (charade) 17 Barrow (charade) 19 Camel (charade/deletion) 23 Ore (deletion)

Mini Puzzle 6: Solution

```
A I R H E A D ▢ M A I L S
L ▢ E ▢ R ▢ I ▢ A ▢ N ▢ A
L E A ▢ R E P U T E D L Y
B ▢ C ▢ O ▢ ▢ I ▢ E ▢ E
U T T E R ▢ F I S H F O R
T ▢ I ▢ ▢ L ▢ S ▢ A ▢ S
▢ C O M P L I M E N T S ▢
E ▢ N ▢ R ▢ N ▢ ▢ I ▢ A
D E A L O U T ▢ P A G E D
I ▢ R ▢ D ▢ ▢ O ▢ A ▢ R
S P I T I T O U T ▢ B I O
O ▢ E ▢ G ▢ A ▢ T ▢ L ▢ I
N A S T Y ▢ K E Y W E S T
```

Across

1 Airhead (container) 5 Mails (homophone) 8 Lea (deletion) 9 Reputedly (anagram) 10 Utter (double meaning) 11,12 Fish for compliments (pun) 16 Deal out (deletion/charade) 17 Paged (charade) 18 Spit it out (rebus) 20 Bio (code) 21 Nasty (deletion) 22 Key West (double meaning)

Down

1 All but (anagram/container) 2 Reactionaries (compound anagram/charade) 3 Error (deletion) 4 Dip (double meaning) 5 Matisse (charade/anagram) 6 Indefatigable (anagram) 7 Sayers (double meaning) 11 Flint (charade) 13 Prodigy (container/alternation) 14 Edison (reversal) 15 Adroit (charade/container) 17 Potty (double meaning) 19 Oak (deletion)

A Word of Thanks

Between 1-Across and Chapter 33, a lot of different minds have helped to realise this book. First I'd like to thank Sophie Cunningham, the *Meanjin* editor, who wanted to hear the noise inside my head. Teasing the essay into a book, I was ably guided by my two simpatico agents – Jenny Darling and Donica Bettanin.

Publisher Sue Hines encouraged the story to reach its potential, even if that meant a few more pages. And when it came to fine-tuning the jam, I was blessed by the best in editors – Ann Lennox and Annette Sayers – plus proofreader Lisa Foulis.

At the *Sydney Morning Herald*, I cherish the humour and wisdom of Harriet Veitch, Lynne Cairncross, Susan Wyndham, Jack Ames, Ron Nichols, Deb Shaw, the Taylor clan and every other vigilante to occupy the puzzle desk. And of course, I remain in the debt of Lindsey Browne, and his erudite other, Elspeth.

Thanks to Chris Dodds for unlocking another dimension, John Holgate for our nights on the tiles, and Ben Ball for that genial brainstorm. Three cheers for the three poets too – Roger McGough, Peter Valentine and Bluey the Shearer – whose verses grace these pages.

While on poetry, I wish to applaud the mystery men and

women whose work underpins this book. From Aardvark to Virgilius, these are the clue-mongers whose lyrics have mesmerised for decades. I'm grateful to their editors (in particular Hugh Stephenson and Colin Inman) for allowing me to share with you the wealth of wit and guile.

In this regard, a special mention to Shirl O'Brien and David Stickley. Reversing the import trend, these two locals both fashion clues for UK papers, as Auster and Styx respectively.

And a big hooray for the genius of Emily Cox and Henry Rathvon. In league with Henry Hook, these three Americans are cryptic pioneers.

Let me also raise a glass of aquavit (because I love those letters) to Francis Heaney, Will Shortz, Ben Tausig, Merl Reagle and every other arch-fiend to push the crossword envelope. On the blog front, the champions remain Amy Reynaldo and Michael Sharp, while the team at Fifteen Squared in the UK is a constant joy to follow. Here in Australia, the crews at Deef and Trippers keep a vital chat ongoing.

Scrabblers, editors, colleagues – this rap could run forever, but I sense that familiar puzzle urge to be brief. So let me close on thanking those closest – Tracy, Finn, Tess and a dog called Tim: your love and willingness to walk beside me have seen puzzles turn into answers.

David Astle (alias DA)
www.davidastle.com